Rethinking Management

Thanks to Doug and Ralph for encouraging me to take myself seriously, and teaching me to think. To Karen and Nick, good colleagues, for their constant input of ideas, support and friendship.

First and last to Nikki, Rosa and George for being with me every step of the way.

Rethinking Management

Radical Insights from the Complexity Sciences

CHRIS MOWLES
University of Hertfordshire Business School, UK

Routledge
Taylor & Francis Group

LONDON AND NEW YORK

First published 2011 by Gower Publishing

2 Park Square, Milton Park, Abingdon, Oxon OX14 4RN
711 Third Avenue, New York, NY 10017, USA

Routledge is an imprint of the Taylor & Francis Group, an informa business

First issued in paperback 2016

Gower Applied Business Research
Our programme provides leaders, practitioners, scholars and researchers with thought provoking, cutting edge books that combine conceptual insights, interdisciplinary rigour and practical relevance in key areas of business and management.

British Library Cataloguing in Publication Data
Mowles, Chris.

    Rethinking management : radical insights from complexity science.
    1. Management. 2. Management – Practice.
    I. Title
    658–dc22

Library of Congress Cataloging-in-Publication Data
Mowles, Chris.
    Rethinking management : radical insights from complexity science / Chris Mowles.
       p. cm.
    Includes bibliographical references and index.
    ISBN 978-1-4094-2933-3 (hardback : alk. paper)
  1. Management. 2. Leadership. 3. Strategic planning. 4. Performance – Management. I. Title.

    HD31. M69 2011
    658–dc22

                                      2011016171

ISBN 978-1-4094-2933-3 (hbk)
ISBN 978-1-138-24556-3 (pbk)

Contents

Foreword

Ralph Stacey

This book makes an important contribution to thinking about organisations and their management through very insightful analyses of the way managers have come to think. It presents a rigorous critique of current conventional management wisdom in a very accessible way so spanning the divide between academic and popular management books. To an unusual degree, Chris Mowles uses his own experience of management, drawing on both his 'successes' and 'failures', to ground theory in actual, rather than idealised, practice. The book works with the creative tension of theory and practice and in so doing it presents a significant challenge to managerialist claims. He talks about his own growing dissatisfaction and unease with dominant ideas about his own practice, that of consulting to organisations, and proposes to explore instead the insights for managers provided by marginalised concepts of emergence, paradox and complexity in social processes.

The book immediately confronts the criticism it has already attracted. The main criticism is that the book provides no management tools, techniques, frameworks or conventional prescriptions. The reason for this lack is made quite clear: what pass for tools, techniques, and frameworks are in fact highly abstract, generalised and idealised prescriptions which are not supported by any rigorous evidence. However, what the book does provide is insight into the ordinary, everyday politics of organisational life. Management is not a science but it is a political practice. Many ideas are provided about how to manage in realistic circumstances. The claim is that reflection on ordinary daily interaction is at the heart of what a manager, or a consultant, could be usefully doing. The author is trying to model the ways of working that he believes are increasingly necessary in modern organisations and what he is modelling is how he pays attention to live, local interactions between engaged participants. He shows that what happens between people, whether it goes well or badly, is more important for thinking of how to improve performance than trying to develop tools or frameworks. His own work is that of encouraging managers to pay attention to the kinds of interaction they are caught in and this includes the strong feelings they often experience.

What the book presents resonates far more with my experience than conventional management literature and I believe many readers will have the same experience.

Ralph Stacey
Business School, University of Hertfordshire
9 December 2010

Preface

Although many people have become interested by the complexity sciences and their possible application to the field of organisational studies and management, there is still a tendency to assume that complexity is something we can get on top of. It is another thing to manage, where manage has come to mean control. This usually manifests itself in a call for 'tools' which can then be 'applied' to organisations so that managers might 'harness' complexity or perhaps 'unleash emergence' to the benefit of creativity and innovation. Without these things, some groups of managers occasionally charge me, then insights from the complexity sciences are in no way 'practical' or 'concrete', merely theoretical.

Since this book deals with the phenomenon of the burgeoning number of prescriptions for how to manage, I suppose that this call for 'practical' tools should no longer surprise me. However, I am sometimes left wondering whether what I am really being asked is not about the practicality or otherwise of what I am saying, but why it does not appear familiar to my questioners: why can it not be reduced to a two-by-two grid or framework like the ones they are used to? It can be a destabilising idea that there are limits to managerial control and that complex organisational situations may require complex ways of thinking about them. It seems to me also to problematise currently taken for granted ideas about what is practical and useful.

But new, more complex ways of thinking about and researching organisations have arisen as a result of taking the radical insights from the complexity sciences seriously, and the ideas have been taken up in very practical ways. For example, the ideas set out in this book, complex responsive processes of relating, which have been developed over a period of 20 years by Ralph Stacey, Doug Griffin and Patricia Shaw have now given rise to a number of academic programmes. The first of which is the Masters/Doctor of Management (MA/DMan) programme at the University of Hertfordshire (UH), where Ralph Stacey and Doug Griffin are still Professors. The DMan programme has been running for more than ten years and has produced 51 graduates, 39 of which are at doctoral level. Programme participants are practising managers from a variety of backgrounds, from directors of hospitals or companies, through to organisational consultants and university professors, who study part time and take what they are doing at work as the subject and object of their research. They are asked to write about complex situations in which they find themselves at work, and in the process of doing so to discuss their developing understanding of their situation with other colleagues also on the doctoral progamme. They are then required to locate what they are thinking and writing in a broader discourse of management theory, sociology, philosophy and psychology. The programme draws on both the natural and the social sciences, and is run in a residential setting where programme participants explore their ideas in large and small groups, and where the research cohort itself, as a temporary organisation, becomes a method of research in and of itself.

Over a period of three years, programme participants develop a thesis which comprises four projects and a synopsis. The thesis describes the development of their thinking and management practice as they become more skilful at paying attention to, and describing the quality of their participation at work. The programme is aimed at supporting programme participants to be better managers, and to expose them to the necessary discipline of academic research. It begins then to bring together the generative poles of theory and practice.

The ideas have been similarly taken up particularly in academic institutions in Holland, Denmark and Norway, and in some institutions in the UK on academic programmes where there has been an interest in the radical implications of complex responsive processes of relating and a corresponding dissatisfaction with more orthodox ways of understanding management. In all these cases managers are encouraged to take their experience at work seriously and to think about how they are co-creating the complex dynamic of stability and change at work.

One might argue, then, that taking the radical implications of the complexity sciences seriously does lead to new, practical ways of working and researching by managers, and continues to do so. But in the programme at UH and in other institutions there is belief that the way of making a difference is not to reduce and simplify. Rather, programme participants are required to think about what they are doing in rigorous ways, and they are required continuously to consider how they are thinking about what they are doing, and to go on opening up their enquiries. This is a very different discipline from learning other people's prescriptions and I think also requires more from those of us who make their living teaching in business schools.

Chris Mowles
Oxford
April 2011

1

Why Write This Book?

There are tens of thousands of books on management, ranging from more popular books available in airport bookshops which offer shortcuts for busy managers through to more academic, even critical management texts. The first popular category of books may still be written by academics, usually from north American business schools, and will usually contain words such as 'clear', 'successful', 'secrets', 'effective', and increasingly 'evidence-based'. The point of buying these books is presumably to gain access to nuggets of wisdom which have been boiled down by academics and presented in a way that is accessible and digestible. There is usually a broad appeal to common sense, and practicality and sometimes to spirituality and values. Some of these books are driven by current fads in management, and confusingly, there is even a genre of books which purport to counter faddism to reveal the 'real truth' about management (for example, Pozner and Kouzes, 2010). The more academic management books are not necessarily easily accessible to practising managers and are sometimes geared more towards other academics than intelligent managers with some time, but not with all the time in the world. Current management literature is certainly a many-layered phenomenon with a plethora of genres and competing truth claims.

In many ways then, it is a brave author who dares to declare that what they are saying is in any way radical or different, and particularly if he then goes on not to offer any prescriptions, grids, frameworks, tools or best practice tips offering to make managers more successful or more effective. Instead this book attempts to do two things: it tries to engage with the practice of management as experienced by managers in a variety of organisations and by myself, and it tries to theorise from this experience. But rather than offering idealised, rule-like prescriptions for how to go about managing people and getting things done in organisations, it tries instead to generalise from practice drawing on specific examples in particular contexts, and further it tries to explore how management generalisations get taken up in practice and some of the difficulties that arise as a consequence. This book tries to hang on to the generative tension between theory and practice by enquiring into what managers actually do in organisations. It asks what some of the consequences are of pursuing some taken for granted ways of understanding what they are doing. By writing in this way I am trying to write about management grounded in the experience of managing, and I am trying to encourage managers to think more about how they are thinking and experiencing their day-to-day work. I am assuming that action, thinking, feeling and speaking are all different phases of getting things done: that what we experience informs the way we talk about what we are doing, which is concurrently informing our thinking, which in turn influences further action and speaking about our activities.

I hope it will become clearer during the course of the book why it is important to write about the experience of managing, but as an introduction I think it is necessary to explain how I myself came to management and what my experiences of organisational life have been. As my explanation develops I will begin to demonstrate the method that I will be using throughout this book.

Developing as an Organisational Development (OD) Consultant

My first introduction to the world of management theory was when I was signed up for a Diploma in Management Studies (DMS) at the business department of the local university. I was a youngish manager in the public sector, and the managerial revolution that had washed over Mrs Thatcher's Britain was now rippling through public services, and thereafter into the not-for-profit sector.

Like many other managers who were being sent off on management courses, we were being prepared for the new managerial age that was said to be long overdue in the public sector. We were exposed to a wide range of theories that had been taken up with enthusiasm in the private sector and were thought to apply in similar measure in any sector. In the module on operations, for example, I learnt to apply Michael Porter's (1985) value chain analysis over the services we were offering in my department. The value chain was a way of systematically breaking down a production process into its constituent parts, inputs, manufacturing process, outputs, as a means for managers to identify how they could 'add value' to each of the production stages to enhance customer satisfaction and therefore increase profit. This expression, 'add value', has now passed into common usage in contemporary Britain and is used by many managers I come across, although mostly they have no idea of the provenance of the phrase and have never read Michael Porter, or Karl Marx and Adam Smith upon whose original thinking Porter, as a classical economist, derived his thinking. At the time my colleagues and I, still new to management, were quite sceptical about the relevance of this Harvard Business School Professor's ideas derived from private sector industry and from economics to the public services where we were managing. Nonetheless, it was introduced to us relatively unproblematically by the academics, and in the absence of our having any other theory of how we should work in a sector which historically was considered weak on management, we ourselves became quite enthusiastic about it. It enabled us as new managers to appear as though we knew what we were talking about, and to offer a framework for understanding the work processes we were engaged in. We never questioned to what extent it might be possible to talk about adding value to public services nor noticed the growing primacy of economics as a way of interpreting the world.

Meanwhile I learned that personnel departments were in transition to becoming human resource departments as a way of maximising the benefit to the organisation of the people who worked for it. This was another way of considering people as 'human capital' for whatever enterprise an organisation was undertaking. People were at the centre of business and needed to be taken seriously if they were to 'buy in' to the organisational mission and strategy – the days of command and control were over and it became important to win over hearts and minds. The enterprise was no longer something that was deemed to be an antagonistic undertaking, something that managers would propose and workers would oppose, but was something that could be shared, each of us striving to put the 'customer' first. Increasingly workplaces were about sharing vision and values and putting aside our differences for the good of the organisation. This was an interesting development for me as an ex-trade union shop steward, since I had always assumed that the interests of workers and managers were not necessarily shared. Of this I still needed convincing.

Additionally, the Director of the department where I was working had come across Peters and Waterman's *In Search of Excellence* (1982), and had started to send round cryptic memos telling us that we should 'stick to the knitting' and that we should develop 'loose/tight' properties in the services for which we were responsible. Although we were serious about our jobs and wanted to do our best for the clients we were working with, we had no idea what these prescriptions might mean, and knitting jokes abounded in the department for a number of weeks.

This was my first exposure to the already burgeoning management literature where there were a certain number of lessons to follow, in Peters and Waterman's case eight, that would guarantee success. After a time as a manager, I began to be drawn into internal consultancy within the department, and thereafter, as the market for consultancy began to expand in the private and public sectors, into external consultancy where these sorts of ideas and approaches seemed to have some cachet with the people I was working with. I had often read the books and they had not, and this gave me something of a head start. I began in the game by being half a step ahead of the people I was working with. They trusted me to know what it was I was talking about.

Over the course of the next decade I undertook consultancies across the private, public and third sectors which included strategic planning, evaluations, organisational review and organisational development (OD), the last of which was the subject of a burgeoning literature. I became one of a myriad practitioners who styled themselves OD consultants. OD is a very broad church of concepts drawing on psychological and humanistic theories and systems dynamics (principal adherents would be thinkers such as Argyris, 1982, 1990; Schein, 1987; Senge, 1990) which nonetheless is now practised in a way which has a number of assumptions in common. These are that an organisation can be thought of as a whole, or a system made up of different sub-systems. What interests contemporary OD practitioners is the way the parts are interacting and the relationships between them, not all of which are knowable. The organisation is taken to be a self-influencing system that arises out of the interaction of the different parts. It is not always possible to know how intervening on one part of the system will affect the other parts, since cause and effect can be separated by distance and time. However, it is possible for the organisation understood as a system to evolve into a different state. An organisational consultant who thinks of themselves as an OD practitioner can make an analysis of the organisation and by intervening on certain leverage points can act as a midwife to the new equilibrium state, which is more suited to the environment the organisation now finds itself in. Sometimes OD practitioners use metaphysical descriptions to describe this process such as when the organisation, understood as a self-regulating system, is described as a 'living, breathing, whole', or an organism. This particular phrasing reflects the origin of much systems theory from the biological sciences (von Bertalanffy, 1968): the implication is that the OD practitioner is some kind of doctor making a rigorous diagnosis which can bring the organisational organism back to health. In bringing over theories from the natural sciences which have proved so successful in both medicine and engineering, there is a tendency to clothe organisational theory in the language of natural science, a phenomenon I will be exploring in the course of this book.

At the heart of systems dynamics is an essential contradiction: on the one hand the organisation is thought of as a self-regulating system which evolves continuously into new states of greater harmony with its new environment. On the other hand, managers and/or consultants are thought to have a unique role in identifying, choosing, and propelling the organisation and its employees to this new desired state. The organisation is self-regulating and controlled by managers at the same time. Where the role of managers is to choose an ideal future for the organisation, and to develop a motivating vision to excite employees, the function of the consultant is to help the manager design the appropriate organisational systems for the organisation to evolve towards this ideal. One of these systems is thought to be the organisational values, which is the preserve of managers to articulate and for others to adopt and share through a process of discussion. A very common invitation to OD consultants is to help change the organisational 'culture', which is usually thought of as the enacted values of all staff, so that it becomes more fitting for the imagined future than the current one is deemed to be. There is usually a great emphasis on agreement, harmony and alignment towards an idealised future, and consultants often use the vocabulary of gap-closing between the inappropriate state we currently find ourselves in, and the ideally adapted state to which we aspire. I will be exploring each of these concepts, culture, vision, values as we proceed through the book.

During my time as an OD consultant, evaluator and facilitator, I have used and promoted a lot of these theories in my work in organisations. However, a number of difficulties began to arise for me in my practice. The first of these was the implied ability of the outside consultant to come up with an accurate 'diagnosis' of what was required and for this to lead to a remedy which would be guaranteed to work. My difficulty frequently occurred in contexts where I was invited to facilitate only one- or two-day away-days, as though this would be enough for me to understand what was going on in an organisation so that I could help. I felt under pressure to get it right: in an environment where there were more and more people offering what I had to offer, there was an increased tendency for consultants to claim that what they could bring would guarantee increased organisational effectiveness. Our methods would 'work'. However, instead of being able to close a gap, I found that the distance between what we promised and what we were able to achieve, particularly in the time frame that managers were prepared to commit to any investigative process, began to widen significantly. It was very difficult to know what was going on. Although I could always claim that I was making some difference to the organisations I was working with, it became increasingly clear to me that there were no organisational levers, or intervention points which could bring about the changes that we all said that we wanted in the way that we wanted them. I could see that sometimes my interventions were effective and sometimes they were not so effective, and I did not always know why there was a difference.

In fact, the more I ran facilitation events or intervened in organisations, the more I realised that I had little idea about what was really happening day to day in any organisation I was working with. It is possible on occasion to get glimpses of the rich hinterland of experience and history that staff bring with them during such interventions, but in general it is not usually these histories that are valued by the methods OD practitioners use, since they are drawn to more abstract idealising towards an organisational vision or mission, or sharing values. Systems theories are predicated on the concept of getting organisations to work in similar ways. OD methods suggest an ideal state, comprising eight characteristics of excellence or five systems disciplines, which employees are invited to take up, or on which they are encouraged to converge. My job, then, was less about enquiring into what they were doing and more about telling them what they ought to be doing from my unique perspective of being a detached observer who could compare their efforts with the ideal. On a number of occasions I was invited back to the same organisation some months after an event that I had facilitated or an intervention I had made, only to find myself confronting very similar problems manifesting themselves in different ways. Had I not prescribed the right advice? Had the employees not taken the medicine, or had they shortened the course of treatment?

On a number of occasions the intervention I had designed with managers was disrupted by some unforeseen confrontation between members of staff, or a well-articulated objection to the schema or framework that I was offering. What was clear to me was that bringing people together to talk about ostensibly neutral subjects like strategy or evaluation often provoked very strong feelings amongst those who had gathered together to discuss, including me. Sometimes these strong feelings were directed at me. When outbursts occurred I had to work with the expectation that this kind of intervention had created, that somehow I would keep the show on the road irrespective of what was happening, and I would fulfil the objectives that we had determined in advance. To do otherwise, to address the nature of the objection being raised or to enquire into the difficulty between employees, would be to act unprofessionally. As temporary leader in my role as consultant, I had to show that I was in charge and could 'manage conflict'. Increasingly I felt as though I was expected to be some kind of performer, to distract from what we needed to talk about with a box of tricks, slides containing grids, frameworks and principles to which we could all bend our efforts and find an ideal way of working together. We could not be wasting our time, turning the away-day into a 'talking shop' and getting distracted. It was not the 'little things' that were important, such as day-to-day disagreements, or the petty relationships that irk us in the workplace, but the 'big picture', the future towards which we all aspired. My job was to keep employees focused on the big picture, and not to let them get diverted by the here and now. But what exactly was I covering over by working in this way?

Systems or Complex Patterning?

Over a period of time I lost confidence in the models I was using because of the anxiety that they began to provoke in me every time they were probed, or every time I had to struggle to exert control over unruly and argumentative groups. It began to feel like a kind of game-playing, one where I had too much responsibility and too little power, or where I was presumed to have the kind of expertise that I had begun to doubt. I was also finding it difficult to keep up with the number of models that seemed to be appearing on the market, and their different, sometimes proprietary methods which required a licence or a franchise to operate. As the domain of management began to diversify, so too did the consultancy profession, with any number of different and sometimes conflicting methods claiming to provide what it was that we were all looking for. It was, as Minztberg, Ahlstrand and Lampel had observed in the field of strategy (1998), a real jungle of competing ideas all of which seemed to be suggesting a slightly different ideal and way of working, and none of which I found myself very comfortable with.

During my time on the Diploma in Management Studies many years previously one of the lecturers had introduced us to the ideas of Ralph Stacey who in the early 1990s had begun to write about the complexity sciences and the way they could offer analogies for thinking about the process of organising. Stacey has developed his ideas over the course of nearly twenty years, but for the last decade or so Stacey (2005, 2007, 2009) and colleagues at the Complexity and Management Centre, University of Hertfordshire (Stacey, Griffin and Shaw, 2000; Stacey and Griffin, 2005) have developed an interest in processes of communicative interaction between people and the potential that they have for transformation. Change, they argue, does not arise as a consequence of abstract idealising, but in the daily exploration of similarities and differences as people co-operate and compete in the workplace. In doing so Stacey and colleagues have mounted a radical critique of systems theory, arguing that organisations are not systems at all but the ongoing patterning of power and ideology as they emerge in local conversation. In arguing that this patterning arises from complex responsive processes of relating between engaged, interdependent people, Stacey and colleagues argue that there is nowhere for a manager to stand outside these processes as some kind of detached observer, intervening to bring about 'alignment' or to reset the 'system' towards some kind of ideal. Rather, both managers and consultants are themselves participants in the ongoing patterning of relations that they seek to change. Although some participants, managers and leaders, clearly have greater ability to influence the patterning that arises than others, what transpires will be the unplanned interweaving of everyone's intentions, which will follow no overall plan or blueprint. The ongoing interaction between people will inevitably provoke strong reactions and feelings as they negotiate with each other about how to go on, and this is an important aspect of the work to which one should pay attention. It is these ideas that I will exploring more fully in this book. For now it is probably enough to say that I joined the programme at Hertfordshire, completed my doctorate and now teach on the same programme.

I will be setting out a perspective that is critical of the dominant discourse of OD and systems thinking, and which offers instead an alternative that explores theories of emergence, paradox and complexity as they arise in social processes. The book explores what people do in organisations when they are working together and how they take up and make sense of management concepts that are ubiquitous no matter in what sector one might now find oneself working. These concepts constitute a body of ideas which is usually termed 'managerialism'; that is to say, an ideology that claims a unique role and expertise for an increasingly large cadre of managers. So, in the private, public and third sectors, many managers will have gone on similar kinds of management and leadership development programmes as the one I did, will engage in strategic planning and in doing so will have set out their vision, mission and values statements, will have had their performance managed by others and will engage with consultants to help sort out one type of organisational problem or another using diagnostic tools and frameworks. In doing so they will probably have worked with some of the management ideas that I have begun to sketch out above, and which now inform what it is that they are doing. This is not to say that management is practised everywhere the same: each sector has its own particular characteristics, but there has been a convergence in the kinds of concepts that are taken up by managers wherever they practise. These are everyday, taken for granted ideas and activities in organisations to which we have grown so accustomed that it would be hard to imagine organisational life without them. What I intend to do in this book is to explore more fully the thinking which underpins these kinds of management methods, and how they actually work out in practice. How helpful are they, and what kinds of problems arise as a consequence of taking them up?

In the course of this book I will be setting out a case, developed from my experience as a manager and consultant, that many of the management approaches that are taken for granted in organisations, and which are taught on management courses and replicated by management consultants, actually get in the way of doing good work and hinder rather than help. They promise what they cannot deliver because they are predicated on ideas of predictability and control and imply powers of intervention on the part of managers and consultants which they cannot possess. People in organisations do not fit into two-by-two grids, and are not parts of wholes. The interweaving of intentions, hopes, aspirations and behaviour of people who are both inside and outside organisations, who behave both rationally and irrationally, will bring about outcomes which no one has predicted and which no one has planned.

I will go on to argue that not only is the promise of management largely unfulfilled, but management methods often distract from the day-to-day fluctuations in relationships between people and the way they are making sense of what it is they are doing. It is in these everyday exchanges, I will argue, that the beginnings of transformative change are really happening. Management frameworks are often pursued with such anxiety on the part of managers about 'getting it right', and often with some degree of rigour, that the process can leave employees feeling unrecognised and ignored. This can prove deeply frustrating and dispiriting to everyone concerned. It can also lead to recrimination within organisations if conclusions are drawn that some planned change in organisations has been unsuccessful because employees were not operating the model properly or have not been trying hard enough. Both managers and consultants get drawn into playing a game they can never win. The thing about grids, tools and frameworks is that they are often convincing in their logic, reassuring in their certainty, powerful in their way of reducing complex phenomena and representing them in simple schemata, but ultimately they are decontextualised, reductive and misleading. They exclude as much as they include and without history, context and the particularities of what consultants and managers have to deal with in their situation, they can prove unhelpful.

By engaging with the daily practice of managers in organisations this book tries to explore contemporary management theory as it is practised in organisations in a number of different ways. In doing so, it will be posing a challenge to managerialist claims. One of my approaches will be to use narrative as a method, the reasons for using narrative and reflection on narrative I will discuss in Chapter 3. What this means practically then, is that I will write about an episode of organisational life that I have been engaged in with others, either as a consultant or manager, a trustee or director, and then will explore what this might mean for the people I am working with in terms of organisational theory and the kinds of thinking that underpin it. I will then go on to add different ways of understanding the same experience drawing on insights from the complexity sciences, as well as those academics like Stacey, and other philosophers and sociologists who have also grappled with complex social processes in their work. In the process of doing this I am trying to generalise from the particular, which brings with it its own difficulties which need addressing. In the end, though, this book will stand or fall on the degree of resonance that readers find in it with their own experience of working in organisations, and the extent to which they find what I am writing about compelling and illuminating, which I imagine will be varied.

The reason for suspecting that it might be varied is that in the course of writing this book and other articles, which I have submitted for publication, mostly successfully, I have encountered some strong reactions. The way I have gone about discussing management in organisations and the ideas I have been using have clearly provoked some reviewers: people seem either to be very enthused by what I have written or, just as likely to take a violent dislike to it. As part of the justification for why I think this book is necessary, particularly given the plethora of management and organisational writing that is available elsewhere which I mentioned above, I think it is important to engage with both parties and to try and probe what I think is aggravating or exciting them. I do this not with the intention of excusing or justifying myself, but as a way of further setting out the thinking behind the book and what I think it is and is not possible to do when writing and thinking about the experience of organising.

What exactly is it about the nature of the ideas in this book that seems to provoke so? There are three main criticisms that are levelled at what I have written and that my colleagues have encountered too. These are:

1.   There are no grids, tables or frameworks or prescriptions for what managers should do. Where are the 'tools' which managers can use?

2.   Linked to the first point, the examples given in what I have been writing about are too negative and do not make enough of a case for management.

3.   There is too much sociology and philosophy included in the critique: the views in this book are more useful for historians of management or sociologists, but not managers.

I will deal with each of the criticisms sequentially.

1. There are no grids, tables or frameworks or prescriptions for what to do and the critique offers nothing by way of 'tools' for managers.

This particular criticism seems to arise most sharply from academics who make their living teaching in business schools, and who, presumably spend a lot of their time teaching such grids and frameworks to their students. One academic reviewer recommended me to read *Built to Last: Successful Habits of Visionary Companies* by Collins and Porras (2005), since it was 'terrific', particularly as synthesised in a monograph the authors had written translating their lessons from the private to the public sectors. It supposedly offered a helpful antidote to what I had written. I am grateful for this recommendation since I think it is a good example of the kind of management book that I was alluding to earlier in this chapter, and it sets out exactly what I am concerned not to do in this book. It raises many of the organisational concepts the provenance of which I explore in later chapters, such as vision, values, and the role of leaders and managers. Although my book is very unlikely to be an airport bookshop purchase like *Built to Last* and I am not attempting to write anything like the same thing, it is nonetheless worth dwelling a while on my reviewer's recommendation and thinking about the kind of understanding of management and the role of managers it represents.

Collins and Porras' book is in many ways a significant achievement: it has sold millions of copies worldwide and has been translated into 16 languages. This kind of blockbuster success is similar to that achieved by Peters and Waterman (*In Search of Excellence*, 1982) and Stephen Covey's *The Seven Habits of Highly Effective People* (1999), which shares a similar-sounding title of Collins and Porras' work. All three develop from a similar formula. This involves carrying out a large number of interviews with big name managers, or managers working in (usually American) companies which are world famous, generalising from them, then representing these generalisations in some kind of highly shaped or arresting format. There may be seven habits, or five lessons (in the case of Peter Senge (1990), a fourth very popular author, there are five disciplines), or three things to remember. The idea then, is to abstract from years of probably turbulent company history which is stripped away to produce a small number of memorable rules for other managers to follow which are applicable in any company or organisation operating in any context.

In Collins and Porras' case, there are a number of characteristics that highly successful, or what the authors call 'visionary' companies share, which are articulated as prescriptions:

1. Be a clock builder not a timekeeper: all successful companies focused on building their organisations so that it would run 'smooth as a clock'.

2. Have a clear set of values which should be timeless and only amended in extreme circumstances.

3. Preserve the company's core ideology, although unlike the values the ideology can be changed over time.

4. Set Big Hairy Audacious Goals (BHAG) – alongside day-to-day shifts in ideology there needs to be an accompanying project of setting longer term audacious goals that are seen to be 'paradigm shifting' (such as sending a man to the moon).

5. Have a cult-like culture – everyone one who comes to work for the company should be indoctrinated into the company like being infected with a disease. It is imperative that staff create a 'tight fit' with others in the company.

6. Try and use things that work – this prescription encourages companies to keep abreast of, or anticipate changes.

7. Make the core ideology/values a reality – this is achieved by encouraging everyone to align across the organisation.

This book has particular recommendations, but is also recognisable as a set of prescriptions which both conforms to and shapes expectations about what management books should contain: it is part of a long-established and repeated trend in management thinking. The book contains advice which is sufficiently generalised and idealised as to be almost gnomic. And in producing such sententious recommendations business books of this kind are close to self-help or even religious literature, since they are offering rule-like precepts, disciplines by which managers should live their lives. In some cases it can be hard to disagree with what the authors say – who, for example, could disagree with the idea of keeping what works or needing to continue to innovate? – but equally hard to know how to take them up. Other prescriptions are much more contentious and draw little attention to the kinds of consequences that would ensue from ruthlessly excluding those who do not agree with company ideology. The authors are explicit that the company should be run like a cult with all the concomitant manipulation that this implies, a concept which we will explore later in Chapter 6 on values. Although Collins and Porras have suffered a similar experience to Peters and Waterman in the sense that many of the companies they have written about have not done so well over the period since the book was written, this seems to have done little to deter people from buying it. The combination of tough love, heroic determination and manipulation clearly has strong resonance with the millions of people buying the book, and for the academics and business consultants who use it, or recommend that others do.

What does this then tell us about the prevailing understanding of management as a profession? How might we account for the book's success, at least in terms of the number of copies sold? I will be exploring both these questions during the course of the book looking both at the ways that the orthodox theories of management get taken up, replicated and perpetuated, and the way that idealised concepts can be understood as a way of appealing to the religious imagination of people who work in increasingly instrumentalised and flattened organisations. In the chapters on vision and values I will also be claiming that appeals to the religious imagination are often taken up as forms of social control.

During the course of this book I intend engaging with the ideology that underpins the kind of recommendations that authors like Collins and Porras are making. In using the word ideology I am responding to the way that the authors themselves use the word and turn to the moral philosopher Alasdair MacIntyre's definition of the term as a way of further explaining it. In an essay discussing scientific method as taken up in the social sciences, MacIntyre argues that in any given situation there are contestable understandings about what is really happening:

> It is a central feature of established social orders that they tend to embody in their social institutions denials of the centrality of conflict, argument, contestability and unpredictability in human life; and it is a central feature of most social theories that they share this characteristic with most social orders ... social victory at this deep level is the achievement of inducing those who participate in the practice to agree in conceptualising their activities in such a way that one of the contestable interpretations no longer appears contestable, but simply how things are – 'the facts'.
>
> (MacIntyre in Knight, 1998: 58–59)

MacIntyre does not necessarily impute any motives to those advancing an ideology, nor does he think that ideologies must be wholly untrue. However, they are always put forward in a way that tries to cover over contestability and conflict to present a particular view of the world as the only view. The particular belief that much contemporary management literature is sustaining is the unique ability of managers and leaders to intervene in organisational life to bring about intended consequences, a belief that has developed into what is now termed by critical writers 'managerialism'. Much of the vocabulary of managerialism is evident in Collins and Porras' book and in this particular case it also cloaks the manager with heroism too. The manager is an undaunted figure driving for continuous improvement, never put off by the half-baked efforts of others, ruthless enough to weed out those employees not completely committed to what the company is doing, and is continuously moving forwards towards an idealised future. By creating the right conditions in an organisation the manager or leader (and the distinction between the two is something we might explore later on) shapes the future. Of course, not all management literature supports this kind of thinking, and there is a substantial minority who are critical of it (Alvesson, Bridgeman and Willmott, 2009; Thompson and McHugh, 2009; Tsoukas, 2004; Wilmott, 1993, 2003). However, as a dominant set of themes in the resources available to managers, it is not surprising that they have a significant effect on practice as well as shaping the expectation about what management literature should look like. Who wouldn't want to be a management hero, particularly with the rewards and status which are accorded to people we have come to understand as such?

As far as the academic who reviewed my work is concerned, there are a number of other strengths of this kind of approach. First, the authors of many contemporary management books carry out face to face interviews with successful business leaders: according to my particular academic reviewer, this makes their work empirical. These interviews are nearly always taken at face value: there is little critical enquiry or doubt expressed about the way that 'top managers' present their world views and whether they might be influenced by the very heroic literature that we have been discussing during the last section. To a degree the discussion around what management is, is intensely self-referential as I will be demonstrating in the book. Second, the recommendations are helpful to managers looking for solutions to their organisational problems because they simplify and present a recipe for success developed out of the richness of other people's experience. Third, ideas are presented in a way which is easily understandable. It has become a tradition in contemporary management literature to use systems diagrams, schemata or the ubiquitous four square matrixes (the Ansoff matrix (1957), the Boston Consulting Group matrix) to present findings in easily assimilable ways which are then thought to be 'practical' for other managers to help them know how to act. These kinds of representations lend themselves to management education understood as training, where the provision of tools and schemata is intended to try and reduce uncertainty and reduce blame for unpredictable outcomes. I am contrasting training with education and unashamedly privileging the latter revealing my own ideological conviction that education is best undertaken supporting people to think for themselves rather than simply learning what others want to tell them.

To write a book such as my own, then, which engages not in neat but reductive abstractions but the daily messy reality of what people do every day in organisations, is clearly a break from the paradigm set by many popular management books. Rather than providing rules I am asking questions. Instead of adopting a tone of certainty I am encouraging radical doubt. Instead of simplifying I am pointing to the fact that everyday life in organisations is complex and uncertain. By exploring everyday concepts used in managerialism it will be an invitation to the reader to think about how they are thinking. And thinking, as the political theorist Hannah Arendt wrote in a famous essay (1971), has a tendency to unravel what it is we are thinking about.

And while we are thinking about prescriptions and recommendations, what is the basis for my academic reviewer believing that there is a case for making prescriptions for others to follow? Just how successful are generalised, abstract models and schemata for helping managers and consultants to make sense of organisational life? It is my contention that many contemporary books on management, replete with recipes for success, are analytical, concrete, logical, convincing and wrong.

WHAT IS THE EVIDENCE BASE FOR MANAGEMENT PRESCRIPTIONS?

In recent books both Khurana (2007) and Stacey (2010) have documented how management has developed as a profession, and how it has struggled to gain respectability, authority and legitimacy. Professionalisation brings with it the social rewards and privileges of respect and status, and Khurana charts how American business leaders since the end of the nineteenth century tried to elevate the profession of management above the vulgar activity of mere profit-making. At the end of the nineteenth century even the business community was sceptical that entrepreneurship could ever be taught, but Khurana argues that the drive for legitimacy and purpose led the business vanguard to the founding of business schools in universities. Between the rise of research universities in the United States, the impetus towards professionalism for the practice of management and contemporary optimism about the civilising potential of science, it made sense to found management schools as departments in universities and to establish it as being a science-based discipline. Frederick W. Taylor, one of the founding fathers of scientific management, was enthusiastic about the possibilities:

> Under scientific management arbitrary power, arbitrary dictation, ceases and every single subject, large and small, becomes the question for scientific investigations, for reduction to law ... The man at the head of the business under scientific management is governed by rules and laws which have been developed through hundreds of experiments just as much as the workman is, and the standards which have been developed are equitable.
>
> (Bendix, 1956: 278)

It is commonly thought that Taylor developed his thinking about scientific management as a way of dominating workers: to the contrary, he had quite utopian aspirations for management as a means of liberating them and establishing industrial harmony as all sides agreed upon the one best way of undertaking the work. Although management methods and thinking have developed during the last hundred years beyond Taylor's experiments which broke industrial processes down into small, measurable segments, nonetheless the themes of this kind of approach are still evident today. Many contemporary management methods are predicated on ideas of rule-following understood as best practice, and the interests of employees and managers are presumed to converge around an agreed vision and values. Management is a neutral, technical discipline that rises above politics, affect and subjectivity and can be practised in similar ways across different organisational domains and contexts.

Technical disciplines surely require 'tools' which is what I think my critical reviewer was alluding to. The manager can intervene with her tools in an organisation in the same way a mechanic can adjust an engine, or a doctor uses a stethoscope to listen to a patient's heart. The manager stands detached from the organisation they are part of and act upon it as a scientist conducts an experiment.

There have been a number of recent explicit attempts to bring over disciplines from the natural sciences through a turn to 'evidence based management' (Rousseau, 2006; Pfeffer and Sutton, 2006). Denise Rousseau, recently elected President of the American Academy of Management, draws on an analogy with evidence-based medicine as a 'success story' in her article advocating for evidence-based management and sums up the key concepts of what the practice would look like:

- learning about cause–effect connections in professional practices;

- isolating the variations that *measurably* affect desired outcomes;

- creating a culture of evidence-based decision-making and research participation; and

- using information-sharing communities to reduce overuse, underuse, and misuse of specific practices (Rousseau, 2006: 259–260).

A hundred years after Taylor was putting forward similar ideas, Rousseau is still writing into the same tradition, believing that it is possible to derive law-like generalisations from the practice of management in organisations, to 'measure' what works, to identify independent variables and by doing so to instil 'best practice'. Pfeffer and Sutton are slightly more sceptical than Rousseau in the sense that they have a much more nuanced understanding of what we might take to be evidence in the domain of social practices. They document the dizzying array of academic articles, advice and frameworks which all claim to offer advice on management practice and note how contradictory many of them are. They are critical of strategic planning and sceptical about the weight attached to the performance of heroic CEOs. Indeed, they take issue with Collins and Porras' idea that you should routinely fire people who do not conform to the company's ideology or hit performance targets, but they nonetheless conclude that it is not the lack of evidence for what works which is the problem, but weak sifting of the evidence, poor implementation or poor systems. They themselves produce nine principles of evidence-based management advising managers to stick with the 'facts'. Pfeffer and Sutton try to have it both ways, pointing out on the one hand that the prescriptions for good management are many, and yet on the other hand recommending that managers stick with what works and producing in time honoured form their own prescriptions. This is an example of the kind of double-think that would have impressed Orwell as scholars produce prescriptions about not having prescriptions.

So what does work? How robust is the evidence base for management, and what would a fact in management look like?

Stacey (2009) carries out a review of different studies which investigate how successful a number of management methods have been in improving organisational performance. In the process of doing so he considers studies of strategic planning, Total Quality Management (TQM), and Human Resource Management, as well as the generic proposition that one can learn lessons from studying successful companies. Stacey's conclusions are that the evidence base for particular management techniques is often weak and contradictory. For example, one review by Boyne and Walker (2002) of 19 studies of TQM concluded that there was no comprehensive support for the idea that TQM improves company performance. They go on to point out that governments around the world continue to introduce TQM into their public sectors without there being a clear evidence base for doing so. Meanwhile Eskilsdon (2006) carried out a survey of 150 company turnarounds in the USA and concluded that TQM implementation strategies had limited impact. Stacey is sceptical of the claim that lessons can be derived from supposedly successful companies, observing that the average life expectancy of any organisation is roughly 40 years, and as they flourish and fade away, any randomly selected population of organisations is likely to produce those that are successful and those that are not: success is time-bound, as other critics of both Peters and Waterman's excellent companies, or Collins and Porras' companies built to last have pointed out. Stacey draws the conclusion that there is no comprehensive, reliable evidence base for many of the dominant management prescriptions.

In his consideration of the teaching of leadership in many US business schools including Harvard Business School, his own employer, Khurana reaches the same conclusion:

> *From a scholarly perspective, then, leadership as a body of knowledge after decades of scholarly attention under the social science research lens ... remains without a widely accepted theoretical framework or a cumulative empirical understanding leading to a usable body of knowledge. Moreover, the probability that leadership studies will make significant strides in developing a fundamental knowledge base is fairly low.*
>
> *(Khurana, 2007: 357)*

Similarly, in an article that reviewed all digitally-accessible management journal articles up to 2008, Reay, Whitney and Kohn (2009) attempted to answer the question 'What's the evidence for evidence-based management?' In doing so they were interested in two levels of enquiry: how good is the evidence adduced in so-called evidence-based journal articles, and what is the evidence that taking up evidence-based management works? Their conclusions are that the majority of articles pointing to the importance of evidence-based management are themselves weak in adducing evidence, and similarly weak in making the case that evidence-based management really does improve organisational performance (and from the perspective they are taking Reay, Whitney and Kohn assume that the highest form of evidence we might adduce is derived from large-scale randomised control trials, a method which is widely used in medicine):

> *First, we see that there are a large number of articles devoted to the topic, but most encourage adoption of EBMgt based on opinion and anecdotal information. This is really not sufficient evidence on which to base managerial decisions, any more than we would encourage physicians to change their practice based on opinions and anecdotes.*
>
> *(2009: 17)*

However, Reay, Whitney and Kohn do not give up on evidence-based management and see promising signs of local successes of good practice, which they still think might work elsewhere if knowledge could be adequately transferred. They also believe that an increased attention by managers to evidence and a greater ability to assess it would likely lead to better management practice.

In Chapter 8 on performance management I review the evidence that it makes any difference to organisational performance and adduce scholars who argue that its efficacy is still partial, contested and inconclusive.

If we acknowledge what Stacey (2009), Khurana (2007) and Reay, Whitney and Kohn (2009) have to say, as well as a number of other scholars critical of the managerialist project we might begin to wonder at the way that certain management methods get taken up and replicated as though there were a good reason for doing so. We would have to ask ourselves why people become so wedded to the methods that they are using when there seems to be so little evidential basis for doing so, and why it provokes such strong feelings, like those of my reviewer, when these methods are called into question.

So the short answer to my academic reviewer, which I will explore at greater length in the course of the book, is that there are no grids, frameworks or prescriptions for what managers should do in this book because I have found no research basis for including any, neither as an academic nor as a practitioner. The conceptual premise of many contemporary management methods is that the practice of management is a science, and that it is possible to identify generalisable rules for managers to apply in all circumstances with predictable results with an if-then causality. In this book I will be giving an alternative account, that what happens in organisations is context-dependent, constrained by history and non-linear. Human beings have a tendency to act in particular ways, but the exact way their different intentions interweave is unpredictable, and that the manager or consultant is a co-participant in any organisational process. They have no unique overview or ability to change the 'system as a whole'. I understand that this might be a difficult set of assumptions to work with if one made one's living teaching managers what to do in a conventional business school. It raises questions about what it means to be professional, and makes problematic the notion of expertise and dealing with the unknown. It is a potentially destabilising claim, particularly for those scholars who stake their truth claim on having produced some generalisable recipe for success.

2. The examples are too negative and do not make enough of a case for management – the cult of positivity

Sometimes when I am talking to groups of managers there is a tendency for them to swing to the opposite end of the spectrum if I suggest that there are problems with the theoretical underpinnings of strategic planning, or if I question conventional theories of leadership. They conclude, wrongly, that I am suggesting that they should not make plans at all, or that if I question the degree of control that leaders really exert then they assume that I am saying that leaders should do nothing and just 'let things emerge'. I hope it will be clear to readers of this book that I am saying neither such thing. On the contrary I make the case that managers should participate actively with others to try and bring about what they intend, make plans, direct others and do all the things that managers are supposed to do, but with a good deal of questioning about the kinds of methods they may be obliged to use, and what they cover over and inhibit. I hope this book is both an invitation to think about how managers are thinking and experiencing (although thought is also experience), as well as a request to take seriously what actually happens when we undertake management activities with others, including our affective responses. The last is also important data for considering whether we are working skilfully and is not something that can simply be disregarded or 'managed'.

It is probably a fair observation that in writing which concerns itself with taking a critical or oppositional view of more orthodox ways of understanding the world there may be a tendency to over-egg the pudding and to choose examples from working life where orthodoxies have been challenged spectacularly. However, I think it is important to include these, since they occur much more frequently than much contemporary management literature would have us believe. And in taking a critical position I find myself agreeing with the political philosopher Raymond Geuss when he says that:

> ... *any society has a tendency to try to mobilise human inertia in order to protect itself as much as possible from radical change, and one main way in which this can be done is through the effort to impose the requirement of 'positivity' or 'constructiveness' on potential critics: you can't criticise the police system, the system of labour law, the organisation of the health services etc., unless you have a full elaborated, positive alternative to propose.*

> (2008: 96)

To impose a criterion of positivity, Geuss argues, is to try and dictate the terms on which you are prepared to be criticised, and thus control the debate. As I indicated earlier, I am in no doubt that writing about management and the processes of organising is a struggle over ideology, and ideology is an attempt to confirm a particular set of power relations. I hope that in the course of this book I will provide enough recognisable examples of what happens when some of the conventional prescriptions are taken up actively in organisations for the reader to appreciate the strength of my argument, irrespective of whether I can produce something alternative in terms which they might be familiar.

Contemporary management theories sometimes contribute to the thread of breezy positivity and instrumentalism in contemporary life, particularly when they appear to borrow from sales techniques and suggest that the role of the manager is to turn all negatives to positives, and that all aspects of human endeavour can be managed. In this respect there is a very close proximity between management orthodoxy and the burgeoning shelves of self-help literature. Management methods, we are told, are a way of turning everything to the good, of bringing about positive change, of managing conflict and mobilising talent: to borrow from Collins and Porras, relentless self-improvement with the aim of doing better and better, forever into the future. The popular facilitation method Appreciative Inquiry (AI) (Cooperrider and Whitney, 2005) is based on a similar assumption, that by enquiring into the good, one can bring about the good. AI draws on a long tradition of humanistic and utopian thought which suggests that by tapping into their 'inner' potential, humans can bring about radical, positive transformation with and for others. To a degree this is a way of warding off critique, since even critique needs to be 'positive', although positive for whom is left a little unclear.

In this book I support the view that all human interaction has the potential to be transformative, but also go on to argue that the potential for both positive and negative consequences will arise at the same time. And what we consider to be positive is also an ideological judgement. For example, in this book I discuss episodes in organisational life where we have been exploring conflict rather than trying to 'manage' it. From the perspective of AI choosing to work with the strong and sometimes negative feelings arising from conflict might be viewed as a failure to discover the positive. If one were to take the view that creativity in organisations is also accompanied by destruction, however, one would be accepting that conflict, negativity and crisis are part and parcel of human interaction and cannot always be turned to the good.

In developing an alternative theory of what managers do and claiming that this is rooted in the day-to-day messy reality, I am suggesting that managers might develop greater confidence about working with uncertainty. This will involve accepting that human experience is inevitably both positive and negative depending on how one makes sense of it. To claim otherwise or to adduce some superhuman skill in managers to turn everything to the positive is to set them up for failure. In writing about organisations, however, it is also important to mention that most managers are doing their best, working with an imperfect grasp of imperfect theories of management. There is no criminal intent, and many managers are obliged to work with methods and frameworks with which they may have little sympathy themselves.

However, in comparison with the offer of hearty recipes for success, this book may seem like an anaemic and meat-free alternative.

3. There is too much sociology and philosophy: this book is more useful for historians of management or sociologists, but not managers

It is understandable and expected that in any academic domain scholars will allude to the work of other scholars in their field. Without this process of mutual referral it would be hard for any academic discipline to develop. At the same time, a body of literature can become self-referential and justify the case it is making on the basis that others have made the same case. The argument I was making above on the lack of evidential support for most management methods is a good example, where there is a strong incentive, both professional and financial, for continuing to sustain the argument for managerialism, although at the same time as making the pitch that the particular method being offered is more effective than all the others. Many management scholars and business schools have a big stake in the game they are describing and have an interest in amplifying that game. Of course, I have no less of a stake and make my living in the same way, although I would argue that I do so in opposition to the dominant way of thinking rather in support of it. Rather than amplifying the game and trying to speed it up, my intention is to try and draw attention to the way that the game is being played, how the rules affect the course of play and who benefits. To do this is to risk having one's bona fides called into question, as I have experienced from some of the reviews of the articles and chapters I have written previously.

Thankfully, I am joining a substantial minority of scholars, who, from one perspective or another take a critical view of managerialism, and in doing so often draw on traditions of scholarship outside the domain into which they are writing. It is to this minority tradition that I aim to make a small contribution.

Just to make my own ideological convictions clearer. In drawing on analogies from the complexity sciences I am exploring the consequences for managerial practice of dealing with uncertainty, rather than certainty. As I do so the work of Stacey and colleagues will often be my guide. The arguments for drawing on the sociology of Norbert Elias (1939/1991, 1939/2000), and Pierre Bourdieu and L. Wacquant (1992); Bourdieu (1977) amongst others, is because of their particular interest in the processes of power relating and the way that this gives rise to both predictable and unpredictable social patterning over time. In turning to philosophers in the American pragmatist tradition, such as G.H. Mead (1934) and John Dewey (2005), and the political theorist Hannah Arendt (1958) I am doing so because of their patient attention to everyday experience, their interest in the paradox of the particular and the general, and their identification of the importance of negotiation, conflict and politics in helping us go on together. Mead in particular has rooted a theory of transformative change in everyday communicative interaction. This coincides with my own interest in everyday practices in organisations. I will also adduce contemporary theories of management, but this will often be to compare and contrast these with how other scholars in different traditions have written about the same phenomena. In acknowledging a reviewer who praised what I have written I also intend signalling more clearly to readers when I am about to embark upon a more philosophical section of what I am writing.

All of the thinkers I have adduced above as my guides in writing about the process of organising are less interested in rules and the supposed foundations from which they emerge, than in social practises. In pursuing their enquiry into experience, social interaction and what informs it, they draw on a philosophical tradition that can be traced back to Heraclitus by way of Hegel. In taking an interest in the dialectic of self and other, order and disorder, the known and the unknown, in process, these thinkers do pose a challenge to what would be termed a realist position of many contemporary management writers, perhaps including my academic critic. Realists think that rules can be discovered which govern the way human beings relate, and these will be able to be applied irrespective of context, history and time. To quote Tsoukas (2004) on the realist perspective:

Ontologically, it assumes a pre-given world. Epistemologically, it is based on the belief that only pure thinking can yield reliable knowledge, by allowing a deductive approach. And praxeologically it adheres to instrumental action: actors follow explicit rules or apply explicit precepts in order to achieve their goals. Action is driven by reliable prior knowledge.

(Tsoukas, 2004: 361)

Throughout this book I will be discussing whether we do, in fact, think before acting on the basis of theories of the world deduced from 'facts', rather than thinking on the basis of action. By drawing on insights from the complexity sciences and the philosophers and sociologists outlined above I will be making an alternative case that organisations are unique, that generalised tendencies to act get taken up in particular ways according to context and history. By writing about what I have experienced in organisations I will be trying to demonstrate a different form of empiricism and an iterative understanding of time. If management is a kind of practical and political action, a practice, then time is rendered more complex than the if-then causality espoused by a more realist approach to management, where we are often impelled relentlessly and sequentially towards an idealised future. In following Alasdair MacIntyre (1981), who has written about the importance of understanding professions to be historically and socially evolving practices, I am also making the case that we need to take into account the past as much as the future. For MacIntyre a practice understood as a living tradition is 'an historically extended, socially embodied argument …' (ibid.: 222). Time, then, is iterative as we anticipate future possibilities which the past has made available to the present. The practice involves a continuous conversation between practitioners about what we take to be the good, as we will discover later in this book.

So offering a critique of dominant ways of understanding management and arguing that it cannot be reduced to rules and prescriptions does not mean to imply that there is nothing to say about management and managing. But it does mean that we need to look for different ways of doing so.

Conclusions and Structure of the Book

In this chapter I have outlined how it was that I first got drawn into management and consultancy as part of a general social shift towards the ideological view that managers and the profession of management has a unique role in bringing about transformative change in organisations, and by inference, in society. I have accepted the term coined by others that we might refer to this ideology as 'managerialism'. I have drawn attention to the ways in which managerialism has been so successful that it would be impossible now to take part in organisational life without bumping up against one or other of the taken for granted methods, such as strategic planning or performance management. The claims of managerialism are often rooted in concepts brought over from the natural sciences, although there is also a good degree of hype, faddism and blind faith. But some very prevalent ideas are that management is a science, and the manager and/or consultant is a detached, objective observer of organisations, who can use highly abstract tools and frameworks largely derived from systems thinking to diagnose organisational 'problems' and recommend and implement wholesale 'solutions'. These methods are rooted in theories of linear cause and effect, and predicated on ideas of predictability and control. In the use of these abstract models, people and what they do in their everyday predictable and unpredictable interactions with others, largely disappear. I have described my own experience as a manager and consultant who has both used and promoted these ideas.

In beginning to unpick the claims made for management I have found, with other critics, that there are not many grounds for thinking that most management methods are derived from a secure evidential base, or even that there is likely to be one, particularly as evidence is understood from a natural science perspective. I have found myself intrigued by the experience of airing this critique along with others, when I have encountered very strong reactions from other scholars working in more orthodox managerial environments to what I have to say. One might conclude that any profession confident of its intellectual heritage would not feel so easily provoked.

My own discomfort with the methods and ideas I have been using led me to discover the work of others who have pursued the radical implications of assuming that that the world is inherently unpredictable. How is it that there is stability and instability at the same time, and yet most contemporary management methods presume only the former? What, then, is the role of a manager and consultant if they are working with predictability and unpredictability at the same time? How do employees make sense of everyday uncertainty, and how might their managers support them? If the organisation is not a 'system', then what is it? In the remainder of this book I will begin to explore some of these issues.

The second chapter treats the nature of consultancy, since it is as a consultant that I am now often invited into organisations. What is it that people think they are getting when they contract a consultant or facilitator, and how do I, and others, understand the process that we are engaged in together? The chapter takes up the idea that an appreciation of politics, understood as people's daily attempts to co-operate and compete in the workplace to get things done, is fundamental to understanding the role of a consultant.

Chapter 3 reflects further on the methods I am using in my work and in this book, and locates them in a broader research tradition. The chapter makes the case that managers could also think of themselves as researchers and participants in the processes in which they are engaged, rather than as detached observers. By paying attention to the way that population-wide patterning arises in organisations and the part that they have to play in this, is one of the central roles of managers and leaders.

Chapter 4 investigates leadership and deconstructs some of the contemporary discourse on what leaders are and what they do. It argues that much contemporary literature on leadership is profoundly contradictory and at the same time hopelessly idealises the role of leader. The chapter calls into question the separation of leadership from management and argues that leaders are as constrained as everyone else in the organisational context. If leaders can never live up to the idealisation, what is it that they can do? The chapter argues that leadership is a social and improvisational activity that arises in groups of people whose identities arise in acts of mutual recognition.

Chapters 5, 6 and 7 take up the tripartite vision/mission, values and strategy to explore the thinking that underpins much strategic planning which is widely practised in many organisations. Vision and values are also themes of tremendous idealisation in dominant management texts and are at the same time taken up instrumentally, as though they are tools of management. There is usually a great emphasis placed on the need for employees to align their behaviour and values with those described by senior managers. These chapters argue that vision, values and strategy are inevitably themes which will be contested and struggled over by employees, and it is in these struggles that innovation and novelty arises rather than through the planned interventions of calculating managers.

Chapter 8 reflects upon performance management and discusses how possible it is to judge the performance of individuals who work in groups.

Arguing against the dominant understanding of performance as an individual act, the chapter describes how one might understand it as a social and group activity which demands a very different interpretation of what we might mean by the word 'performance'.

Chapter 9 is a summary of the book and looks to draw some conclusions from the preceding chapters. The only way that it is helpful to think of management as a science is if we also take up the non-linear sciences. To do so automatically problematises the simple prescriptions and if-then causality of much contemporary management discourse. The way we pay attention to how we are participating in the ongoing patterning of interactions between us and our colleagues will help us develop a much more reality-congruent understanding of management as practice.

Above all this book is an encouragement to practising managers and consultants to take seriously what they are doing and to notice what happens when they are doing it.

References

Alvesson, M., Bridgeman, T. and Willmott, H. (2009) *The Oxford Handbook of Critical Management Studies*, Oxford: Oxford University Press.

Ansoff, I. (1957) Strategies for diversification, *Harvard Business Review*, 35(5) Sept–Oct: 113–124.

Arendt, H. (1958) *The Human Condition*, Chicago: University of Chicago Press.

—— (1971) Thinking and moral considerations: A lecture, *Social Research*, 38(3): 417–446.

Argyris, C. (1982) *Reasoning, Learning and Action: Individual and Organisational*, San Francisco: Jossey Bass.

—— (1990) *Overcoming Organizational Defensives: Facilitating Organizational Learning*, Needham Heights, MA: Alleyn and Bacon.

Bendix, R. (1956/2001) *Work and Authority in Industry: Managerial Ideologies in the Course of Industrialisation*, New Brunswick, NJ: Transaction.

Boyne, A.G. and Walker, R.M. (2002) Total quality management and performance: An evaluation of the evidence and lessons for research on public organizations, *Public Performance and Management Review*, 26(2): 111–130.

Bourdieu, P. (1977) *Outline of a Theory of Practice*, Cambridge: Cambridge University Press.

—— and Wacquant, L. (1992) *An Invitation to Reflexive Sociology*, Chicago: University of Chicago Press.

Chia, R.C.H. and Holt, R. (2009) *Strategy without Design: The Silent Efficacy of Indirect Action*, Cambridge: Cambridge University Press.

Collins, J. and Porras, J. (2005) *Built to Last: Successful Habits of Visionary Companies*, New York: Random House.

Cooperrider, D. and Whitney, D. (2005) *Appreciative Inquiry: A Positive Revolution in Change*, New York: Berrett-Koehler.

Covey, S. (1999) *The Seven Habits of Highly Effective People*, London: Simon and Schuster.

Dewey, J. (2005) *The Quest for Certainty: A Study of the Relation of Knowledge and Action*, New York: Kessinger.

Elias, N. (1939/1991). *The Society of Individuals*. Oxford: Blackwell.

—— (1939/2000) *The Civilising Process*. Oxford: Blackwell.

Eskildson, L. (2006) TQM's role in corporate success: Analyzing the evidence, *National Productivity Review*, 14(4): 25–38.

Geuss, R. (2008) *Philosophy and Real Politics*, Woodstock: Prince University Press.

Khurana, R. (2007) *From Higher Aims to Hired Hands: The Social Transformation of American Business Schools and the Unfulfilled Promise of Management as a Profession*, Princeton NJ: Princeton University Press.

Knight, K. (ed.) (1998) *The MacIntyre Reader*, Cambridge: Polity Press.

MacIntyre, A. (1981) *After Virtue*, London: Duckworth.

—— (1998) Social science methodology as the ideology of bureaucratic authority, in Knight, K. (ed.) *The MacIntyre Reader*, Cambridge: Polity Press.

Mead, G.H. (1934) *Mind, Self and Society from the Standpoint of a Social Behaviourist*, Chicago: University of Chicago Press.

Mintzberg, H., Ahlstrand B. and Lampel, J. (1998) *Strategy Safari: The Complete Guide Through the Wilds of Strategic Management*, Edinburgh: Pearson.

Peters, T. and Waterman, R. (1982) *In Search of Excellence: Lessons from America's Best-run Companies*, New York: Harper Business.

Pfeffer, J. and Sutton, R. (2006) *Hard Facts, Dangerous Half-Truths, and Total Nonsense: Profiting from Evidence-based Management*, Boston MA: Harvard Business School Press.

Porter, M. (1985) *Competitive Advantage*, New York: The Free Press.

Pozner, B. and Kouzes, J. (2010) *The Truth about Leadership: The No-fads, Heart-of-the-Matter Facts You Need to Know*, San Francisco: Jossey Bass.

Reay, T., Whitney, B. and Kohn, K. (2009) What's the evidence on evidence-based management? *Academy of Management Perspectives*, 23(4): 5–18.

Rousseau, D. (2006) Is there such a thing as 'evidence based management'?, *Academy of Management Review*, 31(2): 256–269.

Schein, E. (1987) *Process Consultation, vol. 1: Its role in Organization Development. Process Consultation; Vol. 2: Lessons for Managers and Consultants*, Reading, MA: Addison-Wesley.

Senge, P. (1990) *The Fifth Discipline: The Art and Practice of the Learning Organisation*, London: Transworld.

Stacey, R. (2007) *Strategic Management and Organisational Dynamics: The Challenge of Complexity*, 5th edition, London: Prentice Hall.

—— (2010) *Complexity and Organizational Reality: Uncertainty and the Need to Rethink Management after the Collapse of Investment Capitalism*, London: Routledge.

—— (ed.) (2005) *Experiencing Emergence in Organisations: Local Interaction and the Emergence of the Global Pattern*, London: Routledge.

—— and Griffin, D. (eds) (2005) *A Complexity Perspective on Researching Organisations . Taking Experience Seriously*, London: Routledge.

——, Griffin, D. and Shaw, P. (2000) *Complexity and Management: Fad or Radical Challenge to Systems Thinking?*, London: Routledge.

Thompson, P. and McHugh, D. (2009) *Work Organisations: A Critical Approach*, Basingstoke: Palgrave Macmillan

Tsoukas, H. (2004) *Complex Knowledge: Studies in Organizational Epistemology*, Oxford: Oxford University Press.

Von Bertalanffy, L. (1968) *General System Theory: Foundations, Development, Applications*, New York: George Braziller.

Willmott, H. (1993) Strength is ignorance; Slavery is freedom: Managing culture in modern organizations, *Journal of Management Studies*, 30(4): 515–552.

—— (2003) Renewing *Strength:* Corporate culture revisited, *M@n@gement*, 6(3): 73–87.

2

Consultancy as Practical Engagement in Organisational Politics

This chapter will investigate how consultancy is commonly understood and what this means for practice and will question what is it that consultants think they are doing when they are undertaking a consultancy intervention. Although the chapter focuses on consultancy, there are of course contingent implications for managers and leaders who are often acting in an internal consultancy role as they work to support their colleagues in achieving whatever it is they are supposed to be achieving. Many of the skills and areas of expertise claimed by contemporary consultants are similar to those assumed to be possessed by a good manager or leader.

In Chapter 1 I argued that the dominant theory of consultancy or managerial intervention in organisations is based on systems dynamics, where there is an assumption both that an organisation is a self-regulating system and that the consultant/manager is a detached, objective observer who can intervene to help staff bring about specific and necessary change. The two things are thought possible at the same time. The change is often thought to be required to bring the organisation into a new equilibrium state within a changed environment. Many Organisational Development (OD) practitioners would not claim to understand all the linkages between one part of the system and another, nor would they necessarily claim that they are linear connections. However, they still ascribe to themselves the power of analysis and intervention which will lead to greater organisational health. As midwives in the transition from one state to another, consultants anticipate encountering resistance from employees who, for one reason or another, will oppose the change. This is often referred to as the 'soft' side of OD: the feelings and motivations of employees who are wedded to a now outdated way of behaving, but who need to adopt more appropriate behaviours. In their practice the consultant is thought to be able to rise above, or be objective about organisational politics: either this or they are encouraged to behave 'authentically', creating relationships of trust and honesty which dissolve interpersonal difficulties. Resistant employees can be convinced that the changes are necessary and will 'buy in' to them when they have them rationally explained. Just as the manager can choose which change is required to adapt to environmental changes, so the consultant can choose the way they behave with the client and which intervention is most appropriate.

As an alternative I will be making the case that an organisation is not a self-regulating system, and that an OD practitioner only has a limited ability to choose how to behave. The strong push and pull that arises from the way that employees are already actively engaged with each other in fluctuating relationships of power, which I consider organisational politics, is as likely to condition the behaviour of the consultant as the other way round. I will argue that the consultant is actively engaged in this political life from the moment they start the contractual discussion with their employers, and this engagement severely constrains what it is possible for them to do. Rather than being a detached observer, they are drawn into being temporary co-participants in the ongoing discussion in organisations, as they become caught up in the strong patterning which severely limits their choosing. And rather than being objective, if by this term it is implied that they are somehow separate from what is going on, I will argue that what consultants bring is difference to the habitual patterning of the interactions between people in the organisation into which they have been invited. In bringing difference they are directly affecting the relationships of power of which they have become a temporary part. By paying attention to the ways in which consultants find themselves caught up in the everyday politics of organisational life, including noticing the strong feelings that events provoke in them and others, I argue, consultants can help staff in organisations gain greater detachment from their habitual patterns of behaviour even as they are caught up in them.

Definitive Guides to Consultancy

A good example of the dominant way of thinking about consultancy is to be found in the book entitled *The Seven Cs of Consulting: the Definitive Guide to the Consulting Process* (Cope, 2003) which has endorsements from Ernst and Young consultants and the Institute of Management Consultants. Cope is conscious that consultants have a bad reputation, that they cannot always deliver what it is that they promise, but believes also that with more systematic ways of working, the seven 'C's (client, clarify, create, change, confirm, continue, close) they can achieve sustainable, measurable results for their clients. The change project will have 'added value', a phrase I remarked upon in the first chapter. At each stage of the project life cycle, which proceeds in sequential fashion from one stage to the next, Cope produces a large number of ladders, charts, grids and frameworks to help the consultant stay on top of the change project, to detect problems or opposition to the project before they happen, and to keep it on track. Change has to be 'driven' in an organisation, and it is senior managers who do so, aided by consultants. Just as an aside, it is interesting to note how we are in familiar territory with much management literature with the seven steps to success.

In writing about the change process Cope is always trying to achieve balance between the dualisms he finds in organisational life: for example, it is important to find the balance between 'head', the logical self, and 'heart', the emotional self. People can be divided into those who like tight structures and those who like loose ones (an echo of Peters and Waterman's (1982) *In Search of Excellence* mentioned in Chapter 1.

Organisations have espoused values and actual practices which may be different (an implicit reference to the work of Argyris, 1982 who writes extensively about organisations where staff have 'espoused theories' on the one hand, but theories that they actually put into practice on the other, 'theories in use', which are usually different). In bringing his dualisms into equilibrium he demonstrates an overt understanding of organisations as a system in search of homeostasis. The consultant is the Archimedean point through which all contradictions and views are resolved:

> *Your goal is to bring together all the players' perspectives to give a sense of balance to the measurement process. As any boating enthusiast will appreciate, it is impossible to get an accurate bearing by taking a single point of reference, since a true position can only be determined by taking two independent references. It is through this process of triangulation that a true position is derived and it is by the same process that you can confirm that the correct output has been achieved.*
>
> (Cope, 2003: 209)

The consultant is a kind of organisational sailor or scientist, who, in an objective way, measures, diagnoses, triangulates and gives a true picture.

Cope demonstrates the kind of realist understanding of the world that I alluded to in the previous chapter in the quotation from Tsoukas (2004) where there is an assumption that the consultant is not part of what they are moved to comment upon, but is somehow separate from it.

In his chapter on change, Cope draws extensively on Senge (1990) to argue that an organisation is a self-regulating system which naturally gravitates to a state of equilibrium where order naturally arises out of disorder. There may be natural resistance on the part of employees to accept that change is needed, but there is always a D spot, a decision point, where employees consciously or unconsciously decide to set aside their old attitudes and decide to adopt new ones. According to Senge, this is a question of surfacing your existing 'mental models' and adopting the new required ones. The central role of the consultant in all of this is as explainer, giving the 'resisters' sufficient information for them to realise that change is needed. Cope only mentions politics once explicitly and power not at all in the course of describing the change process in which a consultant is engaged. Politics is a 'system' to which employees are attuned, so if a consultant or manager is introducing change which employees will suffer from then it is important to sell it to them in a non-threatening way. If a new computer system will bring about redundancies then it is best to present this to the people affected by telling them about the benefits, although it is not entirely clear what the benefits would be to people who are laid off by a change. It is in these passages of the book that Cope tends towards the metaphysical, hitching quasi-scientific language to highly abstract concepts. So it behoves a consultant to 'map the energy used to drive change' (p. 237) to assess whether the change will continue after the consultant leaves. If the consultant concludes that it will not continue then they need to look for other 'energy sources'. Tapping into these energy sources, selling the change in a convincing way, aligning the change with the political system, will all bring about the desired result, which is 'embedded into the behaviours or management systems'.

Throughout Cope is straddling the contradiction that the organisation he is working with is self-regulating, as though it were an organism in its own right, but at the same time he is working to choose with managers the archetype to which the organisation should evolve. Both the manager and the consultant they employ are choosing, and their choice will be so persuasive that most organisational employees will be rationally convinced of the necessity for change. As they become convinced they will relinquish their old paradigms for understanding the world and adopt new ones as they become enthusiastic about their new shared future. Cope never reveals whether he has any doubts about the changes he recommends to his clients, or whether he has ever come across employees reluctant to recognise how the proposed changes are good for them.

A Different Experience of Consultancy

In what follows I will describe my own experience of organisational change as a consultant and will go on to explore how other consultants have made sense of their experience in more challenging circumstances than Cope describes.

I was part of a team of consultants who had been contracted to evaluate the work of a UN organisation in the Middle East and then make recommendations as a result of the evaluation as to how they might organise themselves differently. The original contract had been awarded to a well-known research institution in the UK, but they did not have the resources to undertake the consultancy themselves, so they subcontracted it to someone they had worked with before. He in turn assembled a group of consultants who had never worked together before, of which I was one. In effect, the UN organisation contracted with the research institution, which sub-contracted to an independent consultant as team leader, who sub-contracted to me and some others.

We were brought together as a team by the team leader because we were deemed to have complementary skills: we comprised a group who could analyse the financial, managerial and operational performance of the UN organisation. In the event, we spent very little time talking together about the work before embarking on it, since it was due to be completed to a very short time scale. The UN organisation had still not finalised the terms of reference with the research institute, which had still not fully agreed the ways of working with the team leader, who had not had time to bring us together as a team to discuss the what and the how of our working together.

In my experience this is a very characteristic piece of consultancy in the sense that the team carrying out the work is often at a number of removes from the managers originally specifying and contracting the work. In many contemporary organisations work is contracted out, and the team carrying out the work may be at a number of removes from the original conversation specifying what was intended.

As we began working together in the Middle East, conflicts began to open up on a number of fronts. The UN organisation itself was completely dependent upon funding from the American government and from the EU who did not always agree on priorities: managers in the organisation were under constant criticism from the governments of the countries in which it worked, who were likely to side with the US, the EU or with neither. The UN organisation, which had a huge and extensive operation, was often operating with inadequate funds, and struggled to pay its staff on time. Whatever the senior managers decided, they would displease somebody. As a consequence they were used to responding very defensively to what were often attacks on their judgement and competence. They understood the evaluation we were undertaking to be one such attack, so they did their utmost to frustrate what we were doing. This included questioning the terms of reference for the evaluation: by the time we were completing the work we were on our eighth draft of the terms of reference which were still not agreed. In addition they queried almost every proposal we made to them suggesting ways of undertaking the work. So, for example, we proposed to them we met the managers together in groups as well as one to one, so that we could encourage the group to reflect on each other's interpretation of what had happened. The managers with whom we were negotiating this idea showed overt hostility to the suggestion, and when we did eventually manage to meet with one or two groups of managers they did their best to frustrate the discussion by presenting their actions and the decisions they had made as being the best possible in the circumstances.

It was not just the work with the managers in the UN organisation which was conflictual. As a group of consultants we rapidly discovered that despite our 'complementary skills' and our experience, we had very different ways of working and completely different ideas about what was needed. One consultant was an experienced group facilitator who had spent some time in the US and wanted to facilitate a group of managers by throwing around a red plastic heart to encourage them to 'speak from the heart'. Two other British consultants were bitterly opposed to working this way with a group of managers that they perceived to be hostile and unforgiving, but were unable to say this aloud. They were unable to speak from the heart.

From beginning to end of this particular consultancy we were engaged together in a struggle over what we were doing and how we might understand what we were doing. We were partly responding to the sense of being besieged that the managers of the UN organisation were expressing in their dealings with us, but in addition we had our own difficulties of finding a way to work together.

Politics as a Condition for Everyday Organising

In the narrative I have described above we were engaged in negotiation with each other as a group of consultants from the moment we started working together, and struggled to negotiate what it was we were supposed to be doing with the client. We could not agree the best way of proceeding in either situation. This is a rather extreme example of my 15 years of consultancy experience, but it is by no means unusual. So, referring back to Cope and his treatise on carrying out definitive consultancies at the beginning of the chapter, one might have been left with the idea after reading him that somehow it is obvious what is needed to proceed in organisational life. The exercise of evaluating and assessing is commonly understood to be a neutral, technical process carried out by objective outsiders, and would yield data that would be convincing about what is needed for an organisation to change. Instead, the process of evaluating and assessing is often experienced as a profoundly disturbing activity by those working in organisations who may fiercely resist, particularly if it challenges the stories they have been telling themselves about what it is that they think they are engaged in.

Here is an example from another consultant who undertook a consultancy for the British government. David Mosse (2006) gives a vivid demonstration of what can happen when a consultant begins to describe what he thinks is happening when it runs counter to received interpretations, particularly if these interpretations are informed by what I described as the dominant discourse in Chapter 1. Mosse, an anthropologist by training, was involved over a ten-year period as a consultant to a project funded by the British government in India. As part of his method for researching for his book *Cultivating Development* (Mosse, 2005) he started to share his writing with the colleagues he had worked with on the project and quickly found a bitter reaction from them:

> I was astonished by the strength of the emotion conveyed through e-mail, telephone conversations and eventually face to face, about a book which to all its independent readers did not appear to defame or malign the reputation of anyone. Nor was there any plausible explanation of how the book would damage organisations (the Department for International Development or the project agency), destroy the programme, or its routes to funding.
>
> (Mosse, 2006)

Since Mosse was writing from his perspective as an academic anthropologist one of the offences he seemed to have committed with his colleagues was a refusal to give sufficient acknowledgement of managerial interpretations of what was happening in the project:

> ... the ethnography was read from a managerial perspective. It was unnecessary and embarrassing because it refused to explain outcomes in terms of design, and evaded the expectation that problems should really only be analysed in relation to solutions. It did not provide a proper project history of implementation, learning and improvement, which should reveal a progressive narrowing of the gap between intention, action and outcomes.
>
> (Mosse, 2006)

Mosse experienced a similar kind of reaction to the one I described in the first chapter at the hands of my academic reviewer. Managerialist ways of thinking assume a realist interpretation of the world, one which is susceptible to technical tools for improvement. What Mosse was doing was to call into question the ideas of predictability and control through the panoply of managerial tools and frameworks by writing about what he actually saw happening rather than what was supposed to be happening, and in doing so he invited opprobrium. This might lead one to the conclusion that the invitation to the consultant is only a partial one: there is often little freedom to call into question the way the work is being framed, but one is rather asked to lend weight to it by adding 'expertise', or experience from elsewhere. The experience that is being sought often amounts to more of the same processes which may have caused the organisational difficulties in the first place. As a consultant there is a limit to which one can call the existing situation into question.

As a consultant myself I am often struck by the irony of situations I find myself in when a contractor asks for support during a particular phase of being stuck, which dominant ways of understanding management have not moved on, and to which they may even have contributed. And yet at the same time there is an inevitable expectation that I will use more orthodox management approaches for discussing and thinking through what it is that I am being asked to deal with. I say 'inevitable' in the sense that often there is no standing outside the way we see the world. In order to have succeeded to become senior managers in organisations, they will have become fluent in the language and concepts that underpin systemic approaches to management. One of the assumptions at the heart of the current orthodoxy is that the processes of organising are improvable, often towards an abstract and idealised end point. Current stuckness can be perceived as a failure of professionalism, an inability to 'close the gap' between where people are and where they think they would like to be. When managers think of their organisation as 'parts' and 'wholes' they are sometimes drawn into talking about 'a disconnect' between them. As a consultant I am invited to connect up the parts to form a coherent whole, and to help close the gap between the current messiness and the idealised future. Sometimes the terms of reference for a consultancy are so tightly constrained by these ways of thinking that it is hard to know how to work. Terms of reference may sometimes specify both the way the work should be carried out, as well as the kinds of findings the consultant is likely to uncover along the way as well as the kinds of 'tools' and frameworks they are required to use.

And yet, in spite of an appeal for help, contractors, and the managers and staff they work with, often vigorously defend their ways of working in the manner that is described above. Sometimes the last thing one is able to do as an outsider is to draw attention to what is going on, and to do so is to invite opprobrium or criticism of one's level of professionalism. And yet, as I have pointed out previously, there are few evidential grounds for proceeding on the basis that understanding an organisation as a self-organising system is likely to be successful. Potentially this faces the consultant or manager with a double bind: when systemic ways of managing are deemed to have failed very often the invitation to the consultant is to try and make them more systemic, to connect up more parts, to try harder with the current understanding. However, drawing attention to the limitations of this way of thinking can be identity-threatening for managers and can provoke strong emotions and a strong reaction against the consultant or manager. This is what I mean by the strong ideological claims of much current management practice. It is often very difficult to begin to articulate a different way of understanding what it is that we find ourselves doing together.

This causes something of a practical as well as an ethical dilemma for consultants who are enjoined by more orthodox writers on consultancy to do the following:

> *A consultant should be free from an organisation's internal politics and able to provide clear, constructive advice from a detached and objective perspective.*
>
> *(Rowley and Rubin, 2006)*

If we take Mosse's experience as a guide, and the experience I myself describe above, then the relationship between the consultant and contractor is clearly not as straightforward as Rowley and Rubin describe. Consultants are often in no position to be free from the organisation's politics, and are indeed severely constrained by them. Nor is it straightforward what would constitute 'objective' and 'constructive' advice in any given circumstance. I would contend that there is no rising above the internal politics of an organisation one is invited into. The moment one engages in a discussion about what the work might involve, one has entered into the domain of politics and the way the client sees the world, irrespective of whether we convince ourselves that we are all working together for the good of the organisation. From the beginning we become pitched into a struggle over what it is we mean by the good, and how we might find a way of being constructive together.

Change Through Power and Affect – A Sociological Input

If my contention is that organisations are not self-organising systems, then what exactly are they? If a manager or consultant is not an objective designer of organisational processes then what are they doing? How do I justify my assertion that power and politics are useful ways of understanding what is happening when people try to achieve things together, and to what would I attribute the strong affective reactions that consultants can provoke and experience when they intervene in organisations? In order to set out my understanding of the kinds of social processes that one can anticipate finding in organisations I would like to take a reasonably lengthy detour into the thinking of the German sociologist Norbert Elias. The reason for doing so is that Elias articulated an emergent theory of social evolution where power and affect are at the core of the explanation of how humankind has developed over time. This does not depend on the idea that society evolves as the result of any group's plan or intention: we have become civilised, Elias argues, because of the interweaving of everyone's intentions, a blindly operating process of which no one is in control. I want to explain Elias' theories in brief as a way of pointing to what I think is happening in organisations, making the case that, because we are interdependent human beings, we are inevitably involved in power relations.

For Elias, the social processes that we find ourselves caught up in and contributing to arise from the autonomous dynamics of the web of relationships in which we are bound to function. This web of relationships is made up of co-operating and competing interdependent people conditioned by the fluctuating power relationships between them, which Elias called a 'figuration'. It is in these figurations, the interweaving of different actions and intentionality mediated by power, that knowledge arises. For Elias there is no mystery about the emergence of social phenomena: they do so from the warp and weft of the actions and intentions of interdependent people over the centuries. This gives rise to recognisable social patterning which tends in a particular direction, but which is still open to an uncommon combination of common events and circumstances which can lead to a completely unexpected outcome. *The Civilising Process* (Elias, 1939/2000) is a sociogenesis of the way that our social structures have evolved over time, and continue to evolve in ways which are both unplanned and unpredictable, but which have also led to changes in the structure of our personalities. In our attempts to co-operate and compete with each other we are both forming, and being formed at the same time, by the societies and groups in which we participate. Elias notes that human societies have developed considerably, but there is no inevitability about progress, since the civilising process can also go into reverse.

In the development of his thinking, Elias reaches right back to the formation of states and the monopolisation of the means of violence by the state, initially through kings and their courts. The imposition of taxation allowed more stable societies to coalesce through the development of institutions. The first stage of the civilising process for Elias is the transition from warrior to courtier as states began to form around kingdoms and courts. Instead of settling disputes that inevitably arise because of competition over power, influence and resources by violent means, courtiers learnt to pursue their own interests in more stable societies and more subtly by political machinations, in their attempts to gain the ear of the king. The king, meanwhile, derived his power by hopping from foot to foot, staying at the centre of a web of relationships, playing off one group against another, feudal lords against the newly emerging middle classes. Gradually societies emerged over time through the ineluctable consequences of co-operation, which led to a greater social stability so that different groups could prosper, but also through competition as different groups sought to push their own interests within the newly emerging stability. Monopolisation of the means of violence is only one way of one group exercising control over another: in a pacified state there are other things to struggle over as Marx noted, such as the monopolisation of the means of production.

Elias supported his case by undertaking an empirical study of the way in which manners developed over time, and understood this to be the differentiation of behaviour between one group and another as a subtle way of seeking status advantage. The development of more refined manners grew out of the competing interests of different groups at court. Additionally he noted that with increasing competition social function becomes more and more differentiated leading in turn to more highly differentiated skills and knowledge:

> *The more differentiated they become, the larger grows the number of functions and thus of people on whom the individual constantly depends in all his actions, from the simplest and most commonplace to the more complex and uncommon. As more and more people must attune their conduct to that of others, the web of actions must be organised more and more strictly and accurately, if each individual action is to fulfil its social function. Individuals are compelled to regulate their conduct in an increasingly differentiated, more even and stable manner.*
>
> (Elias, 1939/2000: 367)

Forms of social control have become internalised over the centuries as societies become increasingly civilised. That is to say, we become socialised into the degree in which we have to hold ourselves in check in order to function in a highly interdependent society. By using the term 'civilised' Elias is attaching no value judgement, but simply means the stabilising effects on both social structure and personality structure that arises from long-term patterning of relations over time.

So the civilising influence of increasing numbers of citizens trying to co-ordinate their actions as well as compete led to a move away from settling disputes by means of the immediate expression of affect, and perhaps violence. Greater advantage was to be gained by increased self control. As societies developed, more and more people became more dependent on each other more of the time. The diminishing of the external threat of violence and the need for greater mutual attunement led to a change in personality structure towards an internally-generated form of self control operating both consciously and unconsciously. Increasing social interdependence can only function if the individual can control themselves in their relations with others, and this is a mechanism that begins to be instilled in us as social beings from a very early age through parenting and education. It operates both self-consciously and blindly as a part of our social conditioning in ways over which we only have limited control.

Because of increased attunement to growing numbers of others, individually and collectively we have developed the ability to take what Elias refers to as a 'detour via detachment'. This is the capacity to reflect on different courses of action that we might take and assess their consequences in relation to others so that we might exercise self-restraint. Using both hindsight and foresight, we distance ourselves from our immediate affective reactions to situations in which we find ourselves. This kind of self-restraint affords greater social advantage as people manoeuvre to advance their own plans over the plans of others. It has also led to the possibility of the development of scientific thinking as we have gradually learned to control our initially overwhelming affective reactions to natural phenomena; Elias refers to the latter as 'magico-mythical thinking'. Previously we might have ascribed mystical agency to frightening natural events. Increasingly, the development of scientific forms of enquiry arising out of a greater propensity for detachment has enabled more durable, reality-congruent explanations of natural phenomena to be formulated. Over time these forms of knowledge become independent of the groups of people who develop them and become autonomous, useful to increasing numbers of people seeking reality-congruent explanations of the world.

When Elias talks about our ability to take a detour via detachment he is not saying the same thing as a realist might: that it is possible to be an objective observer of what is going on and then rationally choose the optimum path for self-advancement. Instead he understands this as a limited but still enhanced ability to notice how one is obliged to play the game one is caught up in, and through doing so, perhaps to gain some advantage. By becoming more detached about what we are doing, we may be able better to predict one or two moves ahead in the game, although this does not mean to say that we will be right. So we are both playing the game and have developed our capacities to notice how we are playing the game with others.

At the same time as we have developed the capacity of greater detachment we are also subject to feelings which operate blindly, 'a wall of deep-rooted fears' instilled in us in the socialisation process that prevents us from causing offence to socially acceptable behaviour. Elias refers to the 'rising tide of guilt and shame' that develops in us in direct proportion to the decreasing threat of external physical control. We learn to subordinate our own impulses more or less successfully. The parenting and educational process which are aimed at curbing excesses of impulse and affect are always imperfect, and thus Elias argues, the process is never without pain and always leaves scars. The patterning of these scars continues to affect adults throughout their lives, if, in coming into conflict with others they open up the wounds that the socialisation process has left. The imperfect socialisation process induces feelings which operate unconsciously, and they often produce collisions with social reality. Pushed and pulled by our own emotions and compulsions, and the automatically instilled self-governance processes into which we are socialised, we bump up against others who are in the same position as we are. If we think that we can control this interaction with appeals to reason or objectivity, Elias argues, we are significantly missing the point.

In the next chapter and in Chapter 7 on strategy I will be examining the similarities between Elias' theory of social evolution and the conclusions of scientists building computer-based models of complex adaptive systems. Both describe non-linear, mutually adapting and self-influencing processes where the patterning which arises is both stable and unstable at the same time and capable of radical and transformative change which no single agent has planned. Both describe global patterning that arises as a consequence of what everyone is doing locally, trying to co-operate and compete with other interdependent agents.

In the meantime, however, I would like to link what Elias is saying to the argument I am developing about the role of consultants in organisations who are invited into organisations where complex games are being played as people co-operate and compete together to get things done. It is inevitable that they will begin to co-operate and compete with the consultant as well, whether the consultant tries to stick to their seven step framework or not. What emerges will not just be as a consequence of what the consultant brings in the way of tools and frameworks, and in some instances their very participation in organisational life will provoke very strong reactions.

Elias on Parts and Wholes

Readers will note the difference that Elias is making with his ideas that social processes are constrained and enabled by the fluctuating figurations of longer and longer chains of interdependent people from the explanation one finds in the dominant discourse that society, or organisations, can be disaggregated into different levels, or comprise parts and wholes. How useful did Elias think the latter explanations were for explaining social phenomena? In his books *What is Sociology* (1978) and *Problems of Involvement and Detachment* (1987) Elias reflects upon the question as to the usefulness of scientific thinking, which has proved so successful for gaining greater control over the natural world, and the degree to which it is also useful for describing the social world. The social world, Elias argues, never stands still, but is continuously morphing and changing as the figurations, the patterning of interdependencies, fluctuate. Sociology, the discipline concerning the study of society which has aspired to becoming more scientific, has done so in the twentieth century by becoming overly reliant on methods derived from the natural sciences. For Elias these unnecessarily reduce process and borrow the disaggregating logic of parts and whole which are inappropriate and inadequate for capturing the flux of human interaction. Time and again, he complains, biological explanations are substituted for sociological ones and they are inadequate to the task (1978: 107). Social processes are not in transition from one static state to another, nor can they be considered to be parts and wholes: to do so is simply to use a mystery to solve a mystery, he argues. He was more concerned to try and study how patterns of inter-relationships change over time, phenomena which our language does not prepare us well for, he argued, since it too has a tendency to reduce process.

The question about the extent to which we might think of management as a science, and the usefulness of scientific methods, and what we might mean by scientific in unique organisational environments are recurring themes in this book to which we will return again and again.

The Consequences for Consultancy

So what might we make of this long digression on Elias when we are thinking about management and consultancy? Previously in this chapter I have been describing the overwhelmingly strong social processes that I and others have found themselves caught up in when undertaking consultancies in organisations, and the powerful emotions that these interventions often provoke both for consultants and those they work with. This, in contrast to more orthodox accounts of consultancy, gives very little account of the profoundly political game that one needs to engage with as a consultant. Power and politics, if they are mentioned at all, are things to be managed or aligned with some other abstraction. We are offered the idea that an organisation is a self-regulating system, drawing on analogies from the biological sciences, which a consultant can operate upon to shift it from one state to another by building relationships of honesty and trust with their contractors. By drawing on the sociology of Elias I am pointing to a different understanding of what might be going on in organisations, understood instead as the interweaving of intention, detachment and blindly operating affect producing a patterning of interactions between people of which no one is in overall control. As we try and achieve things together we will be co-operating and competing at the same time and this is likely to provoke strong feelings in us and in others. Our ability to get things done will be both enabled and constrained by our long chains of interdependencies with others so our ability to 'choose' a future for the organisation or department we happen to be working with will be highly constrained no matter how great the formal authority a manager is supposed to have.

I am recommending Elias' account of the civilising process because for me it offers a more reality-congruent account of what a consultant is likely to be confronted with in any organisational assignment. They are liable to come into an organisation where the patterning of people's actions and intentions have developed over many years to constrain powerfully what it is possible to say and do, both for employees in that organisation and for consultants. The consultant will offer different ways of understanding these phenomena, but their ability to influence those they are working with will depend on their ability to play the game in which they find themselves caught up. Rather than merely affecting the organisation into which they have been invited, consultants are themselves likely to be heavily affected.

Two Different Ideas of How to Work With Power as a Consultant

I am starting from a position that consultancy can make a difference and I would not want to give the impression that consultants can only work in the way that contractors want or oblige them to. However I would also argue that the practice of consultancy is more problematic that the quotation from Rowley and Rubin (2006) above would have us believe and that different evaluative standards are needed than these I found in an article pinned up on a management training centre notice board identifying how one might identify an expert facilitator of groups:

- *Participation is high, goals and objectives are set and are clear, and the process moves along at the right pace.*

- *Good facilitators lead without appearing to.*

- *They know how to trigger and control group dynamics such as discussion and participation.*
  (Roffey Management Institute Bulletin January 2005)

As far as the group I worked with in the consultancy with the UN organisation are concerned, the role of the consultant is far from unproblematic and the idea that they can 'trigger and control' anything without the express co-operation of the group, tendentious. These unproblematic ideas are informed by a body of literature which understands the consultant to stand outside the work of the organisation, to the extent of being able to intervene virtually at will to bring about desired and predictable changes. There is little acknowledgement of the power dynamics to which I am drawing attention, and which are scarce in Cope (2003).

In an article outlining some of the dominant approaches to consultancy (Mowles, 2009) I write a critical commentary on both Edgar Schein (1987) and Peter Block (2000), both of whom have been taken up widely in the domain of organisational consultancy. I am addressing these scholars because they do acknowledge power relations in organisations, although they do so in very different ways. Additionally I want to set out an alternative to the way they think a consultant should be working with power.

Schein is one of the fathers of OD. He understands consultancy intervention as a kind of drama, where the consultant obliges the manager they are working with to act out the 'solutions' to a jointly defined 'problem'. Schein acknowledges that managers are likely to know far more about the context of their organisation than an incoming consultant ever could: in this sense he does not make the same claim as Cope that a consultant can recommend the right intervention to bring about desired changes in organisational life. He does however take his own intervention to be a kind of 'benign manipulation', his own term, to force the manager to do what they have committed to:

> *Staying in the process consultant mode is tantamount to refusing to take centre stage, assuming instead a coaching role. The process consultant keeps the client on centre stage and helps him to continue there by 'forcing' him or benignly manipulating him into to starting to work on his own problem. The helper stays in the audience role, watching with interest and supports the efforts of the client as actor to solve his own problem.*
>
> *(Schein, 1987: 83)*

Here we have Schein clearly demonstrating his belief that organisational process is something that the consultant can to choose step beyond: he is sitting outside the 'boundary' or organisational action as a spectator. I share neither Schein's optimism about the power of the consultant to divert processes towards an anticipated outcome and his belief in 'designing solutions',[1] nor can I ignore the political consequences of my own power in the situations in which I find myself, as I feel Schein does. As a consultant to organisations I am obliged to play the game and am, to a greater or lesser extent, constrained by the rules of that game.

Another popular proponent of the practice of consultancy is Peter Block (2000) who has written probably the best-selling and most widely used treatise on consulting which he has entitled *Flawless Consulting*. Block writes into a more orthodox managerialist understanding of how organisations function, what managers do, and thus what the task of a consultant should be. There is good practice and bad practice, and consultants should tend towards the former and away from the latter. At the beginning of the book he explains why he thinks that perfect consulting is a possibility:

> *My using the term* flawless consulting *may sound presumptuous, but it is not accidental. A basic value underlying the book is that there is in each of us the possibility of perfection. There is a consulting 'pro' inside each of us, and our task is to allow that flawless consultant to emerge. On the surface, this book is about methods and techniques. But each technique carries a consistent message more important than any method – that each act that expresses trust in ourselves and belief in the validity of our own experience is always the right path to follow. Each act that is manipulative or filled with pretense is always self-destructive.*
>
> (Block, 2000: 11)

Although the book is filled with techniques and frameworks and offers the usual separation between 'task' and 'process', which we also encountered with Schein, Block's principal appeal is to the consultant's sense of 'authenticity'; by acting in consonance with our true selves, he argues, we can build trust and maximise our leverage with the client and on the problem we have in hand. It is not clear what Block makes of Schein's reference to 'benign manipulation',

---

1   Schein's emphasis on design, models and representations has been thoroughly critiqued by Shaw (2002).

although he draws on him in the course of the book. Block puts the case that consultants should learn to be comfortable with tension and difficulty and should not fall back on action lists and plans as a way of avoiding these tensions. He enjoins us to watch for changes in the moments that they are happening, through attention and reflection, and to be prepared to change ourselves first, and in doing so he invites us into metaphysical territory:

> *If you look at the great leaders through history, you see a consciousness of their own limitations that was essential to their greatness. From Confucius, Buddha, and Christ, to Lincoln, Gandhi and Martin Luther King – all touched lives because of their presence more than their position. They became archetypes for the right use of power, and one source of their power was their own humility.*
>
> (Block, 2000: 341–342)

Block, like Schein, is concerned with the ethical challenges of being a consultant, and argues that consultants should be values-driven. Rather than using the consultant's power to 'force' the client to adopt a particular role, as does Schein, Block would have us believe that we can choose to give up our power for the good. Block implies that we can aspire to the greatness of religious and world leaders by so doing, although one might argue that he has misunderstood and underestimated both Gandhi and King in respect of their own understanding of power. Although enjoining us to be comfortable with uncertainty and not knowing, on issues of power and values Block himself inhabits a Manichean world, one where there is good practice and bad practice, power for the good and power for the bad. We can have insight into which is which by appealing to our 'inner selves' and trusting our experience.

Both Griffin (2002) and Stacey (Griffin and Stacey (eds), 2005) have drawn attention to the tendency in current management literature to enjoin obedience to a mystical whole, to give up our bad selves for the sake of the greater good, and this thread is also clear in Block's work. Rather than understanding power as the currency of human relating he writes about it as a disposition that one can choose to use or not use. Moreover, Block pays scant attention to the processes that the consultant, the client and everyone that one is working with are caught up in, beyond the incidence of our relating. It also seems unclear to me as to whether giving up one's power, if this indeed were possible, would necessarily result in the good.

Summary of More Orthodox Explanations of Consultancy

The three writers on consultancy that I have discussed in this chapter deal with power in different ways. Cope barely mentions power, and when he does he understands it to be a 'sub-system' which needs aligning with other systems. Political opposition can be managed away with trust and honesty. For Schein it is most important for the client to act and take responsibility for the work in hand, even if it means the consultant forcing the client to address it. The consultant, then, stands outside the process they are observing and wherever possible directs proceedings towards the client's stated goals. In this description the consultant is clearly working with power, but is doing so in a way that implies that the consultant can stand outside the processes they are directing and are largely unaffected by them. Meanwhile Block enjoins authenticity in the relationship between consultant and client, both in terms of encouraging the client to do what they say they really want to and in reflecting on the consultant's ability to support the process; this may involve following one's 'true self' and giving up power for the good.

For me, all of these accounts are inadequate for explaining what it is that I encounter when I am working as a consultant with organisations, and what it is I find myself doing. When I am invited to support a client to contend with an organisational difficulty, I do not always share the client's analysis of what is happening and how we might move it on. Sometimes the negotiation over what we might do is long and protracted. Sometimes the terms of reference for my work can be as inhibiting as they are helpful. Simply supporting the client to implement the 'solution' that they seem to have identified, as Schein suggests, would for me be an inadequate response. Nor do I share both Block and Schein's dualistic view that there is 'good practice' and 'bad practice', the job of the consultant being to steer towards one and away from the other, since the idea of good practice is often not shared. This is not to say that the client and I cannot evaluate together what is more or less helpful for moving things on. Additionally, I do not consider myself all-powerful as does Schein, or powerless in any situation where I find myself working with others, particularly where I am deemed to be an 'expert', rightly or wrongly, by those I am working with. To a greater or lesser degree, consultancy prescriptions from the dominant discourse still cling to the idea that the consultant is detached from the organisation into which they are invited and can choose how they can behave. Although I would agree that a consultant has a different role to play (and part of this is to bring difference) I am going to set out a different understanding of what I think happens.

Consultancy Practice as Radical Engagement

One way of understanding the orthodox literature on consultancy is as an attempt at depoliticising the consultant's role: a consultant is supposed to be above politics, or detached from the client's problems. By presenting consultancy as a technical service, consultants are trying to borrow the clothes of a detached and scientific observer. This decontextualises both the invitation to a consultant and the consultant's offer of help. Driven by an understandable desire to standardise the consultancy service, in the sense of wanting to offer high standards, the risk is of pretending that what works for one organisation will work for all organisations. It is exactly this risk that consultancy practices acknowledge when they claim to offer both advice on 'best practice' organisational tools and frameworks as well as tailoring what they are offering to the specific needs of the organisation they are working with. The consultancy service is both bespoke and off the peg at the same time.

In my digression on Norbert Elias' ideas I have been making the case that it is not helpful to think of an organisation as a system, but rather as the constant patterning and interweaving of intentions which express power relationships. In any consultancy intervention the consultant temporarily joins and contributes to this patterning, and will find themselves caught up in what can be very powerful social processes. Learning to work with this may or may not involve looking for answers outside the organisation, as the pragmatic philosopher John Dewey identified:

> *The more completely the notion of the model is formed outside and irrespective of the specific conditions which the situation of action presents, the less intelligent is the act.*
>
> *(1915: 236–271)*

What concerned Dewey, as it concerns me, is the idea that models for action can necessarily be imported from somewhere else and be useful in the circumstances we are currently dealing with, which, being particular and new, may demand a particular and new approach. We cannot suspend our own judgement by assuming that others have necessarily judged better. So if we could be considered shortsighted if we did not take cognisance of the way in which practice has developed elsewhere, we would also be remiss, in Dewey's terms unintelligent, if we thought these practices would necessarily fit with the context we are dealing with.

And how is it that we decide what circumstances we are dealing with? It would not be possible to give 'constructive advice' to a client without exploring with them the detail of their particular situation, unless we take up the role of an 'expert' who knows best and applies only general rules or principles. In this exploration we are likely to encounter difference, particularly if we call on all the people who are involved in the situation we are trying to move on. In other words, rather than rising above the politics of an organisation, by which I take to mean the differences of interpretation and shifts in power relating which are an inescapable aspect of working with others, I am recommending that we recognise and engage with it. This involves bringing oneself, and others into an encounter with otherness and difference, that I have mentioned previously.

I have drawn attention to the importance of negotiation between the consultant and their contractor which begins from the moment the different parties discuss what it is that is needed. Together we need to negotiate a way of going on together based on an understanding that we may all see the situation differently, and that we have an investment in seeing things the way we do. I am arguing that there is no avoiding becoming part of the power relations between people in the organisation one is working with, and in this sense, there is no avoiding the politics. But as an outsider who has only a temporary stake in the organisation, in that they are only engaged for that particular piece of work, the power relationship between the consultant and staff will be different. This does not necessarily make the relationships more comfortable. But by drawing attention to the different points of view that are present, and by bringing a different perspective themselves, the consultant may be able broaden the understanding of the particular situation that staff in an organisation find themselves in, and by broadening it, alter the way they understand their circumstances. Through this broadening is the potential for change.

So this is how what I am recommending is different from Cope, Schein or Block. All three unproblematically assume that there is an objective place to stand from where a consultant can give detached advice free from the politics of the organisation. Schein assumes the same detachment, but then proceeds to act politically, 'benignly' manipulating the client for 'their own good'. Block recognises the power relationships in organisations but believes it is possible to give up one's power 'for the good'. I am arguing that there is no avoiding the politics. It is the politics that can potentially make the difference. By engaging with and drawing attention to the power relations, the differences that are emerging around conflicting understandings of the process of organising the consultant is working with the particularities that they encounter in the organisation that has contracted them. What I am encouraging is joint reflection on the difficulties that we are experiencing together as a way of making them more explicit to determine how we might go forward together. I consider this to be an ethical expression of consultancy practice, striving to respond to the particular circumstances of what one encounters with others, in the way that Aristotle understood it when he strove to define what it means to act well:

> *When we are discussing actions, although general statements have a wider application, particular statements are closer to the truth. This is because actions are concerned with particular facts, and theories must be brought into harmony with these.*
> (Aristotle, 2004, 1107a: 30–34)

A consultant's ethics can be manifested not so much in adherence to abstract standards such as honesty, transparency or detachment, but by paying attention in a particular way to the circumstances of their client. I do not underestimate the difficulties of doing this, as both my narratives and Mosse's narrative illustrate. There could be strong reactions and resistance to this way of working, which is why it behoves a consultant who intends working in this way to be explicit about how they work.

And it is in the process of drawing attention with others to what is happening that I think that there is the need for the consultant to strive hardest for detachment. We are impelled not just to reflect on what it is that is going on, but to call into question our own reflections. Both reflection and reflexivity are required if we are to consider ourselves, and be considered, co-discussants with the people we are working with, rather than assuming a stance presumed to be that of a detached observer with some kind of undefined expertise. The expertise of a consultant could reside in their ability to help groups in organisations make explicit their differences and join with them in discussing them. One of the things that a consultant might bring is the ability to try to make more visible how employees are thinking about what they are doing as a prerequisite for thinking and acting differently. This is neither an easy process nor necessarily a comfortable one, since it can often provoke strong feelings and often a profound destabilisation of identity as taken-for-granted assumptions are called into question. But in this way the group confirms the consultant's expertise in recognition of their direct experience of it.

Concluding Thoughts on Consultancy and Research

How does any of the above help a consultant or manager know what it is they should be doing? If I am not going to recommend grids and frameworks, the 'what' of organisational consultancy, then how am I recommending a consultant, or a consultant manager to work? The following is a narrative about a piece of work I did recently with some health service managers by means of illustration of what I am talking about.

I have been working for a while with some health service managers in a department of 150 people whose work is distributed geographically. We have been discussing the constant rounds of reform and change that they suffer which is triggered on a weekly basis by senior managers, or by local and national politicians. Some of these seem reasonably thought through and follow causally and coherently from an identified need or from the last initiative, others seem capricious, politically motivated and wild. This leads to rounds of evaluation, organisation and reorganisation. Things are constantly changing and in flux. Sometimes initiatives cut across each other with unpredictable results, sometimes it looks as though drastic service reductions are being planned.

In order to protect the patients for whom they feel responsible, and perhaps their team members, this group of managers I am working with try to engage with each initiative, and as they do so find they are involved in acts of political lobbying and even covert rebellion. One might make the case that they would not be doing their jobs properly if they did not do this They become involved in discussions about how this or that particular service 'improvement' will be carried out in practice, and they begin to influence it this way and that, depending on the strength of their relationships with the managers with whom they are engaged. Their ability to influence their manager will depend a lot on the way their manager manages them.

Middle managers, with whom I am working, are often conducting one set of discussions amongst themselves about what they may or may not achieve, about tactics, and are likely to say other things more publically with their teams. Equally, those responsible for the 'improvements' are themselves engaged in formal and informal discussions about what they intend, what they are prepared to say explicitly about what they intend, and how they will present their ideas to the public. What actually happens will be an interweaving of all these different intentions, with the more powerful having a greater effect on the outcome than the less powerful. Equally, there will be unintended consequences, both unwanted and unexpected, for which no single group will be responsible. There are public transcripts about what is happening alongside multiple hidden transcripts, an idea I will explore later in the book. As a consultant working with the group, I also become involved in these discussions as we explore our points of view on what is happening.

On what basis is it ethical to engage in acts of subversion at work and on what basis am I working with these managers? What any group of managers brings to the service that they manage is a rich and complex understanding of what they are responsible for, which will have emerged from their history of working in their particular department. They will usually understand their department or service much better than the managers who manage them: what they might lack, however, is an appreciation of the broader, more generalised thinking that is behind the wider organisational initiative. Although senior managers are removed from the work, they also have their responsibilities in organising services in ways which they think are best for the service. So by negotiating with peer managers about what would be best to try and conserve as well as change in their particular area of operation at the same time as negotiating with more senior managers about the broader implications of what is being proposed, managers are trying to make wider organisational generalisations, abstract propositions, more particular. And in doing so they can make the difference between a better or worse implemented change or 'improvement'. As peers they will be negotiating together how to engage with the change initiative, and the quality of this discussion will be critical for informing how managers then engage with the broader political process of change.

My role in this is to help the group reflect upon the strong organisational processes in which they are all caught up and over which they have little control, which also begin to arise between us in the group. I am helping them to think about their own contribution to the interactions in which they participate. The power relations which affect their ability to do their jobs are so strong that there is no way that they can 'manage' them, since they are more likely to be managed by them. However, they are not entirely powerless. Instead of reaching for grids and frameworks, however, what I do with the group is to encourage them to think about and discuss their understanding of what they are experiencing with others and with me as we discuss the issues together. Interestingly the way people are managed outside this meeting surfaces in our discussion: group members take up particular stances or form particular interpretations partly arising out of the way they themselves have previously experienced management. The way we are working together, and my role, become objects of discussion too. Together we begin to see new possibilities as we continuously reinterpret what we are experiencing in this process of reflection. I am trying to help them in a very practical way to cope with whatever they face in their jobs on a daily basis. One of the experiences that we have together is that it is possible to discuss differences without things necessarily unravelling between us – to a degree this might give them confidence to negotiate further with their managers. The experience of coming to see the complexity of what they are engaged in, to take in Elias' terms a 'detour via detachment' may enable each of them to act more skilfully in their particular work environments where they take up their role in the game again.

This is what I understand my role to be in this particular circumstance. We are using the experience of organising that this group of managers has as a natural part of doing their jobs and we treat this as significant data worthy of detached reflection. This includes not just the abstract processes of change, restructuring perhaps, or new system introduction, but also their colleagues' reactions to these changes and how they themselves are feeling about them. For some it is their first realisation of how caught up in the changes they have become, and how emotionally charged it is for them. I engage with them as an equal participant in discussing what all of this might mean, and in discussing together we are, in Elias' terms, trying to become more detached about our involvement. We are discussing how we are coming to influence the games in which we participate, and how we are influenced by them.

In the following chapter I intend to explore what taking an experiential view of organisational life would mean for the process of researching organisations, picking up and developing the themes of politics and power further.

References

Argyris, C. (1982) *Reasoning, Learning and Action: Individual and Organisational,* San Fransisco: Jossey Bass.
Aristotle (2004) *The Nicomachean Ethics,* Barnes, J. (ed.) (2004), London: Penguin.
Block, P. (2000) *Flawless Consulting,* San Francisco: Jossey Bass.
Cope, M. (2003) *The Seven Cs of Consulting: The Definitive Guide to the Consulting Process,* London: Financial Times/Prentice Hall.

Dewey, J. (1915) The logic of judgements of practice, in Hickman, L.A. and Alexander, T.M. (eds) (1998) *The Essential Dewey: Vol. 2, Ethics, Logic, Psychology*, Indianapolis: Indiana University Press.

Elias, N. (1939/2000) *The Civilising Process*, Oxford: Blackwell.

—— (1978) *What is Sociology?*, New York: Columbia University Press.

—— (1987) Problems of involvement and detachment, in Elias, N., Schröter, M. (ed.) and Jephcott, E. (trans.), *Involvement and Detachment,* Oxford: Basil Blackwell.

Griffin, D. (2002) *The Emergence of Leadership: Linking Self-organisation and Ethics*, London: Routledge.

—— and Stacey, R. (eds) (2005) *Complexity and the Experience of Leading Organisations*, London: Routledge.

Mosse, D. (2005) *Cultivating Development: An Ethnography of Aid Policy and Practice*, London: Pluto.

—— (2006) Anti-social anthropology? Objectivity, objection, and the ethnography of public policy and professional communities, *Journal of the Royal Anthropological Institute*, 12(4): 935–956.

Mowles, C. (2009) Consultancy as temporary leadership: Negotiating power in everyday practice, *International Journal of Learning and Change*, 3(3): 281–293.

Rowley, J. and Rubin, F. (2006) *Effective Consultancies in Development and Humanitarian Programmes*, Oxford: Oxfam Publications:.

Schein, E. (1987) *Process Consultation, Vol. 1: Its role in Organization Development. Process Consultation, Vol. 2: Lessons for Managers and Consultants*, Reading, MA: Addison-Wesley.

Senge, P. (1990) *The Fifth Discipline: the Art and Practice of the Learning Organisation*, London: Transworld.

Shaw, P. (2002) *Changing Conversations in Organisations: A Complexity Approach to Change*, London: Routledge.

3

Leaders, Managers and Consultants as Researchers: Using the Self as an Instrument of Research

Introduction

In Chapter 2, I explored the importance of politics and power for the consultant who becomes a temporary participant in the patterning of relations and discussion in any organisation into which they are invited. I also offered a critique of the idea of a consultant or manager as someone who somehow stands outside this patterning and by being objective can offer some kind of 'diagnosis' of what is 'really going on'. In much contemporary management literature managers are also thought to be 'system designers', Senge (1990), which implies not only that an organisation can be thought of as a 'system' but that a manager has the ability to be part of and separate from the system which is being designed. There is no indication in such theories how it is possible to reconcile the notion of a free individual choosing what kind of intervention to make at the same time as assuming that there is an equally independent, self-regulating 'whole' organisation upon which one is acting. As an alternative I started to argue, drawing particularly on the work of Norbert Elias, that both consultants and managers are forming and being formed by the web of relations into which they are acting, and are constrained in what they are able to understand and do.

In this chapter I will continue with the argument as to why it is an important insight to think of leaders, managers and consultants as co-participants in the process of organising with others and explore what this might mean for the way that they undertake research into what they are doing. If there is no place to stand 'outside' of what is going on using idealisations and abstractions, how is it possible to form a view about how to act? On what basis is a leader planning and intervening in an organisation to bring about changes? Is a rejection of the idea that an organisation is a system equivalent to saying that there is no point in making plans? To a large extent this argument turns on what it is we think an organisation is, how it arises and how we think change comes about. It will mean forming a view about the agency of leaders, managers and consultants and what it is and is not possible for them to bring about in co-operation with others.

Local Interaction and Global Patterning – A Theoretical Input

Previously I explored Norbert Elias' explanation of how social patterning arises from the interweaving of intentions and actions of interdependent people, who are competing and co-operating with each other over many centuries. There are regularities in social interaction which we shape and are shaped by, but which operate autonomously from our individual and collective intentions even as they are formed by them. In developing the theory of complex responsive processes with colleagues, Stacey (2000, 2007; Stacey, Griffin and Shaw, 2002) has drawn extensively on the work of Elias and has done so motivated by the similarities he has found between Elias' theories of sociogenesis, how complex social patterning emerges unpredictably, and his own exploration of insights from the complexity sciences, which point to a similar phenomenon.

Along with a variety of other authors, Stacey has been intrigued by the question of how order and disorder, local and global are related and how novelty emerges in the interaction between the two. He poses a unique challenge to prevailing ideas of predictability and control which he thinks underpin much contemporary management theory by drawing on the implications he derives from an emerging discipline of modelling complex social phenomena using agent-based computer experiments. These agent-based models have been developed to demonstrate what has come to be known as complex adaptive systems theory.

A complex adaptive system, as modelled by a computer programme, consists of a large number of interacting entities called agents which operate according to a set of rules guiding their interactions with other agents. In these experiments agents are pre-programmed bit-strings, and the bit-strings interact with and respond to each other according to their programmes or 'intentions'. So rather than being referenced to a plan or blueprint operating outside the system, agents are self-organising, iterating and then re-iterating their mutually responsive activities. As the programme develops over time it begins to demonstrate radical structural change as a result of the many local interactions that are occurring between self-organising agents. In other words, novelty arises as a result of the self-organising processes that are evolving minute by minute. The system begins to evolve in a way which could not have been predicted in advance of running the programme, even though the rules of engagement have been determined by the computer programmer. As the programme plays out it begins to demonstrate how radical change arises in a system operating in a paradoxical dynamic of stability and instability at the same time. In the system of interacting agents small local variations in responses between agents can escalate into large population-wide changes which destroy some forms and create others. But the novelty in the emerging global patterns arises only if the agents differ from each other: diversity is a prerequisite for novel forms to emerge.

Stacey realises the limitations of borrowing from computer-based simulations and applying them to organisational life. He accepts the argument from some critics that these experiments may tell us more about programming that they do about human life. He is adamant that he is not claiming, as some management scholars do, that organisations are complex adaptive systems. So for example, a management theorist like Margaret Wheatley (1999) takes the analogy with complex adaptive systems theory literally, and this leads her to suggest that managers should develop simple rules for staff to follow so that they can attune to some implicit harmony of the universe. Stacey rejects this view as being highly reductive, but what interests him about the emerging global patterning is that it is both ordered and disordered at the same time, and arises unpredictably and entirely without any plan, blueprint or some overall guiding controller. He thinks this insight has radical implications for thinking about management in organisations:

> These findings are of major importance, in my view, because they challenge the dominant discourse's most fundamental assumptions. From a complexity perspective, harmony and consensus cannot be equated with success, and unpredictability is fundamentally unavoidable, making it impossible to talk about being in control. The 'whole' is not designed or chosen in advance because it emerges in local interaction. Such emergence is in no way a matter of chance because what emerges does so precisely because of what all the agents are doing or not doing.
>
> (Stacey, 2007: 237)

For Stacey human agents are not analogous to interacting bit-strings but are diverse, unique, conscious and self-conscious beings. Because of their diversity they are highly unlikely to interpret any simple rules the same way, nor would he believe in a manager's ability to devise the rules in the first place. By prescribing that leaders should run their organisations according to 'simple rules', as though insights from the complexity sciences could be directly applied to organisations, Wheatley is still assuming that a manager can stand outside the processes of interaction to devise an intervention that brings about a pre-reflected result. From Stacey's perspective the move to instrumentalise the radical implications of insights from the complexity sciences is entirely to miss the point.

In Stacey's view what is common to both the radical implications of complex adaptive systems theory and the sociology of Norbert Elias is that they provide a coherent explanation of how global patterning arises out of local interaction without separating them out onto different 'levels'. There is no need to think in terms of an organisation as a self-regulating metaphysical entity separate from the actions of individual members of staff or managers. An organisation arises purely out of the activities, intentions, idealisations and the attempts to make meaning of the many employees who join together with the intention of achieving something collectively. In what Elias would refer to as a figuration, or web of people engaged in fluctuating and asymmetric power relations co-operating in their undertaking and competing over meaning and ideology, the organisation *becomes*. In subsequent chapters I will explore the importance of these power relationships and how they affect what it is and is not possible to say and do.

Additionally, Stacey argues, on the basis of accepting these implications there is then a strong case for taking seriously the patterning of local interaction between interdependent people as they adapt to each other and articulate what it is that they think is going on in the collective enterprise:

> *Strategy as a population-wide pattern of action cannot be chosen by anyone but rather emerges in the interplay of individual intentions and choices in local interactions …. All* anyone *can ever do, no matter how powerful, is engage intentionally, and as skilfully as possible, in local interaction, dealing with the consequences as they emerge.*
>
> (2007: 239)

It is important to note what a radical departure this is from the understanding of a leader, or a group of senior managers as having the power to design an organisation's future, or rearrange its culture, or change an organisation's 'direction.' Even a leader of a big enterprise, Stacey would argue, is only directly engaged with a very small proportion of the employees for whom they are responsible and it is in these local interactions that the generalisations that we might call 'strategy' emerge. We will return to the subject of strategy and the insights that might be gained from investigating mathematical modelling of complex social phenomena in Chapter 7.

The medium of engagement between staff engaged in competitive and co-operative interaction to achieve things together is embodied communication. By talking, discussing, taking turns, gesturing and responding to each other, recognising and misrecognising each other, staff in organisations are structuring what they do as themes and narratives of organising arise between them. Staff make sense together in both abstract and particular ways and contribute to organisational narratives about what is going on. They take up more abstract themes of organising, the organisation's vision, mission and strategy, but can only do so locally, in particular situations with particular others. Organisational activity, then, is always local, no matter how senior are the staff who are working, and it always involves communication. But it is from the many, many local communicative interactions that the global organisational patterning arises, which in turn constrains and informs the local interactions.

The analogy that Stacey is making with agent-based models which demonstrate complex adaptive systems theory is that it is from the actions of many, many employees organising locally with particular others that global organisational patterns emerge, and these global patterns are in turn taken up as generalisations in local interaction between staff. This may seem at first quite a difficult concept since it turns on the idea of paradox, which is very different from the assumptions in what I have been calling the dominant literature on management. In the latter it is possible for the leader of manager both to be an independent observer and designer of an organisation, and to be part of the unfolding of that design. The leader is at one stage outside the organisation as a detached observer, and then at another stage is inside the organisation subject to the effects of their design. With Stacey's formulation there is no splitting of the paradox: the leader or manager is forming and being formed by the global patterning *both at the same time*. In participating locally with powerful others, leaders and senior managers are contributing to the formulation of organising themes which get taken up by employees in the organisation. These organising themes are already shaped by the history of interaction within organisation, and the way that they are further taken up by employees in their myriad interactions with each other continue to influence the way that senior managers develop their ideas. Local and global phenomena are present both at the same time in all interactions in the organisation.

In thinking about organisations by analogy with insights from the complexity sciences and trying to maintain their radical implications Stacey has arrived at a similar conclusion about the importance of language and conversation, but from a different perspective, to the ethnomethodologist Boden (1994). Stacey's oeuvre has a much broader canvas than just language, since the ideas he has developed with Griffin and Shaw (2005) in the body of thought termed complex responsive processes of relating details the way in which engaged, responsive human bodies are engaged in fluctuating and paradoxical figurations with each other in iterative patterns of power and ideology. I will elaborate some of these ideas further in future chapters, but for the purposes of this chapter I will investigate the similarities and differences between Stacey's conclusions about language and conversation and Boden's views, who works from an ethnomethodological tradition. Ethnomethodology is form of research which takes a particular interest in the way that people account for the social situations they find themselves contributing to, and for this reason focuses heavily on language that the objects of research use to describe their everyday situations. Boden also thinks of organisations as arising out of an emergent, daily process of people coming together to try and achieve things collectively. Rather than privileging an abstract, broad brush discussion of structures and systems, she pays attention instead to what people do and what they say about what they do:

> To understand the profound orderliness of social life requires not aggregation and abstraction but attention to the finegrained details of moment-to-moment existence, and to their temporal, spatial and profoundly sequential organisation.
>
> (1994: 65)

I am also assuming, with Stacey and Boden, that what we have come to call structure and strategy is not something separate from people's everyday activities with each other, but it arises out of these activities, paradoxically formed by them, and forming them both at the same time. Language is at the core of the process of organising as people describe and interpret the key questions of organisational life: who are we and who are we becoming:

> *People* ... talk *their way to solutions,* talk *themselves into working*
> *agreements,* talk *their organizational coalitions,* talk *their organizational*
> *agendas, and, occasionally talk* through *or* past *each other.*
>
> (Boden, 1994: 52, emphasis in original)

There is nothing mystical or inexplicable about these diurnal processes which structure people's daily interactions with each other, and thus the shape of the organisation's work. An organisation is not some separate entity superimposed on people's daily life, it arises out of it as people take up organisational themes in their conversations with each other.

What I take from both Stacey and Boden is the insight that the particular details of people's interaction in an organisation is not a distraction from the 'bigger picture', but rather it is the way in which the bigger picture is formed. There will be a regularity to the way in which people come together to talk about what it is they think they are doing formed by their history of interactions and by the broader organisational themes that they may have shaped over months or years, and which in turn has shaped their responses. Equally, each interaction, be it a business meeting or planning workshop, will be a unique manifestation of these broader organisational themes because of the particular people involved and the context in which they meet. There is the potential for both stability and change at the same time because of the coming together of habitual organisational themes taken up in new circumstances with different people. Familiar themes are taken up in groups of people, who by engaging with them both sustain and potentially transform them at the same time.

To research an organisation understood as patterning and repatterning of people's communicative interactions requires that the researcher uses methods which pay attention to exactly this local interplay, as I will explore in the following example. In what follows I will narrate an episode of organisational life in which I was directly involved, will reflect on some of the themes that I think emerge from the episode, and will then reflect on the process of reflecting and the methods that this employs.

Working with a Group on Strategy

I was asked recently to facilitate a three-day workshop in the UK and a four-day workshop in Latin America for a large British multinational organisation drawing in 30 people from around the globe. The workshops were intended to develop two of the organisation's strategic aims in fulfilment of their broader strategy, which had been designed by the top management team.

In the first piece of work in the UK I had been given an outline agenda for the three days we would be spending together which my contractor had referred to as a workshop 'roadmap'. He told me that he has used this kind of outline before, which was quite detailed and had aims and objectives for every single session. In the event I had not followed this road map religiously but had spent my time negotiating intensely every step of the way with the participants. In this sense I felt I was working against received wisdom about what it means to be a facilitator and consultant, which I explored in the previous chapter.

Whilst recognising that I was most probably working with a group of people who would have this set of expectations of me, I nonetheless proceeded in a way that constantly opened things up for discussion and negotiation; the order we might discuss things, the way we might discuss them, and whether other things had arisen in the course of the discussion so far that had affected our original plans. At the same time I had to bear in mind what it was that my contractors expected of me. I also needed to work with the expectation that I would bring them to point where they had produced something that looked to them like a recognisable strategy. I was conscious that one of the unspoken things we were dealing with was the anxiety about 'delivering the outputs', a set of ideas and intentions that would pass muster for what this particular organisation understood strategy to be. Through this constant negotiation of the way that we undertook the task together, which was mediated by whether we would produce something of the right quality and on time, small opportunities had opened up for discussing things differently. The original order of the workshop changed, and we did indeed address questions that arose in the course of discussion. By the last day I did not feel that the outcome of the three days was significantly affected by the way I had worked, at least in the shape and tenor of the concluding strategic statements, and this was partly because the most senior manager present had acted unilaterally towards the end of the workshop to rewrite other people's efforts into a document that she felt was expected by her managers. But I could see at least the glimmerings of difference that had emerged both through things that were included in the statement and the way participants had joined in to present it.

As a result of this experience I proceeded to carry out my role in a similar way in the second workshop in Latin America. It was the same contractor who had experienced me working before who had asked me back on the basis of the perceived success of what had taken place previously. I began by negotiating very mildly on the first day about the extension of an activity which some of the participants had not completed. The very act of rescheduling, however, seemed to trigger enormous anxiety in a vocal minority of the participants that we would not 'deliver our outputs' on time. This manifested itself in their criticising the way the workshop had been planned in general, and my role as a facilitator in particular. Although I thought I had acted to open up possibilities for the participants themselves to exercise influence they seemed viscerally opposed to doing so. Their criticism was couched in terms of my not being in control of the workshop, which points to their strong expectation about what facilitators are there to do.

The remaining days turned into a struggle over the way I did my job, with participants seeming to want me to set them tighter and tighter objectives with less and less time to fulfil them. As I did so, guided by my contractor, they seemed to react to the increasing constraints by acting out in ill-disciplined ways, turning up late in the mornings for the start of proceedings, talking over each other and not keeping to time despite their requests that I should be a more disciplined time keeper. Participants wandered in and out of the workshop as it preceded, even senior members of staff, making and taking mobile phone calls, and were rude to each other and to me. What I was tempted to do, but was prevented by my contractor from so doing, was to draw attention to what was happening in the room. I put this to my contractor and a small group of participants that we had formed in order to act as a reference group for the event. My contractor thought that to ask the group to reflect on what was happening in the room would be 'unfair' to the participants, since they were not accustomed to reflecting on their own actions.

Thoroughly depressed and demoralised, I undertook the rest of the consultancy trying to hold on to whatever shreds of dignity I could maintain, asking for guidance at every stage from my contractor and the reference group, in order to work in a way that they felt they could recognise. For me it became a lifeless and mechanical performance, an act, where I was pretending to be the kind of facilitator they expected me to be, although it was clear to me and to them that I was not doing this credibly.

Reflections on what Happened

Previously in this chapter I have made the case that the global patterning of interaction in an organisation arises from the way in which people relate to each other in their day-to-day work, which in turn reproduces the global patterning. The particular quality and nature of this global patterning may be what some people refer to as organisational 'culture'. In this particular organisation I was aware of a good degree of anxiety about producing 'outputs', although there was much less clarity about what adequate 'outputs' would look like. So great was this anxiety that it began to have a dominating effect on the way that people related to each other, and to the way that they related to me. To borrow from the language that I have been developing earlier in the chapter, it became a narrative theme organising the experience of all of us participating in the workshop – the way participants in the workshop began to articulate their anxiety began to shape what was happening for all of us. For most participants the anxiety about producing results in the workshop led them to behave in ways where they tried to exert control over the situation, and over me. The patterning of this collective effort to control resulted in a very constraining dynamic operating in the group which ultimately no one was in control of, not even the facilitator, and it led a number of participants to behave in ways which might appear counter-intuitive or even irrational to an outsider. It undermined the ability to discuss what we had come to do as we became more and more preoccupied with our emotional reactions to each other.

It is exactly this process of affect, strong feeling, blindly driving social interaction that we began to explore in the previous chapter drawing on Elias (1939/2000). Many participants in the group clearly had expectations of me and what I was supposed to be doing to which they were so committed that it overcame their self-restraint. They demanded that I direct them, to organise each session in a particular way with clear objectives, and for me to have a clear sense of when we had achieved them. They wanted me to manipulate them towards this end. To this extent, our expectations of what I was there to do clearly differed and we were unable to find ways of exploring that difference. I was concerned about the strategy we were producing as a group because of the difficulty of having open discussion which had become so constrained by our struggles over influence. In this particular event it became impossible to differ and discuss the difference.

I was concerned to discuss what was happening in the group: for me it was an important area of enquiry. My contractor, however, was both unwilling and unable to find time to talk about what we found ourselves caught up in. Just recently in other consultancies a number of managers and consultants have made a similar point of telling me that they do not read much and have little time to think about the work that they are doing. They tell me they are practical people. Sometimes they are the same managers who also find it difficult to find time to sit down with their staff to reflect on what it is they are doing together. If they invite me to join them when they do find half a day, or a day (rarely more than this) there is often much talk about how this is a 'luxury', how we really need to make this time count, how we need to be sure that this is not just a 'talking shop.' Even reflective time has to be oriented towards 'outputs' or 'results', without there being any clear idea about what a result might look like.

Staff and managers in organisations have a tendency to suggest in many organisational settings that conflict can and should be 'managed', that staff should align their efforts and their aspirations in order to effect a kind of organisational unity, and that by doing so the efforts of everyone will be enhanced. This is an idealised portrayal of what happens in the day-to-day in organisations, and I believe it attempts to cover over people's everyday lived experience of working together with others which will involve both co-operation and conflict. I regard this as a missed opportunity for leaders and managers who are appealing to an abstract idea of organising at the expense of paying attention to what is actually happening. My contention is that managers in organisations should be investigating and researching the complexity they are part of, rather than dismissing it as a distraction from idealised ends. The situation I described above was one which it seemed to me would have benefited from the kind of reflection to which I am drawing attention, when we might have asked ourselves: 'What on earth is going on here? And why have we become so obsessed with producing outputs.'

I am developing the argument the reflection with others on the day-to-day process of organising is at the heart of what a manager and consultant could be doing by way of research, since it is daily interaction, and reflection on action, that different ways of interacting can be discovered. I am making the case that paying attention to the experience of working together, noticing the habitual patterning that we contribute to in our dealings with others, allows for the potential transformation of that experience.

What are the grounds for thinking this and on what theories would I be drawing to put these ideas forward?

Philosophical Interlude – on the Need for Reflection and Reflexivity

The pragmatic philosopher George Herbert Mead also enquired into how it is that we become aware of ourselves in a social context, and how we co-ordinate our activities as separate but interdependent selves. How do global social patterns arise from our daily interactions without recourse to metaphysical explanations or abstract wholes? If I am arguing against the idea that change comes about simply by managers and leaders choosing what should happen, then what is going on and how might I begin to reinterpret the incidents that I have described above?

Mead was interested in the way that we anticipate, respond to and potentially transform the interactions we have with other people. He developed his theories, heavily influenced by natural science and in particular Darwin's theory of evolution, to explain the continuous emergence of the novel:

> *There is always some sort of novelty about what happens in the most*
> *common place sort of an experience and the most ordinary sort of an*
> *action, always a tang of novelty about whatever takes place. That novelty*
> *is something which cannot possibly be predicted ... Even what can be*
> *predicted – that you are going to meet your friend at the station, that*
> *you are going to read a book – always carries with it something which*
> *is different from what could possibly have been anticipated. Novelty is*
> *always present ... with every breath we are stepping into a world that*
> *has a novel element in it.*
>
> *(1936: 116)*

Where Elias was concerned with describing long-term patterns of human interaction and the effect these had on our growing ability to 'take a detour via detachment', Mead was concerned more with moment by moment interaction – how patterns of behaviour repeat themselves (and if they didn't there would be no continuity in social life) but also how they are potentially changed. Because of our physiology he argued, we are uniquely able to take ourselves as objects to ourselves, to see ourselves as others might see us. The paradoxical interaction between the self and other is the locus of both continuity and change and is the basis for Mead's explanation of how the local informs the global and vice versa. The reader will note how Mead too is working with the idea of paradox as a way of reaching for explanations which keep the generative tension between local and global, self and other. Equally, at the core of his ideas, and the phenomenon that differentiates us from other species, is the phenomenon of language.

In *Mind, Self and Society* (1934) Mead reflected upon this unique reflexive ability and explored how it contributed to the idea of mind, our sense of self and our co-ordination with other selves, what we call society. Like Elias,

Mead in no sense intended these three perspectives on mind, self and society to be thought of as occurring separately on different 'levels', rather he thought of them being different phases of the same process. Taken together it is, like Elias' processual theories, a radically social and evolutionary view of the formation of our sense of mind, our sense of self, and the production and reproduction of society.

For Mead our interactions with others are a conversation of gesture and response, a communication of what Mead terms 'significant symbols'. A symbol is significant when it implicitly arouses in an individual making it the same responses which it explicitly arouses in others. For Mead there is no separation between mind and body: he does not think of arousal as being a purely mental or alternatively a bodily response, but both at the same time. Interacting with other people calls out feeling states in us and in others, to which we respond. Feelings are the irreducible core of experience, not some kind of add-on or distraction from being rational. Feelings are what make rationality possible, as the neuroscientist Damasio (1999) has pointed out. The communication of significant symbols is possible between individuals of the same social group, or between an individual and him or herself, in the form of an internalised conversation. The symbols are generally understood by all the members of the same social group and without this it would not be possible for us to be able to communicate with each other. However, the meaning of a significant symbol does not lie in the gesture of one individual alone, but only when it is taken together with the response of the individual being gestured to. Meaning arises iteratively and temporally as we gesture and respond to each other and to ourselves.

Just to pause on that point for a moment and reinforce it. Mead is saying that we are not fully aware of the meaning of what we are saying until we have said it and have taken together our own response to what we call out in ourselves, and the response of the person (people) to whom we are gesturing. In this lies the possibility of surprising ourselves, and surprising others. Whatever we intend, our gestures are not always interpreted as we think they might be. There is no pure packet of meaning being conveyed from me to another person, and we cannot be in control of how others respond to what we do and say. We cannot know in advance what resonance our words and actions have for others. And here lies the possibility for small differences to emerge between humans engaged in gesturing and responding to each other as our gestures call out sometimes surprising responses in others which in turn call out potentially surprising responses in ourselves. One of the enjoyable aspects of a good conversation, then, is that it can sometimes take surprising twists and turns and can become a stimulating improvisation between two or more people.

So we are engaged, says Mead, in a conversation of gestures. The gesturer is responding and adjusting both to what they are saying as they say it, and to the response of the other to whom they are gesturing. It is in these subtle mutual adjustments using shared symbols of significance that both stability and change are possible within daily communication. Without significant symbols we would not be able to communicate, at the same time the act of communication is a social process involving mutually adapting communicators where there is room for variation and spontaneity. The internalisation of our experience of external conversations of gesture and response with other individuals, our ability to have an internal 'conversation' with ourselves, is what we would term 'thinking'. For Mead, mind arises from our ability to turn experience back to ourselves, or reflexivity: it is through our reflexive ability, our ability to generate an internal conversation of gestures with ourselves that we experience mind. As individuals we have a constant internal conversation about what we think is going on which affects the way that we interact with others, who are similarly engaged in an internal conversation.

Additionally, Mead argues, our sense of self is only possible in a society of other selves. Our emerging, spontaneous sense of self, what Mead terms the 'I' continuously comes up against our sense of a 'generalised other', a 'me', or an idea of what others would think of us. We do not simply act in the moment, but are able to contemplate how others see us acting, which conditions our actions. We are capable of surprising ourselves in the way that we act and speak just as much as we are capable of surprising others. Again it would be reductive to think that Mead intends us to split these two processes out: first there is an 'I' and then there is a 'me' response. Rather Mead understands them as inseparable, dialectical phases of the same act. The image that he uses is of a rolling two-tone ball which may reveal one side only but is never separated from the other side. This ability both to be an agent and to understand ourselves as an agent is how self-consciousness arises in our interactions with others, but also explains how social processes are present in us.

> Every individual self within a given society of social community reflects in its organised structure the whole relational pattern of organised social behaviour which that society of community exhibits or is carrying on, and its organised structure is constituted by this pattern; but since each of these individual selves reflects a uniquely different aspect or perspective of this pattern in its structure ...

*the structure of each is differently constituted by this pattern from the
way in which the structure of any other is so constituted.*

(Mead, 1934: 202)

We become who we are because we are born into a particular society with a
particular social structure which we learn through a process of socialisation to
adapt to as a 'generalised other'. But our response to the general patterning of
social behaviour and structure is unique: it is in this paradox that both stability
and change, general social themes and particular responses to them, are
possible. This is a very similar understanding to the process of individualisation
that Elias describes in *The Civilising Process* which can only place within the
constraints that society places upon us:

*The coexistence of people, the intertwining of intentions and plans,
the bonds they place on each other, all these, far from destroying
individuality, provide the medium in which it can develop. They set the
individual limits, but at the same time give him greater or lesser scope.
The social fabric in this sense forms the substratum from which and
into which the individual constantly spins and weaves his purposes.*

(1939/2000: 543)

Both Mead and Elias think of the self as arising in the interactions with
other selves, and that this interaction has the potential for both predictability
and unpredictability. Predictability lies in the fact that we do not continuously
invent everything anew, but inherit language, concepts, ways of behaving
that form the society into which we are born. Unpredictability arises from our
own unique response to the generalisations that we inherit in the company of
others. For Mead there are some great minds who make a significant difference
to thinking or to social processes, like Einstein, but he sees this only as an
extreme example of what is happening continuously in our daily processes of
interaction with others as we make unique but minute variations to the stable
patterning in which we find ourselves acting.

It is worth pointing out that many of Mead's theories of the paradoxical coexistence of a sense of 'I' and a generalised understanding of a 'me' arising at
the same time is borne out by a large amount of contemporary brain research
which is articulated by scholars such as Ramachandran (2011), and Damasio
(2010). For example Ramachandran points to the way in which we become self-
conscious, that is to say how we become conscious of how others are conscious
of us. We are able to take ourselves as objects to ourselves, and imagine also

how we figure in the consciousness of others. He develops his argument on the basis of the assumption of 'mirror neurones' in the brain which allow us to adopt tentatively the standpoint of another, which can also be turned back on ourselves.

The third aspect of Mead's understanding of social relating, after mind and self, concerns the emergence of society. Central to this is Mead's idea of a social object. Social objects do not have any existence outside social acts, and in this sense are different from natural objects. Rather what he intended by the term is a generalised tendency to act in a particular way by large numbers of interdependent people. So the workshops that I facilitated in the UK and in Latin America could be thought of in Mead's terms as social objects, in the sense that the people attending them would have had general expectations about what would happen there and how they should behave in that general kind of context. The exact form a social object takes, however, depends upon the way that participants in the social object adapt and respond to each other and struggle over what Mead referred to as 'the life process of the group'. From Mead's perspective we are dealing with something very complex when humans come together to achieve something together. As individuals they are gesturing and responding to others, and to themselves through an internalised dialogue, using significant symbols in a way that calls for subtle mutual adaptation. This is taking place within a generalised group activity, a workshop, which is being realised in the interactions between engaged participants. Irrespective of the intentions of those planning the workshop, such as my contractor and I, the exact form the workshop took would depend on how we gestured and responded to each other, how we anticipated and responded to each other, and how we struggled over the 'life process of the group' and the patterning that arose as a consequence.

Summary of the Argument so far and the Consequences for Research

What I take from my investigation of Stacey as he explores the significance of insights from the complexity sciences and Mead's theories of the emergence of the social self is the importance of our daily, local engagement with others which enacts the potential for both continuity and change at the same time. At the heart of these concepts is the idea of paradox, that in our particular encounters with others we are always taking up generalised social themes bodily and through our communicative interaction with others, which we are forming just as we are being formed. Rather than paying attention to global patterns of organisational life and thinking of them as being fixed superstructures into which all activity 'fits', I am concerned to focus on the way in which we gesture and respond to each other and talk the organisation into existence. I am taking the view that there is no organisation separate from the way we work together in the here and now and the way we come to talk about it. As we gesture and respond to each other we are replicating generalised ways of behaving and talking, but at the same time our own unique responses to each other have the potential for transforming them. When I meet together with others in an organisational context we each have expectations of how the meeting may proceed from our experience of previous meetings and as we take up familiar themes and ideas, but at the same time because of the particular course of mutual adaptation that takes place, each meeting has the potential for surprise and novelty. It is also the case that the people organising together can repeat previous patterns of interaction over and over again in ways which can become stuck, reducing the opportunities for novelty and surprise. The second incident I described in the narrative in Latin America is a good example of stuck patterns, where every time I attempted to negotiate and explore I was prevented from doing so.

For the reasons I have begun to set out, this book tries to pay attention to what actually happens as people try to organise together, to understand from the perspectives of the people I am working with what it is they think they are doing. I am doing so based on the theory that the global patterning that we might take to be an organisation arises out of many, many interactions, but that these interactions are informed by the global patterning. Enquiring into particular examples, events where a particular patterning of interaction has arisen, provides the data for reflecting on the more general themes that one can encounter in the organisation into which one is acting. In this chapter I have described a number of incidents that happened with colleagues in Latin America and in the UK in narrative form and have started to use them as the basis for reflection. In the narrative I am paying particular attention to affect, both my own and other people's, as well as noting the language that people use to describe what they are doing, or the theories that they allude to in organising themselves. In doing so I am guided by Elias, Stacey and Mead who value not abstract, static concepts of organisation, but the process of organisational becoming, how organisations arise in the day-to-day engagement between people.

I am offering this way of working as a form of qualitative social research in the phenomenological and hermeneutic traditions, which shares some things in common with ethnomethodology, which I have demonstrated by drawing on Boden (1994). In common with ethnomethodology I am interested in the specific, the contextual and the micro. However, in addition I am also interested in affect, power relations expressed as organisational politics, and the paradoxical interplay of the local and global patterning. For I share a critique of ethnomethodology in common with the French sociologist Bourdieu (1977) when he argues that paying attention to the contextual does not necessarily give the researcher an insight into the conditions that allowed for the contextual to occur. As Alvesson and Sköldberg (2009) have also noted the ethnomethodologist's attention seems to waver just at the point that research starts to get interesting if we were also eager to enquire into the broader social patterning that has formed the actors in the first place.

Putting it more simply, by phenomenological I understand to mean the process of addressing phenomena that arise in the process of my engaging with others without my ascribing to them abstract ways of thinking or categorisations that commonly get taken up in writing about organisations. By hermeneutic, I intend the idea that once I have written about my experiences of working with others in narrative form, I will then attempt to interpret what it is I am experiencing using a broader tradition of thought of management theory, sociology and philosophy.

Narrative is broadly accepted in sociological research as being a method well suited to capturing some of the complexity of what researchers are dealing with (Atkins, 2008; Czarniawska, 2004; Tsoukas and Hatch, 2001). However, I will be making no claims that the narrative that I am writing is 'fact'. What I write differs from fiction in the sense that I have not intentionally set out to substitute an artistic and imaginative rendering of the experiences that I thought I had with others, but I also make no claims that what I am describing is 'the truth'. Nor will I be making claims that this is ethnomethodological research in the sense that Garfinkel (1967) meant it and the example I gave above from Deirdre Boden's work. That is to say, unlike Boden I have not systematically kept notes of every interaction that I was engaged with as a form of micro study. The narratives I write are an episode of organisational life that somehow struck me as being of consequence to what it was we were dealing with at the time, and I render it to the best of my ability without producing what have come to be understood as case studies in the management literature. In other words, I accept with John Dewey (1958) that my understanding of my own experience will only ever be partial and selective: the narrative I produce will not be particularly polished, or shaped to deliver a pre-reflected educational point. Rather, it is intended to be rich, evocative and full of possibilities, or as Alvesson and Sköldberg (2009: 305) put it 'rich in points'. I go on to try and explore these possibilities and offer some possible interpretations of them. I choose these narratives because they have significance for me in the patterns of relating that I notice while I am working in organisations, often because they repeat themselves a lot in my engagements with organisations, and I am expecting that they will have similar resonance for the reader, particularly if they are employed in organisations as managers, staff or as consultants. It is the extent of this recognition by the reader, both of the events and the theories that I bring to help explain them, which will test whether this method is convincing or not. As Czarniawska argues, using narrative as a qualitative method hinges on the reader finding what has been written interesting and relevant, rather than valid and scientific.

In writing in this way I am consciously producing something very different from a conventional book on management, as I argued in the first chapter. What I am attempting instead is a form of rich reflection on my own practice with staff in organisations with whom I come into contact, and in this sense I am trying to model the kinds of ways of working that I think are increasingly necessary in contemporary organisations. In this sense, although I offer no grids and frameworks to managers and consultants I am offering them some guidance about what I think is important. Since our dealings with other people are complex and constantly in flux, I am making an argument here that the way we come to think about what we are doing when we act together with others should be equally complex. I am presuming that we cannot stand outside the activities we undertake with others from some privileged vantage point and know with any fixed certainty the truth of what is happening. By paying attention to the local, live interaction between engaged participants in organisational life, partly by using narrative and reflection on narrative I am trying to draw attention to what I consider to be general, recognisable trends in the management of organisations which are worthy of note and comment. I have an expectation that what I write will be recognised by my readers to a greater or lesser extent, because I am attempting to describe what I am judging to be patterns which repeat themselves quite often in organisational life. The most important thing I think I am doing is to draw attention both to the object and method of enquiry.

In this sense what I am doing sits very much within the interpretive or hermeneutic tradition to which I allude above. The philosopher Gadamer (1975), a leading figure in the philosophy of hermeneutics, contrasted the

Socratic process of enquiry with that of scientific method, and it is the latter not the former to which most management books aspire. He made the case that scientific enquiry is teleologically driven by knowledge, and as such creates 'an illusion of experience perfected and replaced by knowledge' (1975/2004: 354). What I think he meant by this is that scientific enquiry is always driven by the desire to end in some kind of knowledge product separate from the people who produced it, some generalisable knowledge, such as, in management terms, a grid or a framework. By doing this, Gadamer argued, it robs human experience of much of its value, which is to be found in the story of how the knowledge emerged and the process of dialectic that contributed to the production of knowledge. The dominant idea of scientific enquiry is to create universal and context-free products that enable us to predict and control nature. In contrast, Gadamer idealised not the product but the process; to be experienced, he argues, means that one is open to more experience. He draws attention to the importance of conversation with others since it enables the Socratic process of questioning, the opening up to otherness, that is not about being in control but about being increasingly undogmatic and questioning further:

> The art of questioning is the art of questioning even further – i.e., the art of thinking. It is called dialectic because it is the art of conducting a real dialogue…. To conduct a conversation means to allow oneself to be conducted by the subject matter to which the partners in the dialogue are oriented … As against the fixity of opinions, questioning makes the objects and all its possibilities fluid. A person skilled in the 'art' of questioning is a person who can prevent questions from being suppressed by the dominant opinion.
>
> (1975/2004: 360–361)

What is most important to Gadamer is the ongoing cycle of enquiry and the continued openness to those with whom one is engaging. The parallel that I would draw with the process of organising is that the patterning that arises in organisations as people interact in asymmetric power relations simply results in more patterning. Narrative enquiry and reflections on the narrative allow for the same process of patterning then patterning further as an attempt at meaning making. Equally, in groups, reflection on what we are engaged in allows us better to understand the patterning to which we are contributing, and which we are forming and being formed by at the same time. Drawing on Socrates and Hegel, Gadamer believes that knowledge arises in the process of question and answer in a way that is driven by the movement between engaged discussants. In writing I am offering a contextualised account of organisational patterning for my interpretation and the further interpretation of the reader.

So here is a principal difference that I am offering between my understanding of what happens in organisations and many of the conventional books on management. I am suggesting that what happens between people every day at work, whether it is perceived to have gone well or badly, is more important for thinking about how to work better together than trying to develop a new tool or framework. I am encouraging managers and consultants to pay attention to the kinds of interaction in which they find themselves caught, including noticing the strong feelings that often get evoked at work including in themselves as managers, as a helpful way of thinking about how they might continue to participate. In doing so, they will be uncovering of some taken for granted ideas about the management of organisation as a means of opening them up to further questioning. As I mentioned in Chapter 1, this is a method to encourage managers and consultants to think about what they are doing, to become reflexive about how they interact with others. I am doing so in the belief that it offers an understanding and methods more appropriate for coming to terms with the complexity of situations that face managers and staff in the day-to-day practice of their work. In other words, instead of encouraging managers and consultants to think of an organisation as a thing that they can act upon and change from one state to another, rather they think of themselves as co-participants, perhaps powerful ones, in the ongoing web of relationships to which they are contributing. To reflect upon how they are contributing, and how their contribution is reflected back to them by the reactions of others, and what happens as a result is important data to take into account when deciding what to do next.

What Does Narrative Enquiry and Reflection Mean for Ideas of 'Objectivity'? Some More Theory

In opting for methods based on narrative enquiry, engagement with others and collective reflection am I not also compromising the idea of 'objectivity'? Shouldn't a manager, and particularly a consultant aspire to being an objective influence on those they choose to work with? What happens to the idea of evidence which a manager or consultant, in their investigations into an organisation, is supposed to be collecting data to develop a case for acting one way or another?

Being able to reflect on what it is we are doing, how we are acting, is a powerful way of seeing. When we undertake this exercise with others, when we reflect together on what we are doing and why, it can create opportunities for renewing our faculty of judgement. When we come back to ourselves, when we are reflexive, we are exercising that faculty which, according to Mead, makes us uniquely human. Being able to draw in others into the process adds another interpretive voice. There is the potential for even greater reflection which allows for expanded possibilities for interpretation and action.

But what might evidence look like in a social context, where there are multiple causes, and those wishing to interpret what is going on have been formed by the very social processes that they wish to comment on? This is what the sociologist Anthony Giddens (1993) has referred to as the 'double hermeneutic', where concepts that have been developed to describe social phenomena then re-enter back into the world from which they were drawn and start to form the social behaviour they were describing. We interpret the world and assimilate and adapt to our own interpretations: we describe and are shaped by our own descriptions. As mentioned earlier, we are not simple rule-following agents but can reflect on our own experience of coming to terms with what is expected of us.

However, just because there are many causes of social phenomena and it is difficult to disentangle them does not mean that we should abandon the idea of evidence altogether. Rather, we might need to take a broader view of both scientific method and data as other social scientists have done. The sociologist Bent Flyvbjerg (2001) argues that social scientists should stop trying to emulate natural scientists and strive instead for what he terms 'phronetic research'. In coining the term 'phronetic' he is drawing on Aristotle's concept of *phronesis*, or practical wisdom. Aristotle used the word *phronesis* to describe the context-specific judgement and wisdom that we bring to bear in navigating our way through specific practical situations. This is very different from the universal, context-independent methods widely used in the natural sciences which are striving for *episteme*, or scientific knowledge as commonly understood in the natural sciences. Both Aristotle and Flyvbjerg are clear that in paying attention to our practices and trying to describe them we are not being scientific, if we take a narrow interpretation of what being scientific means, since our reaction to the demands of a specific context may not be generalisable.

Flyvbjorg gives as an example the ten-year study that he carried on the political process surrounding the development of the transport system in the

Danish city of Aalborg; he calls for a scientific method that draws attention to how power works in specific, concrete situations. He tries to rehabilitate narrative as a way of exploring power relations in context. As with methods more commonly used in the natural sciences he then argues that he should then present his theories to other engaged participants as a way of establishing their truth convergence. He invites contestation and argument just as any natural scientist would in publishing a scientific paper.

Perhaps what social scientists and researchers in organisations are striving for is reality-congruence, rather than correspondence with reality, which, in a permanently shifting world, is never possible. This does not mean abandoning the discipline of research, enquiry and the rigorous presentation of one's findings to broader public argument and contestation. It does not mean abandoning an interest in evidence, even if this 'evidence' is necessarily partial, fragmentary and liable to change.

If we were taking a strict view of what it means to be scientific perhaps we would be striving to be as detached and uninvolved as possible. So if we were looking for invariant properties of what we are observing as a way of producing valid data which would be replicable elsewhere, we would try to have as little influence on what is happening as possible. But how possible would that be when we are encouraging practitioners to interpret what it is that they are involved with, and to intensify that interpretation with others? Intervening or not intervening in the process would have an effect on the outcome of the discussion in organisations. To this degree managers and consultants are both researchers and participants in the research at the same time. They cannot maintain complete detachment from the circumstances they are researching, since their very presence affects the object of their research.

The neo-Kantian philosopher Jurgen Habermas (1983) wrestled with the same set of problems and describes how interpretive social science methods inevitably compromise the idea of objectivity. By participating in interpretation of what is happening, Habermas argues, we automatically give up the privileged position of the superior observer by becoming engaged in communicative exchange. The offering of an interpretation invites a counter-interpretation: we are obliged to give an account to one another of what we think is happening. And all of this can only be done within the particular context which we are discussing: it will be dependent upon this particular experience that we are having together. It can never be context independent. Habermas' ideal was to aspire to a power equivalence between engaged discussants so that each had an equal opportunity to be heard and understood. Less idealistically, one might take the view that such equivalence will never arise, since some people will always be more powerful than others, so we will never know whether a shared interpretation is fully shared.

As Gadamer, Flyvbjorg and Habermas have argued, the process of interpretation produces a different kind of knowledge to that of conventionally understood scientific knowledge, which is presumed to be value and context independent. Interpretive knowledge is leavened by the power relations that arise between engaged participants, and is intended to generate meanings which are constantly opened up to further and further interpretation. It may produce interpretations of what has been going on in this context between these particular people and may have value as a powerful example of a more generalised social phenomenon. Whether it is applicable elsewhere will be subject to further rounds of interpretation and power relations that will render the explanations useful or not.

So what interpretive social science methods have in common with a more orthodox understanding of science is that they can open themselves up to further iterations of accountability: like conventional science, interpretative social science is still obliged to justify itself. There is a continuous dialectic of accounting and re-accounting for what one has learned and how one has learned it. However, there is never any pretence that those offering the interpretation somehow stand outside the process they are interpreting or can offer a final truth. They may be more or less skilful at offering an interpretation of what is happening, but they can make no claims to being 'objective'. Although they might pay attention to how they are influencing the group, indeed this might itself become a subject of interpretation, they are unlikely to be able to give a full account of the way in which this is happening.

In his essay *Problems of Involvement and Detachment*, referred to above and in the previous chapter, Elias described the way in which human beings have been able to be much more detached, in his formulation able to take 'a detour via detachment', about the natural world, but not to the same degree about the social world. Our scientific knowledge of the natural world has become relatively autonomous from the groups of scientists producing it. However, according to Elias we have not achieved a similar detachment about our dealings with each other. We find ourselves caught up in our social involvement driven by affect. Elias laments the way that scientific methods more appropriate to the study of the natural world have been taken up unproblematically in the social sciences, where researchers are 'apt to seize upon these models as on ready-made and authoritative means for gaining certainty, often enough without distinguishing clearly whether it is certainty about something worth knowing or something rather insignificant which they have gained in this way' (1987: 33). Elias warns against the mechanical transfer of models from one scientific discipline to another since it provides a kind of pseudo-detachment, distorts the problems under review and severely limits the kinds of research that is possible. He is keen to establish in the social sciences the same kind of dispassionate observation methods which are used in the natural sciences, but ones which take account of the degree of our involvement. We should become more detached about our involvement, a paradoxical concept which I will explore more fully in the next chapter.

Concluding Thoughts on Researching Organisations

In this chapter I have been continuing with the discussion about how in the OD literature which is used extensively on management courses in business schools it is a fairly unproblematic proposition that managers should gather 'evidence' by carrying out an organisational 'assessment' and offer a 'diagnosis' of what is needed to improve organisational performance. Where once it was common to find the kind of vocabulary which implies a detached scientific observer who can identify invariant properties of what they are observing, now it is just as possible to come across scholars who accept the use of self as instrument in the research process. However, in doing so they sometimes stray into metaphysical territory implying that the researcher is required to attune themselves to the 'essence' of the whole organisation before doing so, or they need to achieve some kind of heightened state of mind. For example, in his latest book Senge (Senge, Scharmer, Jaworski et al., 2005) also uses the idea of the decentred self, but seems to suggest that becoming decentred is akin to achieving an increased state of awareness such as that described in esoteric practices like Tibetan Buddhism. It is a mystical state where the consultant is attuned to some kind of archetype of humanity, an idealised wholeness which can be shared. In making an argument for paying attention to daily interaction I am not presuming that managers and consultants will need any arcane knowledge of skills to do so, although it is certainly the case that they can become more and more practised. Stacey and Griffin (2005) make a comparable critique of Reason and Bradbury's participant enquiry method (2001), where esoteric claims are made about new 'wholes' the participating researcher creates with those they are researching, which are presumed to contribute to emancipatory forms of being and a new consciousness.

Chris Argyris (1993), a very eminent American scholar takes a more empirical approach to organisational research and sets out a variety of methods, including narrative and ethnomethodology which he thinks a researcher will be required to use in order to understand what is going on in an organisation. He has no difficulty in also prescribing quantitative methods where they are helpful in attempts to produce what he calls 'actionable knowledge' for changing the status quo. However, relying just on quantitative methods, he argues, means that researchers tend to ignore meanings being developed by their subjects as well as the processes by which they have come to construct their realities. A consideration of meaning requires an intuitive, subjective and empathetic grasp of the subjects' consciousness (1993: 272) which the aspiration to objectivity does not value. Although Argyris takes a more grounded and methodical position than Senge, he nonetheless aims to produce deterministic knowledge, in his terms knowledge which can reliably bring about the required change in organisations: for this reason he is against too much methodological pluralism since for him using too many methods produces too many answers. Argyris intends to 'close the gap' between what he calls espoused theories and theories in use. In other words, managers in organisations claim to believe in one way of acting, but actually undermine that way of acting because of their defensive routines. Argyris understands his job to be producing the 'right' data which will draw managers' attention to the way that they are sabotaging what they aspire to. He helpfully acknowledges the role of anxiety, defensiveness and politics in organisational life, but puts forward the idea that managers are capable of articulating their defensive routines and in doing so, 'correcting' them. The organisation therefore moves from an imperfect to an improved way of functioning.

I am, of course, similarly concerned with organisational improvement but I am much less certain than Argyris about what constitutes the 'right' data. Unlike me I would claim that he is still operating in a rationalist paradigm where he thinks that we can simply identify and correct our mistakes consciously. I find myself siding with Wittgenstein when he observed that we can never stand outside ourselves and very often what we take for granted is invisible to us, by definition.

Summary of this Chapter and Implications for Consultants and Managers

In summing up the similarities and differences between the position I have set out at the beginning of this chapter and those other scholars whom I have drawn into the discussion, I will attempt a review of what I am putting forward as appropriate research methods. Throughout this book I have offered a critique of the idea that a consultant or manager can be an objective observer standing 'outside' of an organisation to make an assessment and diagnosis of what is 'wrong' in order to offer a prescription for change. However, in decentring the consultant or manager and arguing that they are co-contributors to the processes that they intend researching, I join a number of other scholars who have made similar claims. However, as distinct from Senge et al. (2005) and Reason and Bradbury (2001), I do not think that what I am doing is partaking in a metaphysical or emancipatory experience or feel the need to undergo an esoteric training in order to do this. For me, working with everyday experience is not about experiencing the transcendent. Whilst paying attention to the importance of power, politics and anxiety in organisational life, like Argyris, I do not agree with him that it is possible to consciously identify and give up one's defensive routines to achieve 'actionable' improvement. Nor can I assume that the research I do will generate deterministic outcomes if, after Mead, I assume that my findings are a gesture the full meaning of which will only become apparent once the people I am working with have responded. There is no guarantee that any observation I make, or judgement that I offer will be interpreted or made use of as I intend.

What is required to research organisations, I have argued above, are methods that are consonant with the continuous processes of mutual adaptation, mutual anticipation and meaning-making that occurs when people come together to achieve things. Organisations are not static things but are constantly created and recreated as people co-operate and compete in their daily work. In the midst of this mutual becoming the manager and consultant is a co-contributor to the process and will be trying to exercise what Elias (1987) referred to as detached involvement. As a way of trying to overcome what he regarded as the unnecessary dualism of objectivity and subjectivity, Elias suggested that we engage with the world along a continuum of involvement and detachment. We are both involved and detached at the same time in some amalgam of the two. We can never find ourselves at either end of the continuum, unless we are either a very young baby or psychologically damaged in some way: we can never be completely involved or completely detached.

If I am unconvinced by the argument that the manager is objective, am I putting the case that the manager has nothing to offer, and that they are simply caught up along with everyone else? This is certainly not my view. I am arguing that the manager and consultant, in their daily work, have a particular responsibility for drawing attention to the way that people are co-operating and competing in creating the organisation together in their everyday interactions. I take this view drawing on Stacey, Elias and Mead, that it is in the local interactions between engaged participants that the global patterning, what we might call an organisation, arises. The object of the research is the way that people are narrating the organisation to each other: it focuses on what participants do and say emerging from the gestures and responses they are making to each other in the process of organising, and how they are constraining and enabling each other to shape the work. This daily practice between engaged interdependent people is not separate from the organisation; it is the way the organisation becomes. Drawing attention to processes of interaction and making them objects of discussion in themselves will affect these interactions because of the reflexive capacity of human beings. To carry out research using methods appropriate to how organisations continue to emerge obliges managers and consultants to pay attention to the ways in which they themselves may be affecting what is happening, and to do so in as dispassionate a way as possible, striving to be detached about their involvement.

And in calling for a greater use of the self as an instrument of research, as I have done in the title of this chapter, I am arguing, drawing on Mead and Elias, that the self is inseparable from other selves. I am subject to myself and an object to others: subjectivities do no arise arbitrarily, as Bourdieu (1990) has argued, but from historically developed social processes. By paying attention to my own part in the interactions in which I am participating, taking my own experience seriously, I am also able to say something about the patterning which I am forming, and which is forming me.

References

Alvesson, M. and Sköldberg, K. (2009) *Reflexive Methodology: New Vistas for Qualitative Research*, London: Sage.
Argyris, C. (1990) *Overcoming Organizational Defensives: Facilitating Organizational Learning*, Needham Heights, MA: Alleyn and Bacon.
—— (1993) *Knowledge for Action: A Guide to Overcoming Barriers to Organizational Change*, San Fransisco: Jossey Bass.
—— and Schön, D. (1978*) Organizational Learning: A Theory of Action Perspective*, New York: Addison Wesley.
—— (1995) *Organizational Learning: Theory, Method and Practice*, NJ: Prentice Hall.

Atkins, K. (2008) *Narrative Identity and Moral Identity: A Practical Perspective*, London: Routledge.

Boden, D. (1994) *The Business of Talk: Organization in Action*, Cambridge: Polity Press.

Bourdieu, P. (1977) *Outline of a Theory of Practice*, Cambridge: Cambridge University Press.

—— (1990) *The Logic of Practice*, Cambridge: Polity Press.

Czarniawska, B. (2004) *Narratives in Social Science Research*, London: Sage.

Damasio, A. (1999) *The Feeling of What Happens: Body, Emotion and the Making of Consciousness*, London: Verso.

—— (2010) *Self Comes to Mind: Constructing the Conscious Brain: The Evolution of Consciousness*, London: Heineman.

Dewey, J. (1958) *Experience and Nature*, New York: Dover Publications.

Elias, N. (1939/2000) *The Civilising Process*, Oxford: Basil Blackwell.

—— (1987) Problems of involvement and detachment, in Elias, N. Schröter, M. (ed.), Jephcott, E. (trans.), *Involvement and Detachment*, Oxford: Basil Blackwell.

Flyvbjerg, B. (2001) *Making Social Science Matter: Why Social Enquiry Fails and How It Can Succeed Again*, Cambridge: Cambridge University Press.

Gadamer, H.G. (1975) *Truth and Method*, London: Continuum Books.

Garfinkel, H. (1967) *Studies in Ethnomethodology*, Englewood Cliffs NJ: Prentice Hall.

Giddens, A. (1993) *New Rules of Sociological Method*, Stanford: Stanford University Press.

Habermas, J. (1983) Interpretive social science vs. hermeneuticism, in Haan, N., Bellah, R., Rabinow, P. and Sullivan, W. (eds), *Social Science as Moral Inquiry*, New York: Columbia University Press.

Holland, J. (1998) *Emergence from Chaos to Order*, New York: Oxford University Press.

Mead, G.H. (1934) *Mind, Self and Society from the Standpoint of a Social Behaviourist*, Chicago: University of Chicago Press.

—— (1936) *Movements of Thought in the 19th Century*, Chicago: University of Chicago Press.

—— (1938) *The Philosophy of the Act*, Chicago: University of Chicago.

Ramachandran, V.S. (2011) *The Tell-tale Brain: Unlocking the Mystery of Human Nature*, London: Heineman.

Reason, P. and Bradbury, H. (2001) *Handbook of Action Research: Participant Inquiry and Research*, London: Sage.

Senge, P. (1990) *The Fifth Discipline: The Art and Practice of the Learning Organization*, London: Century.

———, Scharmer, C.O., Jaworksi, J. and Flowers, B.S. (2005) *Presence: Exploring Profound Change in People, Organisations and Society*, London: Nicholas Brealey Publishing.

Shaw, P. (2002) *Changing Conversations in Organizations: A Complexity Approach to Change*, London: Routledge.

Stacey, R. (2000) *Strategic Management and Organisational Dynamics: The Challenge of Complexity*, London: Pearson.

———(2007) *Strategic Management and Organisational Dynamics: The Challenge of Complexity*, 5th edition, London: Routledge.

———, Griffin, D. and Shaw P. (2000) *Complexity and Management: Fad or Radical Challenge to Systems Thinking*, London: Routledge.

——— and Griffin, D. (2005) *A Complexity Perspective on Researching Organizations: Taking Experience Seriously*, London: Routledge.

Tsoukas, H. and Hatch, M.J. (2001) Complex thinking, complex practice: The case for a narrative approach to organizational complexity, *Human Relations*, 54(8): 979–1013.

Wheatley, M. (1999) *A Simpler Way*, New York: Berret-Koehler.

4

Theories of Leadership as Magico-Mythical Thinking

Introduction

In the preceding chapters I have been developing a number of arguments against what I have been terming the dominant discourse of managerialism, and the way that managerialist assumptions are taken up in the prevailing orthodoxy of Organisational Development (OD). I have been calling into question the idea that management can be thought of as a scientific discipline, unless we expand the definition of the term 'scientific' to include the non-linear complexity sciences, the sciences of uncertainty. In other words, social life does not proceed predictably and according to anyone's choosing, no matter how powerful they are. Instead daily communicative interactions between highly social interdependent selves produce continuity and the potential for change both at the same time.

I have been trying to reconnect management to philosophical and sociological debates particularly ones which are concerned to question the idea of objectivity, whether there is anywhere for an 'objective' leader or consultant to stand which is somehow 'outside' the interactions which they seek to affect through their participation. In Chapter 3 I began setting out an argument for the importance of reflective and reflexive research into the everyday process of organising because of what it might tell us about the ways in which the habitual patterning of relationships is being sustained in any organisation. I have been making the case that organisations are not simply broad brush abstractions, but emerge from organisational themes being taken up in particular contexts by particular people at a specific time. The way organisational themes get taken up may be highly repetitive and bolstered by strong appeals to identity and affect, which sustains the current order and makes it difficult to work or speak differently. In other words they are sustained by power relationships. As an alternative I have begun to suggest that paying attention to the way we are thinking, speaking, and acting in organisations, particularly noticing occasions where strong feeling is provoked, is an important part of thinking about how to go on together differently.

In order to do this I have been arguing that leaders, managers and consultants will be required paradoxically to become more detached about their involvement in organisational life. This is no easy thing to achieve given that I have also been pointing to the centrality of politics in the daily negotiations about power between engaged members of staff. Our identities are sustained by the roles that we take up in organisations, and the daily exposure to difference and contestation can be identity-threatening. Our efforts to stave off attempts to destabilise our identities may lead to some of the repeating patterns of behaviour that I have begun to describe in previous chapters. So I am offering a critique of the notion that a manager or consultant can rise above politics, or that it is as a distraction from the work, or that it can somehow be 'aligned' with some higher organisational objective. Instead I am saying that daily politics is the work. The kind of research that I am advocating takes an interest in flux, change and the ways in which the patterning of power relationships between people affects what it is possible to say and do.

As a way of explaining what I mean by this paradoxical proposition of detached involvement and the importance of overcoming the subjective/ objective dualism, I have drawn attention to Norbert Elias' ideas that the growing interdependence between larger and larger numbers of people has led to profound social and psychological changes for human beings. One of the significant psychological changes he outlines is the increased human ability to take a detour via detachment and thus move away from what he terms 'magico-mythical' thinking about nature. Increased detachment requires a greater mastery of affect if humans are not to be caught in the double bind where human knowledge with a high emotional and fantasy content, for example, the idea that storms are caused by angry spirits, leads to a decreased ability to respond to, or control nature, which leads in turn to more affect and fantasy-driven behaviour. While Elias considered that the practice of the natural sciences had largely broken the double bind that people used to get drawn into about events in nature, he was much less confident about our treatment of our social conditions:

> Here, high emotionality of thinking and high exposure to the dangers of that emanate from humans themselves, reinforce and often escalate each other.

> *Moreover, the danger is greatly increased by the fact that people caught in this double bind, but unaware of it, often consider the wishful thinking and emotive knowledge it engenders as entirely 'rational', as reality congruent.*
>
> *(Elias, 1987: 73)*

As someone who had been caught up in both world wars in the twentieth century, and as a Jewish refugee from Nazi Germany, Elias had first-hand experience of humankind's inability to achieve the necessary distance from destructive and potentially catastrophic affect-driven behaviour. Despite this he remained optimistic that greater dispassionate engagement was possible, and with it more robust methods for understanding human interdependence. I am suggesting that the methods I am advocating, paying attention to the ways in which we can get caught up in fantasy-driven thinking and behaviour in organisations, are one way of becoming more reality-congruent about the processes that shape daily organisational life.

The Literature on Leadership

In management literature nowhere is magico-mythical thinking more manifest than in the domain of leadership. There are hundreds of books and articles on leadership, most of which offer contradictory advice and recipes for success. The Stanford business professors Jeffrey Pfeffer and Robert Sutton (2006) have also pointed to the way that the leadership is both prolific and contradictory. We might, with Goleman, Boyatzis and McKee (2004) be encouraged to lead with emotional intelligence, or we might be offered a practical, structured way of leading other people (Waldcock and Kelly-Rawat, 2004). Leadership might, as far as Steven Covey (1999) is concerned, be about principles, and one of these principles is likely to be authenticity (Goffee and Jones, 2006), which raises an interesting conundrum about whether one can learn to be authentic. Pfeffer and Sutton point out that much of the literature on leadership is dealing in half-truths. While it is clear that a leader in a small company can have a huge impact, and there have been some huge influential world leaders, nonetheless many of the claims for leadership and leaders is unsupported by any substantial evidence, a proposition which we will be exploring further in this chapter. I want to take seriously Pfeffer and Sutton's claim that leaders are both in control and not in control of their organisations at the same time, and develop their ideas further by drawing on the complexity sciences, as a colleague of mine Philip Streatfield has done (Streatfield, 2001).

To an extent, books on leadership are an easy target and none of the above books is representative of more serious scholarly books on what we might mean by leadership and how important it is in organisational life. There are some prominent themes about leaders and leadership, however, which appear again and again, such as ideas to do with charisma, transformation and inspiration. Prevalent ideas of inspirational, transformational and visionary leadership are partly derived from the work of presidential biographer James MacGregor Burns (1982, 2003), whose ideas were developed by organisational theorists in search of normative criteria for what makes a good leader (Bass and Riggio, 2006; Kotter, 1990). In doing so they begin to make distinctions between 'transformational' and 'transactional' leadership, and develop a difference between leadership and management which I will explore in greater depth below. For Bass and Riggio, transactional leadership is mundane and day-to-day yet necessary process of leading, whilst transformational leadership is inspired, uplifting and, well, visionary. According to Kotter, whilst management is about predictability and control, leadership is a charismatic process very dependent upon the motivational nature of the leader's vision.

I have remarked before on the tendency for conventional management theory to separate out the experience of managing into dualistic poles: hence we have transformational/transactional, positive/negative, continuity/change, leadership and management. Orthodox management theory privileges the idea of the omniscient manager/leader who can choose to come down on one side of the dualism rather than the other, and can decide in advance of acting how they will behave. So a good leader would be someone who could choose to be transformational, turn things to the positive, decide on change and show themselves to be a leader rather than a manager. In being able to sew all of these things together they will have set out their vision in a coherent and morally convincing, authentic way that demonstrates how they will both inspire and deliver results. It is this dominant way of understanding what leadership is, and what leaders do, which partly explains the way that job advertisements come to be worded similarly, and thus why candidates for leadership posts come to describe themselves in the way they do. It is now taken for granted that a leader has to be visionary, and must set out a compelling narrative of transformation. Nothing less will do.

Leadership – The Critique

Perhaps the paragraphs above tell us as much about the state of the market for books on management as it does about leadership, but it is hard to find a concept that is so much talked about, yet so little based on any theoretical substance. As Nohria and Khurana (2010) state, leadership literature '... employs casual and sometimes self-serving empirical evidence; it is rarely grounded in any well-established empirical tradition. In short, it lacks intellectual rigor.' (2010: 5). Nohria and Khurana argue that leadership has long been marginalised as a serious research domain, since over the last 30 years it has had its critics who point out the weak causal link between leaders and what they do, and organisational performance. From the various perspectives of resource dependence research (Pfeffer and Salancik, 1978; Pfeffer, 1997), institutional research (Powell and DiMaggio, 1991) and organisation ecology research (Carroll and Hannan, 2000) leaders are thought to have a minimal impact on what organisations become. There are a handful of scholars who have remained convinced of the importance of leaders to organisations, and a huge plethora of more popular literature, particularly written by consultants and ex-Chief Executive Officers (CEOs) wishing to cash in on their success.

In *From Higher Aims to Hired Hands,* Khurana (2007) sets out his own views on how leadership came to be seen as a separate discipline from management. He makes the argument that the neo-classical economic revolution of the 1970s and 1980s had a profound effect on the way that business studies were taught, how business schools started to function and thus how managers came to think of themselves. First, economics came to dominate the curriculum with the argument that somehow this made management more 'scientific', since economics is a numbers-based discipline. And second, the particular form of economics that dominated regarded maximising shareholder value as the only significant metric of management and organisational performance. This posed a profound challenge to the previously dominant way of understanding the manager as a member of a discipline whose role was to offer stewardship of the company on behalf of a number of stakeholders. It was, Khurana argued, a wholesale discrediting of the conception of the manager as professional.

At the same time that the Chicago school of economists were developing their ideas that theories of organising were best rooted in economics, management scholars were beginning to describe why managers and managerial autonomy were an obstacle to the maximisation of shareholder interest. In an organisation where ownership and authority are widely dispersed a simpler way of scrutinising management behaviour is needed to 'measure' managerial performance. One way of doing this was to bring about a greater alignment between the interests of executives, managerial 'agents', and the interests of shareholders by offering executives share packages as part of their remuneration: if the company did well then they did well. This realignment was brought about on the basis of an ideology that presumes that the market knows best, and the short-term gain, through 'leveraging' debt onto companies, buy-outs and mergers are in shareholders' best interests. But, according to Khurana, it encouraged executives to act much more explicitly according to short-term gains, and out of self interest. Given the current economic crisis and some of the reasons why it came about, one can begin to appreciate the force of Khurana's argument.

Not only did this way of thinking undermine the traditional understanding of management, and the education of managers as agency theory became widely taken up in north American management schools, but it led to a project to separate out the role of leaders, as opposed to managers, because, in order better to respond to the neoclassical project, they would need to behave differently. A seminal article in the *Harvard Business Review* by Abraham Zaleznick (1977) downgraded the role of managers as mere 'problem solvers', while leaders were said to be more charismatic, generating fresh thinking and attitudes. It is here that we first encounter the very common contemporary conception of leader as visionary. Business schools began to reflect this thinking unproblematically in their courses. Khurana gives as an example the Harvard Business School leadership programme, which understands leadership as a personal journey where leaders cope with 'change by developing a vision of the future for the organization, aligning the organization behind the vision, and motivating the people to achieve the vision'. It is exactly this way of conceiving leadership that we have been critiquing in previous chapters.

Khurana argues that the rise of economic disciplines in management and the prominence of agency theory in the 1980s and 1990s is responsible for undermining the decades-long development of the idea of management as a profession, a manager being someone who is responsible for mediating the competing claims of capital and labour, and being a steward of the company for the common good:

> *Agency theorists, however, dismiss any such framing of managerial work as tenderhearted do-gooding. Agency theory also excludes from consideration any notion of collective identity – a fundamental attribute of profession in any sociological framing of the phenomenon –*

let alone collective responsibility. On the contrary, it frames managerial agents as distinct and dissociated from one another, defining an organisation as simply a nexus of contracts among individuals ... by framing the organisation as a nexus of contracts, agency theory conveniently dispenses with issues of power, coercion and exploitation.
(Khurana, 2007: 324–325)

For Khurana, the emergence of a new discourse on leadership threatened to occlude the very things in which I have taken an interest in this book, power, politics and the daily processes of organising. He blames business schools for the way they have taken up these theories and reproduced them uncritically. Offering his own view of leadership theory and the courses in university which promote them, Khurana is extremely doubtful that leadership studies will ever produce a stable and coherent body of knowledge that will be comprehensively helpful in training future generations of leaders. Quoting another scholar writing as far back as the 1930s, Khurana states that leadership is 'the subject of an extraordinary amount of dogmatically stated nonsense' (ibid: 356). When engaging with theories of management, then, we should be careful to enquire into what is being said, how it is being said, and who benefits.

Similarly from a critical perspective, Mats Alvesson and his co-researcher Stefan Sveningsson (2003a; 2003b) have carried out a number of empirical studies in companies which lead them to problematise the dominant discourse about leadership as a distinct discipline. They have researched the way that contemporary leadership theory, which, as I have tried to demonstrate above, presents leadership as an activity on a high moral plain, concerned with reflecting harmony, voluntarism and shared interest, and involving little or no formal power or coercion, is taken up by managers in practice. When they do so their practice produces inconsistencies and incoherencies that the dominant literature on leadership does not prepare them for. On the one hand managers claim that there is something unique about leadership, which they think involves grand theories of vision, strategy and guidance; on the other hand they are unable to give other than very mundane examples of how they are practising leadership, which the researchers describe as vague and fragile. Alvesson and Sveningsson note how managers' theories of leadership are heavily informed by the literature, which they are nonetheless unable coherently to practise or articulate, but also by policies and procedures adopted by their organisations which support the dominant view. To a degree they are conforming to what they know is expected of them, thus perpetuating inadequate theories of leadership. Nonetheless, although Alvesson and Sveningsson doubt that it is possible to prove what difference theories of leadership make to action in organisations, they do conclude that they have significance for managers' sense of identity:

> *What is considered visionary and strategic leadership might very well*
> *be interpreted as esteem-enhancing identity work for those vulnerable*
> *to – or attracted by – the modern leadership discourse. It may have more*
> *impact on managers' efforts to define who they are – or would like to*
> *be – in ideologically appealing ways than on what they are doing.*
>
> *(2003b)*

The idea of leadership as identity-formation, both of those leading and those disposed to be led, is an interesting area of enquiry. Leadership is understood by managers in the study as offering the potential for adopting a morally superior position and an enhanced image of self. It also induces them to invest ordinary, mundane activities, such as talking to staff in corridors, with both symbolic and even magical properties simply because they are associated with the act of leading.

Meanwhile, in a critical review of contemporary leadership training, Ford and Harding (2007) point out how the identification and standardisation of leadership qualities have coincided with the proliferation of management testing instruments, such as the Myers-Briggs Type Indicator (MBTI) personality assessment, which help respondents identify how closely they conform to ideal personality types. Ford and Harding are demonstrating how the instruments of organisational and human resource development are performative, that is, they help create the conditions they purport to measure, so reinforcing the dominant discourse. In their work Ford and Harding are pointing to some of the ways in which popular, if unsubstantiated ideas about what a leader is and does get perpetuated.

In sum, then, there is a substantial, if minority body of scholarship questioning the link between leadership and organisational performance, problematising the idea that leadership is necessarily distinct from management, and querying whether there will ever be a stable body of knowledge about what leadership is. Paradoxically it seems to be the most written about, yet least understood area of management study.

How Management Education and Training Perpetuates These Ideas

Despite what the preceding management scholars have to say about the poverty of leadership research and how little it can claim for the effect leaders have, or even what makes a good leader, idealisations of leadership persist. As a consequence leadership vocabulary pervades everyday organisational life and creates very strong expectations of what leaders can achieve, yet gives very little indication of the assumptions that inform the discourse. Talk of leadership gives a very good example of what Elias was drawing attention to when he argued that wishful thinking and emotive knowledge can be presented as reality-congruent knowledge. As with many contemporary theories of consultancy which we reviewed in Chapter 2, much current leadership theory ascribes to leaders' abilities to analyse and diagnose 'whole' organisations and make interventions to create a different whole change. It supports the view that leaders can choose what and how to change.

So we have great expectations of leadership, and leaders often have great expectations of themselves. A cursory review of advertisements for director posts reveals how leaders are expected to bring together the metaphysical and the rational, being able on the one hand to 'inspire' teams and bring about transformational change, and 'deliver results' on the other. Leaders are expected to evoke in their followers strong imaginative idealisation and identification at the same time as being firmly rooted in the day-to-day world of work, although it is important to point out that the term 'results' is used unproblematically. In the way that leadership has become idealised, advertisements would also lead us to believe that leaders can motivate, 'deliver' and turn everything to the good at the same time:

> At [X Organisation], we believe that every aspect of our work can lead to a positive outcome. If you share this vision and commitment, then you're exactly what we're looking for.

While the task of leading increasingly complex organisations has become more difficult, many organisations still seem stuck with the notion that competent leaders can turn everything to the good. Inspirational leaders are apparently able to act upon their employees in a way that generates motivation, performance and positive transformational change, all at the same time.

The conventional and dualistic way of thinking about leadership and the tendency to believe that leadership qualities such as 'inspiration' can somehow be distilled, bottled and tested for, has resulted in a proliferation of training and consultancy firms offering courses on inspirational or transformational leadership. These range from courses focusing on charismatic individual qualities, through to approaches which are more critical of the idea of the leader as Great Man, offering instead a skills and competency based training (Pedler, Burgoyne and Boydell, 2003). Visionary leadership has become something that can be taught, or otherwise coached and mentored.

At the same time that we must realise that the range of abilities that we are looking for in our leaders is unattainable, we nonetheless continue to demand them. In this sense we are caught in the kind of double bind thinking that Elias was pointing to. Our idealising tendencies around leadership persist, as does the anxiety around what had become known as a leadership deficit. The perceived leadership deficit arises out of a conviction on the one hand that leaders are required to have these exceptional abilities: meanwhile and on the other hand we realise that this is probably an impossible demand.

For example, in 2005 the Department of Trade and Industry (DTI) of the UK government commissioned some research to produce an 'inspired leadership tool' (2005) available both face to face and online for leaders to develop their skills with a view to 'closing the inspirational leadership gap' in the UK. The following is taken from a slide show for use by Sector Skills Development Agencies (SSDAs), government agencies charged with developing skills for businesses. The first attribute of an inspirational leader is the following:

Dimension 1: Creating the Future

This dimension describes the leader's ability to demonstrate and communicate a shared vision, their capacity to focus on exciting long-term possibilities and share these with others such that they 'catch' this excitement and want to contribute.

The inspirational leadership that the government is seeking, which they hope will lead to greater innovation in the UK, is bound up with individual leaders who can generate infectious excitement, and who can harmonise and align their staff around their vision. The not-for-profit sector has also developed its own equivalent of this, although there is still a tendency to cling to the idea that leaders in the not-for-profit sector will have heroic attributes. However, these will be attributes which are appropriate to the sector: for example

Mintzberg (2006), a very prominent management scholar from Canada gives an example of leaders in West Africa who inspire and motivate because of their humility and thoughtfulness. In other words, 'greatness' in the service sector tends more towards Gandhi than Donald Trump. What commentators in the not-for-profit sector say they are looking for in leaders is essentially the same as the requirement for leaders in the private sector:

> *The question of how to assess what type of leader is best suited to the specific requirements of Non-Governmental Organisations (NGOs) depends on, first, their ability to engage with the external world, and second, their skill at managing performance. … The ability to manage and encourage effective performance is as much about implementing change and transforming an organisation, as it is about managing staff, delegating responsibilities, or introducing new systems.*
>
> *(Hailey, 2006)*

Rather than questioning the assumptions about what leadership might mean in a very different sector, Hailey produces a version of the dominant paradigm that would be acceptable within organisations which have a more pronounced tendency towards the articulation of values and to privilege more participatory ways of working. In NGOs leaders are still expected to unite the twin poles of church and corporation, transformation and results.

Wherever one looks in organisations, no matter in what sector they are based, theories of leadership have converged to a considerable degree.

Caveat

I would not want anyone to read into what I have said above that because the idea of leadership has become impossibly overblown it is fruitless to enquire into the phenomenon of leadership, or even that there is no such thing as inspirational leadership. We have all experienced working with inspirational managers and leaders who have made a profound difference to our understanding of what we are doing, whether they be our teachers at school, our church leader or the head of our department. I have also been employed as a consultant in organisations where there is a clear lack of leadership. It is remarkable how fast things can unravel in organisations which are being badly led, or not being led at all, not just by the chief executive but anywhere in an organisation. However, when referring to organisations being badly led I am also including examples, which I will explore below, where the leader is blindly following some aggrandised notion of what leadership is, heavily informed by current theories of leadership. What I am arguing is that our ideas about leadership have become reduced and formulaic and a pale shadow of what it is that happens when people act as leaders and are recognised as such by the people they are trying to lead. In the process they have also become highly individualised: vision, authenticity, charisma is something a leader 'has' in some kind of immanent form. The idea that leading might be a social phenomenon is very underdeveloped in contemporary literature.

The following is a narrative about a situation that emerged in an organisation I was invited into where a conflict arose about the nature and substance of leadership. It demonstrates the point that I was making above that there has been such a convergence of theories of leadership that they are taken up in many sectors of the economy in similar ways.

Narrative on Leadership

The new leader in X not-for-profit organisation had come from a commercial background and had never worked in the not-for-profit sector before. Some of the trustees who appointed him to the job were also from commercial backgrounds, and it might have been the shared language, or some mutual recognition between them that led them to appoint him to the job ahead of other candidates despite the fact that he had never been a senior manager before, was still very young and knew very little about the sector. He had had personal experience of being a child in care, so he felt he could speak with authority on the organisation's principal area of interest, families and children, in particular children at risk of entering into, or emerging from the 'looked after children' system in the UK, even though he had never been professionally involved with it before. His letter of application contained many of the words and phrases that one has come to expect managers to use when they present themselves to the good: he was a transformational leader with exceptional communication skills; he was able to think out of the box, to motivate and inspire.

Even though he was as yet unfamiliar with the work of the organisation he had come to lead he was clear that there needed to be change. Old ways of doing the work needed to be swept away and replaced with newer, more appropriate ones. This organisation was going to be taken into the twenty-first century. Staff felt antagonised by him and impugned: what was wrong with the way that they had been working? The new chief executive was unable to say what was wrong; he just knew he wanted something different. Since he was a new chief executive, he needed to introduce new ways of working. He would return from visits to the district offices with stories about how managers in the districts supported him in what he was saying and felt that staff at headquarters misunderstood the nature of the work. Because some staff in headquarters felt antagonised by him, they began to challenge his authority. In a heated meeting a junior member of staff called his judgement into question; the chief executive retaliated by taking disciplinary procedures out against her and she signed off sick in distress.

Because of this and other incidents, over a period of time staff began to line up into groups: there were those who wanted to give the new leader a chance and were prepared to back him, although they were not always clear what the new 'direction' was. There were those who were fiercely defensive of the old ways of doing things and opposed the director on everything that he proposed. More than this, they began to question his competence. A third group, although they only formed a group in the sense that they did not belong to either of the other two groups, were intent on getting on with their jobs, and took the line of least resistance in order to do so. Sometimes it looked as though they were siding with the 'pros' and sometimes with the 'antis', although actually what they were doing was talking to anyone who was interested in getting the job done. However, in a polarising environment it was impossible not to see any action, or even a gesture or a side conversation, as contributing to the case of one side or another.

Longer-standing members of staff began to involve members of the trustees with whom they had developed a relationship. These latter were torn about how to intervene: on the one hand they could see that some staff who had been around a while were dissatisfied with the way they were being managed. On the other, they had appointed the new director to bring in a new 'direction' and they were reluctant to appear to have lost courage in the face of resistance. In the end, the chair of the trustees intervened at a staff meeting to point out that the new director enjoyed the confidence of the trustees and other senior managers. As a result, over a period of months, members of staff began to leave.

The trustees offered the chief executive some support in the shape of a consultant who would coach him on a regular basis and offer him support in bringing about the changes that he intended, whatever they might be. The consultant was very experienced with many years spent in the banking sector. He coached the chief executive on his communication skills and counselled him how he should deal with the 'usual suspects' whom he felt would oppose him whatever he proposed. He tried to help the director to lead by coaching him in the standards and language of leadership that we have all come to recognise. He advised the chief executive not to 'score any own-goals', to 'stick to the knitting' and to stand his ground.

It is difficult to know how much the chief executive himself recognised that he was struggling, but one thing that he did that was acknowledged as a good thing by all parties was to appoint a highly experienced programme director to work as his deputy. A number of factors brought the issue to a head over a few months: the work that I was doing with a colleague as consultants began to highlight how far the organisation was drifting, the trustees began to lose patience with his lack of clarity and the constant haemorrhage of staff, and the contrast between the chief executive and his newly appointed programme director became more and more stark. The latter was able to talk about the work in a way that was detailed and convincing. He set out no visions, he did not talk about exciting people, but there was something about his authoritative grasp of the work, and his clear ability to articulate his understanding of what he was doing and why that people came to recognise as leadership. Although he was not using the commonly understood language of leadership he nonetheless did begin to excite people, who were able to see possibilities of taking the work forward that had become occluded over the past 18 months.

After a trustees' meeting where both senior managers had spoken, the Board overcame their uncertainty about how to act. The chief executive had to go.

Reflections on the Narrative

Here is a situation, where an inexperienced manager, with little exposure or apparent previous interest in the sector in which he aspired to lead, was appointed to a leader's role in an organisation. Clearly he had been convincing in the interview, and was able to present himself, using leadership vocabulary that is now taken for granted across different sectors, as a leader who could bring about transformational change. Indeed, this particular leader took up the idea of change in the organisation seemingly as an end in itself without somehow posing the question, change towards what or in the name of what? The fantasy that change is a 'good thing' in and of itself is endemic in organisations in my experience. When I work with leaders in other settings I am often working with their own anxieties about how visionary or charismatic they are, just as I often find myself working with employees who struggle with their tendency to idealise their leaders. The process of idealisation is co-created. With idealisation arises the potential for denigration and disappointment at exactly the same time, as I experienced in the organisation I describe above. With one group fiercely supporting him and another, opposite group questioning his judgement, the organisation was riven. And potentially this dynamic began to happen all over again with the programme director, particularly with the stark contrast he provided with his struggling chief executive, as members of staff began to think of him as their new saviour.

On a recent trip to Zambia I was reminded of this charismatic and evangelical role that leaders are expected to perform for those they lead in the current yoking of church and corporation. Zambians have a strong church tradition and Zambian TV often carries sermons by church leaders who are charismatic and mesmerising speakers, quoting scripture to encourage their congregation to aspire to transformation through the grace of God. On the international news channel at the same time I could witness Barack Obama's campaign to seek the Democratic Presidential nomination greeting his audience with the phrase 'hello believers', and see how his supporters are carrying banners with the slogan 'change we can believe in'. There is a strong religious thread in even those management books that present themselves as most rational: vision, mission, values and transformational change for the good. It is not difficult to see how the vocabulary of leadership strays into religious territory.

How is it that ways of talking about and understanding the role of leaders come to predominate in such a way that it becomes almost impossible to apply for a job, be interviewed or coach others without using this language, no matter how inadequate it is? How is it that the idea of leadership has somehow got separated from the detail of leading whom towards what, and form has come to substitute for substance? How is it that the strongly religious theme of inspirational change persists and yet is so difficult to explore publicly?

Sociological Input: Playing the Game with Bourdieu

The sociologist Pierre Bourdieu addressed some aspects of these questions in his book *Language and Symbolic Power* (1991) in his research into processes of power and domination. Bourdieu coined the term 'fields of specialised production' to describe situations where professionals, in the course of developing their area of work with others, have an interest in playing the 'game' of their professionalism and contributing to the integrity of that game. There is a community of interest where:

> *The struggle tends constantly to produce and reproduce the game and its stakes by reproducing, primarily in those who are directly involved, but not in them alone, the practical commitment to the value of the game and its stakes which defines the recognition of legitimacy.*
>
> *(1991: 58)*

The image of the game to represent human activity is an interesting one and has been used by a number of philosophers and sociologists (Mead, 1934; Elias, 1939/2000) because it is a usefully social and dynamic analogy of the way that we interact with one another. It is a different way of thinking about leadership than the orthodox and dominant assumptions which individualised leadership attributes, as though leadership is a secret ingredient that a leader 'has'. Instead it suggests a dynamic and relational process between people constantly adapting to each other.

Every game has rules by which we operate and must recognise, but at the same time we are constantly obliged to improvise around them, what Bourdieu called 'the necessary improvisation', in order to respond to particular circumstances. The domain of leadership and management is what Bourdieu called 'a field of specialised production'. Any aspiring CEO is caught up in a web of 'specialised producers' who have a stake in continuing to describe the world in the way that they do. They cannot just ignore the rules of the game they are entering for fear of being judged to have called the game they are playing into question. It would be almost impossible to apply for a senior job in an organisation and not use the language that has come to be recognised as being indicative of a competent manager, no matter whether one was able to demonstrate the ability to act in this way or not. To point to the limitations of the language and the concepts behind them is not just to undermine one's own legitimacy, but also the legitimacy of others in the field of specialised production where such discourse has value, and amongst a community of people who have an interest in maintaining that value. No professional who has a stake and status in the game they are playing has an interest in calling the game into question.

Bourdieu sees the social use of language as being akin to a series of exchanges where the object is the accumulation of social capital. For Bourdieu, human interaction is like a market place where we try to extract maximum value and legitimacy from our encounters with others:

In other words, utterances are not only ... signs to be understood and deciphered; they are also signs of wealth *intended to be evaluated and appreciated, and the* signs of authority *intended to be believed and obeyed. Quite apart from the literary (and especially poetic) uses of language, it is rare in everyday life for language to function as a pure instrument of communication.*

(Bourdieu, 1991: 66)

In using the accepted vocabulary in applying for the job of chief executive, the leader in my case study clearly understood the rules of the game he was playing, and did so in a way that was sufficiently convincing for the trustees to offer him the job. He was able to accumulate signs of 'wealth' and 'authority' with the audience he was addressing. What he said was clearly music to their ears, although I am not implying that they had no doubts about him.

The idea of a linguistic marketplace has its own symbolic resonance in increasingly marketised times, and in the process of exchange a seller needs a buyer. This understanding works against a more linear representation of domination where those in power are understood simply to assert what they want and expect to get it. Instead, Bourdieu presents a dynamic where the powerful must persuade and the less powerful must be persuaded:

The value of the utterance depends on the relation of power that is concretely established between the speakers' linguistic competences, understood both as their capacity for appropriation and appreciation; it depends on the capacity of various agents involved in the exchange to impose the criteria of appreciation most favourable to their own products.

(Ibid: 67)

The currency of managerialism is an almost formulaic understanding of the role of leaders expressed in widely recognised language. To speak into this discourse involves demonstrating that one has recognised the value of the language and that one can appropriate it as evidence of one's own worth. Moreover, the suggestion of a linguistic market is also important in understanding the way that conventional management theory, largely written and produced by theorists who take an interest in the private sector and constantly adduce economic theory as a basic assumption of what they are recommending, has come to permeate all sectors of the economy. All organisations are exposed to pressures arising from the dominance of liberal economic thinking and marketisation. In order to establish credibility, many managers believe that they must think and act like managers in the private sector. Wherever I go, from Zambia to Aberdeen, from Bangladesh to Toronto, I am told of the importance of transformational leadership and the necessity for change. There is a universal and dominant currency of management language which one must accumulate in order to be recognised.

Bourdieu would understand this process to be the inevitable response to dominant social trends. In commenting on the professionalisation and bureaucratisation of politics, he remarked that:

> ... the struggle for the monopoly of the development and circulation of the principles of division of the social world is more and more strictly reserved for professionals and for large units of production and circulation, thus excluding de facto the small independent producers (starting with the 'free intellectuals').
>
> (Ibid: 196)

There is a convergence of understanding about market mechanisms and the process of organisational management across all sectors of the economy. As they become ubiquitous so they are harder and harder to oppose. To put forward an alternative understanding of leadership, to worry away at the taken for granted assumptions that are left unexplored in currently accepted formulations, is to risk calling one's own professionalism into question.

Bourdieu was not much interested in how organisations work and as a social activist as well as an academic, felt he had little time for analysing management theory. He was more interested in how processes of domination worked against the interests of the dominated. He was, however, interested in political power, and offered some insights on how politicians mobilise support for the programmes they propose. These insights are useful in helping us to understand the political nature of leadership to which I have been pointing above. Leaders do have to convince. All organisations, particularly ones dedicated to social care and change, need leaders and managers who can mobilise people to be committed to projects which are likely to be difficult and complex. Bourdieu's insights may also start to uncover the differences that staff noticed in the organisation I wrote about above, between the chief executive and programme director.

> *The truth of a promise or a prognosis depends not only on the truthfulness*
> *but also on the authority of the person who utters it – that is, on his*
> *capacity to make people believe in his truthfulness and his authority ...*
> *the words through which the spokesperson endows a group with a will, a*
> *plan, a hope or, quite simply, a future,* does what it says *in so far as the*
> *addressees recognise themselves in it, conferring on it the symbolic and*
> *also material power ... which enables the words to come true.*
>
> (1991: 190–193, emphasis Bourdieu)

Rather than understanding leadership as a series of skills and competences that a leader is endowed with or can learn, Bourdieu begins to sketch out the social basis for leadership through a process of mutual recognition. In order for a leader to establish themselves, they need to speak with an authority, a symbolic and material power, that is recognised by those being addressed. This will inevitably entail the leader speaking into an established discourse which is recognised and shared, but in a way that those invited by the leader will come to understand themselves anew in the dynamic between the leader and the led. According to Bourdieu, a leader's authority can be self-reinforcing in the sense that the process of mutual recognition makes it much more likely that leader's words will come true, thus enhancing the leader's authority. But as we have seen in the narrative about the NGO where I was invited to undertake a consultancy, this is clearly not just a one-way process or even a constant one, particularly if the authority of the leader comes to be idealised. The leader perceived as being authoritative can soon flip over into being recognised as an inauthentic charlatan as in the case of Tony Blair, or from being masterful to being indecisive in the case of Gordon Brown. This suggests that a leader is constantly renegotiating their authority with those they lead: it is not a static given.

In summary, drawing on Bourdieu, we need to be aware of the broader social forces that are manifest in day-to-day interactions: 'the body is in the social world, but the social world is in the body' (1982: 38). When we engage with the concept of leadership we are already acting into a domain where there are certain taken for granted assumptions about what it is that we are talking about which oblige us to play the game in a certain way. In the case of political power, which I would argue is a strong theme in leadership, he draws our attention to the way in which language in a marketised society becomes a form of symbolic capital accumulation, where individuals try to establish the criteria for appreciation most favourable to their 'product'. Certain ways of representing the world have greater value than others amongst a greater concentration of professionals who have a stake in maintaining the value of these representations. In establishing themselves, leaders speak into this discourse in a way that tries to establish their authority in processes of mutual recognition that need to be constantly renewed between leader and those they invite to follow them.

Acknowledging the Religious

Although Bourdieu makes a good case for the way the broader social trends get taken up in everyday interaction between people and reproduced, he does not do justice to the themes of religion and belief that permeate management literature to which I have been drawing attention throughout this book.

The role of religion in public life is expressed differently in countries across the world, with the tendencies of north Americans to make a much more explicit connection between faith and politics, or faith and organising which is much closer to attitudes in developing countries than are those of Europeans. Nonetheless, the themes and language of spirituality and religion are prevalent in contemporary management literature, and there are different ways of understanding this phenomenon. Management theorists of the critical school like Willmott (1993, 2003), would understand this to be a manifestation of the way in which management theory has increasingly tried to colonise the personal in a further manipulative effort to bring about employee conformity. Discussions of organisational 'culture', although apparently involving universals, actually revolve around a narrow set of corporate objectives in the hope that employees will:

> ... discipline themselves with feelings of anxiety, shame and guilt that are aroused when they sense themselves to impugn or fall short of the hallowed values of the corporation.
>
> *(1993: 523)*

However, the Canadian philosopher Charles Taylor (2007) understands contemporary spirituality as another development of our modern sense of self, which he has set out in his earlier work (1989). Although our leading rationalists would denounce religion as some kind of pre-modern form of thought (Dawkins, 2006; Hitchens, 2007) Taylor disagrees, and argues that religious and spiritual attachment is a response to the flattening of the contemporary world brought about by the dominance of two and half centuries of naturalism, scientific methods developed in the study of the natural world. Taylor accuses naturalism of the potential for reducing human experience to being rule governed and purposeless. Although he acknowledges that Western society has become increasingly secular he goes on to make the case that we have become who we have become not through our scientific understanding alone but also through our religious imagination in both secular and non-secular variations. Over time our sense of self has become individualised as well as increasingly diverse. He points to the passages of awe and wonder about nature that bookend Dawkins' diatribes against religion as being a manifestation of what he is alluding to.

If we were to take up Taylor's ideas on the role of the religious in contemporary society then we might understand the appeal of leadership theory to the spiritual as an acknowledgement of our increased rich 'interiority', which may or may not find expression in church. The outlets for our sense of the religious are now many and various, and professional life is potentially one of them. Whether or not our religious imagination is appealed to cynically and with a view to manipulation is open to interpretation, but there can be no doubt that the potential for manipulation is there. We should not be surprised, though, following Taylor, that it has become possible to find a discussion of 'rational' leadership techniques and appeals to belief and transformation cheek by jowl.

The Consequences for the Practice of Leadership

I have been arguing in the course of this chapter for a more nuanced understanding of the process of leading on the basis that more complex times demand more complex responses. However, I have also been pointing out how important it is to acknowledge the dynamic that sustains contemporary understandings of leadership, no matter how reduced, and the panoply of consultancy, coaching and literature that buttress these. At its most formulaic, the contemporary route to leadership involves learning individual skills and techniques for being better able to convince others of one's authority and 'presence'. It also involves being fluent in the language of leadership, and being able to act the part using this vocabulary. Contemporary leaders are invited to master and reproduce the dualisms that have come to make the art of leadership distinct: in other words they must show that they know the difference between the transformational rather than the transactional; they must be in favour of change rather than continuity, be a leader rather than a manager and turn everything to the good. They must be able to reduce complexity to a single and unifying vision, which tends towards the idealisation. In doing so leaders are likely themselves to be idealised. It is very difficult in organisations these days to talk in any other way about what a leader is and does.

I have begun to explore an alternative way of understanding the process of leading with a starting point that there is no stable, coherent body of knowledge about leadership. Leadership literature is often confused and contradictory at least, and helps perpetuate relationships of power which privilege particular groups and their interests. Khurana argues that contemporary theories of leadership have arisen during the ascendancy of an extreme form of liberal capitalism. However, the idea of the leader and leadership is also a highly symbolic concept which helps establish a sense of identity both in the leader and in those being led: it is an inescapable aspect of organising together in groups to try and achieve things together. It is a social and constantly renegotiated process of mutual recognition. Rather than being an act where the skills of the actor are under the spotlight, it is a performance involving the leader and the led in group improvisation. In setting out this alternative I am attempting to recast these dualisms as paradoxes: I am assuming that every situation we encounter has the potential for good and bad, change and continuity, and we may find ourselves acting both as a transformational and a transactional manager/leader at the same time, but we are only likely to know in retrospect how the two have arisen in the particular circumstances we found ourselves acting when we reappraise what we have done together with others. In complex situations where the exact nature of cause and effect breaks down, we cannot be confident in advance of acting that we are going to be only 'transformational'.

The idealising processes that arise as a consequence of leaders attempting to lead are an inevitable, and perhaps an important appeal to our religious imagination that has sometimes led to significant shifts in human behaviour in the struggle for civil rights, or social inclusion for example. However, it is crucial that we become aware of the potential for manipulation that arises at the same time and for leaders to come to reflect on how they co-create the circumstances they find themselves in with others. Management theory may have a legitimate interest in inspirational leadership, but we should be suspicious when theorists try to instrumentalise this potential and reduce and reproduce the supposed characteristics of inspirational leadership for a narrow set of manipulative ends. We can also be critical of the ways in which the current discourse on leadership leads us into magico-mythical thinking where insubstantial nonsense is presented as though it were rational common sense.

Practical Leadership

How might we work with the idea of leadership and come to understand it differently?

I was invited to facilitate a two-day retreat for a senior management team by the team leader. One of the things that exercised him was the fact that individually his colleagues were very competent, but somehow they did not work well together with him as a team. The style of his predecessor had been very different from his, in that she had a much more authoritarian way of working. She was more comfortable dealing with people bilaterally. When the team met together as a group they had learnt to wait for her to tell them what she had decided and had got out of the habit of talking things over together. When the new team leader came into post he would ask them what they thought about something, and they would reply by asking him what he thought. They were forever waiting for him to take the lead.

The team leader decided that the best thing to do was to start the retreat by talking about leadership, and the kind of leadership that the team should be exercising, together and with others. His suggestion was that we should spend the first session defining what we meant by leadership, agreeing it, then working out what that might mean for practice. We would go on to develop a plan for the kinds of leadership we might have in place by a certain point in the future.

A constraint for me in knowing how to work with this group was the fact that they had had a session the previous year, with their last team leader, where things had broken down in the group quite quickly and someone had stormed out of the meeting. I realised that there might be quite a lot of trepidation about this meeting and how it might be run. I wanted to work in a way that would keep people in the room and would engage them.

One of the difficulties that I had with this way of working, of agreeing the meaning of an abstract idea, then proceeding from there, is the notion that a group of people would necessarily agree, or even that it is important to do so. Is it really possible to reach a sufficient degree of understanding for the next steps of working together to be obvious? Many of us would be able to articulate idealised understandings of leadership, but how far does this enable us to lead? There are of course lots of books in train stations or airports setting out simple rules, the six steps to this, or the three ways of being. I was keen not simply to reproduce these tropes in the workshop, where, as in Alvesson and Sveningsson's (2003a, 2003b) examples, we could all agree the theory but would not be able to justify the theory in practice.

How should we lead together, however, in this time and place, in this context, with each other?

I suggested an alternative. Rather than spending so much time in idealising about abstract concepts, team members would give an account to each other of the kinds of things that they are managing at the moment as a way into exploring how they were working together, and how they might go on to support each other. We would deal with questions of real time practice. By taking turns, team members would practise recognising each other as managers and leaders, and would come to understand their role in the group in doing so. We would use this method as a way of experiencing, and reflecting on how the team was leading together, rather than how they 'should' be leading.

I suggested this as a way of working to undermine the way we predominantly understand practice in Western organisations as thought before action. It seems a common-sense approach: first we establish what it is by what we mean in abstract terms, and then this shared understanding enables us to co-ordinate our actions. The alternative I was offering is to understand leadership as a shared experience that we are co-creating as we are working together: reflecting on our actions and giving an account to each other of how we are leading gives us a much better grounded opportunity to come to realise what we mean by leadership. We come to know it when we experience it in the here and now. Theory arises out of practice and informs it, which in turn drives theory. The two are not divorced but arise together and are mutually informing.

In the course of the workshop that is exactly what we had an opportunity to do, to reflect together on our experience of leading, and being led and noticing how leadership arose in different practical situations in the group. It became clear to most members of the group that they were already operating with theories of leadership which they were able to explore with each other and experiment with different options. They came to understand what they were already doing anew.

In writing about leadership in this way I am drawing heavily on Doug Griffin's book *The Emergence of Leadership: Linking Self Organisation and Ethics* (2002) where he argues against a mystical view of what leaders are and do.

Instead he makes the case, drawing on Mead (1934), that it is in processes of communicative interaction between engaged participants that leadership emerges. According to Mead a good leader is one who is able to enter into the attitudes of others, so enhancing connection and interaction between group members. A leader may well be idealised, but this idealisation will be functionalised, made practical and experiential, in the everyday negotiations between people about how to go on together.

Concluding Thoughts on Leadership – Implications for Managers

The domain of leadership seems to me to be a very prominent example of the way in which the management literature on what leadership is and what a leader does has proliferated well beyond the tenuous evidence base to support the many and multifarious assertions. It is a pronounced form of what Norbert Elias (1987) termed magico-mythical thinking. And yet conceptions of the leader as a an authentic visionary who can inspire and motivate because of innate charismatic characteristics that they 'have', while producing results and turning everything to the good has so taken hold across all sectors of the economy and politics that it would be hard to imagine a prospective leader turning up for an interview who was unwilling to speak into this discourse. A little probing reveals some of the historical antecedents of the splitting off of the disciplines of management and leadership which took place at a time of the ascendancy of a particularly pronounced form of liberal capitalism. Just as leaders of organisations began paying themselves more and more and the disparity between rewards for senior managers and everyone else became increasingly marked, both in the US and the UK, so the literature and training courses have proliferated which promote the idea of the innate and immanent nature of transformational leadership. If leadership is a highly prized, almost unique set of individual attributes, then it makes sense to reward highly those few individuals who we believe have these characteristics, otherwise they might go and work elsewhere. Equally, we might all have something of an investment in a belief that whatever secret these unique individuals possess could also be ours. Who would aspire to being a transactional manager if they could be a transformational leader? However, when managers in the research examples quoted in this chapter were asked for examples of their own leadership, they were only able to provide very mundane examples of what they were talking about. Everyday examples of talking to employees in corridors or taking decisions were invested with great symbolic significance by the managers concerned because it was an activity associated with leadership.

And this might give us a clue that the domain of leadership does take us into realms of human experience which draw on our imaginations and our tendency to idealise. Rather than treating scientific, 'measurable' disciplines which can be mastered once and for all time we are dealing with rich, complex value-laden territory which involves concepts such as trust, honesty, legitimacy, authority and authenticity. As a way into this territory I have been suggesting that leadership is not a set of qualities that an individual either has or does not have, but is rather a profoundly social experience that involves processes of mutual recognition between those engaged in working out how to go on together. We experience leadership and recognise ourselves and leaders in the process: it arises in a particular context and between particular groups of people. Although leaders may be idealised, what matters is how the idealisations are taken up between people who are negotiating in the everyday who they are and what they think is going on.

I have been describing a highly social understanding of leadership which takes place in fluid organisations, which are sites of great flux and change. Rather than having some kind of mystical innate ability of predicting highly idealised and utopian end states, I am siding with Mead (1934) who thinks of a leader as an individual who in the process of being socialised, has particularly enhanced abilities of recognising and articulating the potential of the particular patterns of relating in the community in which they are part. They have the ability to take the attitude of a large number of others to themselves and to articulate this in a way in which these others are able to recognise themselves in what is said. It is a highly social, group-oriented ability and is discovered and recreated moment by moment.

References

Alvesson, M. and Sveningsson, S. (2003a) Good visions, bad micro-management and ugly ambiguity: Contradictions of (non-) leadership in a knowledge-intensive organization, *Organization Studies*, 24: 961.
—— (2003b) Managers doing leadership: The extra-ordinarization of the mundane, *Human Relations*, 56(12): 1435–1459.
Bass, B. and Riggio, R. (2006) *Transformational Leadership*, 2nd edition, New York: Lawrence Erlbaum Associates Inc.
Bourdieu, P. (1982) *Leçon sur la Leçon*, Paris: Editions de Minuit.
—— (1991) *Language and Symbolic Power*, Cambridge: Polity Press.

Burgoyne, J., Hirsh. W. and Williams. S. (2004) *The Development of Management and Leadership Capability and Its Contribution to Performance,* London: DES Research Report 560.

Carroll, G. and Hannan, M. (2000) *The Demography of Corporations and Industries,* Princeton NJ: Princeton University Press.

Covey, S. (1999) *Principle Centred Leadership,* New York: Simon and Schuster.

Dawkins, R. (2006) *The God Delusion,* London: Black Swan.

Elias, N. (1939/2000) *The Civilising Process,* Oxford: Blackwell.

—— (1987) *Involvement and Detachment,* Oxford: Blackwell.

Ford, J. and Harding, N. (2007) Move over management: We are all leaders now, *Management Learning,* 38(5): 475–493.

Garrett, J. and Frank, J. (2005) *Inspirational Leadership – Insight to Action – The Development of the Inspired Leadership Tool,* report commissioned for the Department of Trade and Industry.

Goffee, R. and Jones, G. (2006) *Why Should Anyone be Led by You?: What it Takes to be an Authentic Leader,* Boston: Harvard Business School Press.

Goleman, D., Boyatzis, R. and McKee, A. (2004) *Primal Leadership: Learning to Lead with Emotional Intelligence,* Boston: Harvard Business School Press.

Griffin, D. (2002) *The Emergence of Leadership: Linking Self-Organisation and Ethics,* London: Routledge.

Hailey, J. (2006) *NGO Leadership Development: A Review of the Literature,* Praxis Paper 10, Oxford: Intrac.

Hitchens, C. (2007) *God is Not Great: How Religion Poisons Everything,* New York: Atlantic Books.

Khurana, R. (2007) *From Higher Aims to Hired Hands: The Social Transformation of American Business Schools and the Unfulfilled Promise of Management as a Profession,* Princeton NJ: Princeton University Press.

Kotter, J.P. (1990) *A Force for Change: How Leadership Differs from Management,* New York: The Free Press.

MacGregor Burns, J. (1982) *Leadership,* New York: HarperPerennial.

—— (2003) *Transforming Leadership,* New York: Atlantic Books.

Mead, G.H. (1934) *Mind, Self and Society from the Standpoint of a Social Behaviourist,* Chicago: University of Chicago Press.

Mintzberg, H. (2006) Developing leaders, developing countries', *Development in Practice,* 16(1): 4–14.

Mouffe, C. (2005) *On the Political,* London: Routledge.

Nohria, N. and Khurana, R. (eds) (2010) *Handbook of Leadership Theory and Practice: A Harvard Business School Centennial Colloquium,* Boston: Harvard Business School Press.

Pedler, M., Burgoyne, J. and Boydell, T. (2003) *A Manager's Guide to Leadership*, London: McGraw Hill International.

Pfeffer, J. (1997) *New Directions for Organization Theory: Problems and Prospects*, New York: Oxford University Press.

—— and Salancik, G. (1978) *The External Control of Organizations*, New York: Harper and Row.

—— and Sutton, R. (2006) *Hard Facts, Dangerous Half-Truths, and Total Nonsense: Profiting from Evidence-based Management*, Boston MA: Harvard Business School Press.

Powell, W. and DiMaggio, P. (1991) *The New Institutionalism in Organizational Analysis*, Chicago: University of Chicago Press.

Streatfield, P. (2001) *The Paradox of Control in Organizations*, London: Routledge.

The New Inspirational Leadership Index http://www.ssda-mandl.org.uk/files/board_present/Inspirational.leadership.index-SSDA.ppt

Taylor, C. (1989) *Sources of the Self: The Making of Modern Identity*, Cambridge: Cambridge University Press.

—— (2007) *A Secular Age*, Cambridge MA: Harvard Belknap Press.

Waldcock, T. and Kelly-Rawat, S. (2004) *The 18 Challenges of Leadership: A Practical, Structured Way to Develop Your Leadership Talent*, London: Prentice Hall.

Weber, M. (1919/2004) *The Vocation Lectures: Science as a Vocation and Politics as a Vocation*, Owen, D. and Strong, T. (eds), Indianapolis: Hackett Publishing Co.

Willmott, H. (1993) Strength is ignorance, slavery is freedom: Managing culture in modern organizations, *Journal of Management Studies*, 30(4): 515–552.

—— (2003) Renewing strength: corporate culture revisited, *M@n@gement*, 6(3): 73–87.

Zaleznik, A. (1977) Managers and leaders: Are they different?, *Harvard Business Review*, 55(3): 67–78.

5

Charisma and Passion – Visioning the Future

Introduction – Social or Individual?

In this chapter I will discuss further the idea of vision, which I introduced in the previous chapter on leadership. It has become a ubiquitous concept. On the one hand it has a common-sense feel about it, surely everyone knows what we are talking about when we say that an organisation or a leader needs vision, someone who can see where the organisation needs to go; on the other hand we are clearly straying into complex and potentially metaphysical territory with its overtones of the religious and the appeal to employees to believe in and commit to the vision, which we have discussed previously. There is often a strong connection made in contemporary management literature between the idea of vision and emotive states such as 'passion' and 'excitement' which are necessarily evoked in employees if they are to participate fully in the organisational vision. But what exactly is a convincing vision and how does a leader form one? How has it arisen that the concept has taken such a hold and can be so taken for granted when discussing the qualities that boards might be looking for in a leader, or when we are assessing our politicians?

It seems to me that vision is a highly abstract quasi-religious concept that reinforces the idea of leader as charismatic individual and ascribes to them semi-mystical powers. In many ways this seems to sit uncomfortably with the broader set of assumptions about management, that it is a scientific discipline which privileges detached rationality. However, it could be understood as a form of reaction to the perception of cold economic reason that pervades much management theorising, a resacralising of the organisation as a site of spiritual fulfilment, in a society which, as I mentioned in Chapter 4, Charles Taylor (1991) has argued has become 'flattened' in its significance by scientific reason. Vision generation is a way of re-engaging employees emotionally and of appealing to the yearning for some kind of psychological fulfilment, which, in our increasingly secular age, is less likely to be sought from the more traditional sites of spiritual engagement such as religious institutions. In the idea of vision the twin ideas of church and corporation come together. At the same time, however, there is also the potential for manipulation and bullying – the invitation to commit to the vision, in Collins and Porras' terms (2005) to submit to the cult, is also an appeal to conformity and obedience. Visions have disciplinary power. I am not alone in drawing attention to the way in which appeals to the ideal can also be ways of evoking guilt, shame and the potential for exclusion in those appealed to (Wilmott, 1993, 2003). It is a way of covering over dissent.

In what follows I will trace what some of the antecedents of the idea of visioning, and by drawing on some current management literature will show how the concept has been used to buttress the notion of leader as distinct from manager. Thereafter I will explore some of the difficulties and dilemmas around visioning and the way it may be experienced in organisations, leading me to reflect on how we might consider the concept from a more social and emergent perspective. What role does vision play in the complex interweaving of intentions to which I have been alluding throughout the book?

The Leader as Unique Individual

In previous chapters I have written about the way that the dominant orthodoxy on management appeals to two varieties of individualism. The leader, manager or consultant is an objective observer, who from a point of removal from what is happening in organisations, can diagnose what is wrong and produce a remedy. The assumption here is that the leader as scientist has undistorted access to the facts. Or, alternatively there is idea that the decentred leader, one who realises that they must play a role with others, can know how to act by tapping into their inner authenticity (Block, 2000), identifying and changing their mental models (Senge, 1990), admitting to their defensive behaviours (Argyris, 1990) or attuning to an esoteric and metaphysical whole (Senge, Scharmer, Jaworski et al., 2005) as a kind of Jungian archetype. Both of these conceptions of what managers do arise from a highly individualised understanding of a rational self who can choose, control, analyse and intervene both with others and with themselves to bring about pre-reflected and intended outcomes. This has led in turn to management courses which focus on individual character and qualities, skill sets or competences which managers then possess and can use at will.

They can then choose which leadership style to adopt, depending on the circumstances in which they find themselves. Mind and self are understood in cognitive terms as attributes of an individual: they are sub-systems of the body understood as system.

Vision is also predominantly understood to be a skill and facility of individual leaders. Previously associated with prophets and artists, it is the propensity to have some kind of unique insight into the human condition and to the future that separates leaders from managers and supposedly justifies their high rewards. All leaders can be managers, it is often said, but not all managers can be leaders. Visionary leaders are expected to help create the conditions where employees can fulfil themselves, can transcend the mundane. The idea of visionary leadership creates extraordinary anxieties in leaders as well as great expectations in those being led. Whether the concept is justified or not, it is certainly widely accepted as being a prerequisite for aspiring to a leadership position, and for that reason it is important to engage with it. In what follows I will review some of the ways in which vision is treated.

Reviewing the Literature

Zaccaro and Banks (2001) produce a helpful review of how previous scholars on leadership have understood the term vision. For Bennis and Nanus (1986) to choose a direction, a leader must first have developed a mental image of a possible and desirable future state of the organisation. This image, which we will call a vision, may be as vague as a dream, or as precise as a goal or mission. This is a very cognitive way of understanding the envisioning process which occurs to a leader individually. Meanwhile, in an earlier work than the one we have been discussing in Chapter 1, Collins and Porras (1991) consider a vision as consisting in two components: a guiding philosophy that, in the context of expected future environments, leads to a tangible image. For House and Shamir (1993) the vision has an ideological import, although they do not use the word ideology in the sense that I have used it in the first chapter. Charismatic leaders are visionary, they state. More specifically such leaders articulate an ideological goal that describes a better future for followers. This goal is ideological in the sense that the leader asserts that it is the moral right of the followers to realise the goal. Since the vision of the leader is ideological, it is stated in terms of values. House and Shamir produce an interesting cocktail of rights, morality, ideology and values and wrap them all up in what a leader must do in producing a vision. Kirkpatrick and Locke (1996) are in broad agreement with House and Shamir, believing that a vision is a general transcendent ideal that represents shared values; it is often ideological in nature and has moral overtones. Meanwhile, John Kotter (1990) rather disagrees with the previous scholars thinking that vision is not mystical or intangible, but means simply a description of something (an organisation, a corporate culture, a business, a technology, an activity) in the future, in terms of the essence of what it should become. Typically, a vision is specific enough to give real guidance to people, yet vague enough to encourage initiative and to remain relevant under a variety of conditions.

In sifting through these different approaches, Zaccaro and Banks understand leaders to be engaged in direction-setting, where the vision is used to delineate something broad, longer term and ambiguous. Top level managers translate the visions into more specific organisational strategies, middle level managers convert the vision into sub-systems and goals and low level staff translate this into even more short-term goals and work plans. Executives are not responsible for translating their visions into day-to-day activities which is the responsibility of their subordinates. At the top level visions can manifest up to 50 years into the future.

Zaccaro and Banks quite clearly think of an organisation as a system disaggregated into different levels, an idea which we have been engaging throughout this book. The leader, presumably from their unique vantage point at the top of the organisation, can see many years into the future and are able to anticipate both the future state of the organisation and the environment in which it operates. This must be both cogent and ambiguous at the same time. However, the leader is not seen as being responsible for making day-to-day sense of the vision, since this is the preserve of managers lower down the hierarchy.

They distinguish vision as an idealised representation of what the organisation ought to become, as opposed to strategy which is a 'relatively rational analysis of the organisation's resources and capabilities and the dynamics of its operating environment' (2001: 191). According to Zaccaro and Banks, visions reject the status quo and can be thought of as a map of how the organisation and its environment are likely to change over time. Visions are wrapped up with values which convey the 'passion and persuasiveness that effective leaders convey when articulating to their subordinates the desired image they have of their future organisation'. A trigger for a vision is a misalignment between the organisation and its environment, or it is grounded in a 'flickering image the top executive has of the organisation grounded in their values'. The vision is expected to generate high trust and intense loyalty from staff.

There are four stages of envisioning according to Conger and Kanungo (1998):

> *evaluation of the status quo and analysis of the need for change; secondly, articulation of a vision which is discrepant from status quo, but which is thirdly logical, cogent and persuasive. Moreover, fourthly the application of charisma demands innovative and unconventional behaviours on the part of the leader in order to achieve the vision. Considerable risks attach to the leaders if they are to do this, although greater admiration and perceptions of credibility will arise from staff if they do. Vision hinges on the need to perceive a crisis facing the organisation that needs significant change to address.*
>
> *(Ibid.: 191)*

What kinds of skills might we expect such a visionary leader to have, according to Zaccaro and Banks? The skills needed are deductive and inductive reasoning, divergent thinking and information processing skills, good verbal reasoning, and the confidence to put their strongly positive message to their followers. In supporting the idea of the charismatic leader, Zaccaro and Banks are conscious of the difficulty of the dangerous charismatic, like Hitler or Stalin. They deal with this difficulty by suggesting that power may be wielded for good, when it is used on behalf of others, or for bad when it is used to aggrandise the self.

What is the evidence for putting forward the ideas in this chapter? Zaccaro and Banks remain rather ambivalent. On the one hand they admit that their attempts to generate a model from the authors they draw on are speculative: 'empirical evidence for the model is somewhat scant' (2001: 198). On the other hand they quote an article by Shamir, House and Arthur (1993) which claims on the basis of different studies on charismatic leadership:

> *Collectively, these findings indicate that leaders who engage in the theoretical charismatic behaviors produce the theoretical charismatic effects. In addition, they receive higher performance ratings, have more satisfied and more highly motivated followers, and are viewed as more effective leaders by their superiors and followers than others in positions of leadership. Further, the effect size of charismatic leader behavior on*

follower satisfaction and performance is consistently higher than prior
field study findings concerning other leader behavior, generally ranging
well below 0.01 probability of error due to chance, with correlations
frequently ranging in the neighbourhood of 0.50 or better.
                          (Shamir, House and Arthur, 1993: 578–579)

This is the strongest claim by any of the authors quoted above as to the efficacy of visionary and charismatic leadership.

Visionary Leadership – A Critique

The above accounts of visionary leadership contain many of the characteristics of the dominant managerial discourse that we have been reviewing previously. Zaccaro and Banks quite clearly think of an organisation as a system with a boundary which is disaggregated into different levels. The leader can see up to 50 years into the future and is able to anticipate both the future state of the organisation and the environment in which it operates. This anticipation must be both cogent and ambiguous at the same time. In their claim that the leader is not responsible for making day-to-day sense of the vision they solidify the split between leadership and management.

The second characteristic worthy of comment is the strong affect that a leader is supposed to provoke around the idea of change: this is change that only they can see since solipsistically they are in the only position to see it. One can imagine, largely from experience in organisations, that the script goes something like this: change is desperately needed if we are to recover from an otherwise inevitable decline. It will require heroic effort and commitment on everyone's part, not least me, your leader. But if you trust me and put your faith in what I am recommending then the rewards will be great. We need to set ourselves stretch targets, the road will be hard, but I promise it will be very exciting when we get there. Readers may be reminded of the narrative I described in the previous chapter, where the new Chief Executive Officer (CEO) was convinced of the compelling need for change, attempted to persuade members of staff in the organisation that change was a necessity, but was unable to spell out exactly what change he was looking for. The status quo is untenable for visionary leaders. It is also possible to see how this way of understanding the visionary role of leaders might allow them to persist in perverse behaviour. If change is imperative and extraordinary behaviour is required by the leader and those who follow, then resistance to the leader's vision may be experienced by them as confirmation that what they are recommending is needed even more.

Third, we encounter another example of what Alvesson and Sveningsson (2003) referred to in the previous chapter as the extraordinarisation of the mundane. The list of skills and qualities that a leader requires, apart from their ineffable ability to see into the future and conjure a vision, are actually quite ordinary. Surely one might expect to see these skills in any member of staff that an organisation employs, even ones quite junior.

Fourth, it is interesting to note the need to shore these claims up with an appeal to empirical scientific method. Without such claims the literature seems simply to feed off itself, as Clegg, Courpasson and Phillips (2006) notice, which I mentioned in the introductory chapter: visionary leadership must be an important phenomenon purely because other management scholars are writing about it. In making an empirical case Shamir, House and Arthur draw on 35 different studies conducted in very different settings, in a laboratory, in a management game, in a longitudinal survey, in interpretative research, and give no account of how they could have synthesised such methodologically different studies and arrived at such a precise statement about the effectiveness of charismatic leadership. Nor do they account for what Giddens (1993) referred to as the double-hermeneutic: the way in which interpretations of social processes are taken up by the groups being studied. So, for example, the expectation that employees might believe that their leader should be charismatic will undoubtedly influence their satisfaction that their leader does indeed display these tendencies. With so many abstract concepts apparently being 'measured' such as performance and charismatic behaviour, this must surely rate as improbable, self-referential research which never questions the assumptions upon which it rests.

But how would we account for the pervasiveness of the concept of vision, and why do management academics strive so hard to buttress the idea? In what follows I will explore how the religious imagination, a narrow conception of science and vision interconnect. As Elias has observed there is a convergence in the belief that science discovers the truth about the world and the idea of immanent vision. Both are grounded in what is known as foundationalism: that the truth proceeds from an essential ground or foundation.

Philosophical Interlude: Essential Nature, Expressivism and Abstraction

I have drawn attention to how Norbert Elias described our increased capacity over time to take a detour via detachment which has resulted in a historical process of individualisation as longer and longer chains of interdependent people co-operate and compete. Society forms us just as we are forming society. However, our enhanced detachment has gradually produced the conviction that there is an 'inside' and an 'outside':

> ... there is a special satisfaction associated for the individual, at the present stage of the development of self-consciousness, with the idea that he owes everything he regards as unique and essential in himself, to himself alone, to his 'nature' and to no one else. The idea that 'alien' people may play an integral part in the formation of one's individuality seems today almost like an infringement of one's rights over oneself.
>
> (1939/1991: 56–57)

The idea of an essential nature that has sprung into being at birth and is responsible for one's individuality is consistent with the religious idea of the soul, and Elias says, anchors individual qualities in something seemingly eternal and regular. It helps explain to individuals how they think we are connected to nature, which would otherwise be inexplicable to them. Stacey (2007: 62) notes how some of these ideas are taken up in humanistic psychology, with its basic assumption that the main problem of human existence is the alienation of the individual from her or his true self. The influence of humanistic psychology is manifest in management methods which emphasise the way in which staff need to be motivated through the engagement of their emotions and desires. The setting of vision and values by leaders allows employees for fulfil themselves psychologically. However, for Elias (1939/1991: 59) individuality is not something mystical and 'natural' but arises because a person grows up in 'a unique reference-point within a network of society' and due to the fact that our psychological make-up is more malleable than the processes that shape us. Society not only produces the similar and the typical, but also the individual. The analogy that Elias uses is that the individual is both die and coin at the same time. We become individuals only through our social interactions with others.

Charles Taylor, whom I introduced briefly in Chapter 4 and at the beginning of this one, has also drawn attention to our strong modern belief in the individualised self (1989, 1991, 2007) and may offer us further guidance in understanding the seeming contradiction in management literature of the rational manager and the imaginative and visionary discourse. Over a series of works Taylor traces the development of our sense of self: we have developed from what he terms 'porous' selves, where there was little separation in the Middle Ages between us and the environment in which we lived, to being 'buffered selves', where we think of ourselves as having a thick barrier between our 'inner' lives and the outer world. In the Middle Ages we would have found it impossible to conceive of not believing in God and perhaps the spiritual qualities of nature, what Elias termed magico-mythical thinking, yet in the modern age and in many western societies it now seems equally hard to believe. Taylor argues that increased secularism which began with the Enlightenment has not lessened our imaginative desire to be part of something greater than ourselves, to the degree that we are now living in what he calls a 'culture of authenticity' where everyone is expected to commit to personal development and self-expression of our inner nature, where nature is taken to be a source of truth. In his book *Sources of the Self* (1989) Taylor dates this tendency which he calls 'expressivism' to the Romantic period. The Romantics had a reaction against the radical implications of Enlightenment thinking with its 'classical stress on rationalism, tradition and formal harmony' and instead accentuated 'the rights of the individual, of the imagination and of feeling' (1989: 368). To give imaginative expression to something inchoate, like a feeling or a sense of things, is to draw on an idea of some kind of inner unity with nature, with things as they really are:

> *Fulfilling my nature means espousing the inner élan, the voice of impulse, And this makes what was hidden manifest for both myself and others. But this manifestation also helps to define what is to be realised. The direction of this élan wasn't and couldn't be clear prior to this manifestation.*
>
> *(1989: 375)*

Taylor notes the strong influence of biological models on the expressivist turn, where the movement is organic rather than mechanistic as each organism is called upon to unfold what is already enfolded in unity with nature. He sees this as something of a rebellion against a world described by cold formulas and calculations, where the world is understood as operating like a machine. He also draws attention to expressivism's strong appeal to individualism, whereby we can each fulfil our individual destiny which is unique to us by getting in touch with our true nature. Previously, in Chapter 3, we have also pointed to the appeal of Senge, Scharmer, Jaworski et al. (2005) for managers to intuit some profound natural truth in their daily interactions with others.

In his enquiry into what has become of our religious imagination in *A Secular Age*, Taylor puts forward the idea that the call to passion has arisen as a reaction to an age dominated by disengaged reason:

> *Now it appears to many that desiccated reason cannot reach the ultimate truths in any form. What is needed is a subtler language which can make manifest the higher or the divine ... Deeply felt personal insight now becomes our most precious resource.*
>
> *(2007: 489)*

If we were to take up Taylor's argument we may better understand how the professionalisation of management and the appeal to the religious imagination may go hand in hand. The contemporary management discourse on the importance of passion, belief, excitement and faith in the organisational mission as revealed through prophetic insight by the leader, or the top management team is a way of resacralising the workplace as a site of spiritual engagement. It is a foil to understanding the process of organising merely as an activity realising targets and outcomes, placing this activity in the expression of a higher truth. Employees are invited to imagine their efforts as contributing to a greater, truer, noble undertaking.

In his latest book *The Scientific Life: A Moral History of a Late Modern Vocation* (2008), the historian of science Steve Shapin gives some very good examples of this combination of rationality and the yearning for a higher moral representation when he describes the intersection of science and business. On the one hand, Shapin argues, we are invited to believe that one of the characteristics of modernity is that whole swaths of social life have been brought under the sway of impersonal reason. On the other when venture capitalists are brought together with scientists hoping to spin their ideas into successful businesses the quality of scientific thought and rigour are not sufficient for a scientist eliciting venture capital funding. The scientists are encouraged by the supposedly hard-headed VCs (Venture Capitalists) themselves to offer visions of transformation:

> *... public displays of the personal virtues of passion, commitment and vision are looked for as signs that entrepreneurs have a chance of success. Asked about money motivation among entrepreneurs, a VC responded: 'The guy who wants to do it for money? He's going to bail on you when the going gets tough and everyone's going to have tough*

going. These things are built by people who have a passion. You need
people who want to change the world.'

(2008: 295)

In one of the universities that host scientists seeking capital, staff work with them to convey passion and excitement about what they are doing, advising them to abandon dry and academic language and translate their nervousness into bodily gestures of excitement as they give their PowerPoint presentations to potential investors. Presenters are not just required to describe vision and commitment, they are asked to perform it. One of the things that Shapin is pointing to is the importance of the personal, of affect, and of the imagination in situations of highly complexity and uncertainty. It is the bonds between people, he argues, that allow for some greater sense of ease in highly fluctuating environments where the outcome of our activities is not clear. Rather than reaching for grids and frameworks, then, or in the case of the VCs, spreadsheets showing the 0s stacking up on the bottom line, highly professional people still appeal to the bond of their relationships with each other and their ability collectively to bring about a better future.

Vision and Truth

But how is it that we have come to understand vision as truth? The political philosopher Hannah Arendt points out that in the Hebrew tradition truth is received aurally, while for the ancient Greeks it was perceived (1971b: 111). There is a strong causal link in Western thought between knowing and seeing. She noticed that allusions to sight are so imbued in Greek literature that we have taken up the idea of sight as a metaphor for the truth unquestioningly. Arendt draws on the phenomenological philosopher Hans Jonas (2001) who reflected extensively on the sense of sight and its metaphorical and moral implications. According to Jonas, vision is different from the other senses in that hearing, touch and smell operate by our registering change in the environment. We hear a sound and then it passes away:

Only sight therefore provides the sensual basis on which the mind
may conceive of the idea of the eternal, and which never changes and is
always present.

(2001: 145)

Vision has both advantages and disadvantages. On the one hand, Jonas claims, the object perceived is separate from me and thus gains in the concept of objectivity. On the other hand, this gain in objectivity is the very thing that separates us from the casual involvement in the things perceived:

> *Thus vision secures that standing back from the aggressiveness of the world which frees for observation and opens a horizon for elective attention. But it does so at the price of offering a becalmed and abstract of reality denuded of its raw power.*
>
> *(Ibid.: 148)*

So distance and abstraction are the most basic conditions for the functioning of vision. Vision allows us to contemplate the eternal and the distant, the true which can seem as though it is all laid out before us. On the other hand it can appear distant and idealised, separated from the hurly burly of our experience and other objects in our phenomenal world which make their presence known to us by impinging upon us. And in the management literature quoted in the paragraphs above, leaders are not expected to bother with specifying how to reach the vision since this is the preserve of more mundane managers. They reveal truth and communicate their excitement about the possibilities that they have perceived, but the more mundane task of working out how to realise it is left to more junior staff.

Summary

In the paragraphs above I have been exploring some of the literature that tries to explain what might appear to be the metaphysical concept of vision, which is thought to be a requirement for leading today's highly complex organisations. In previous chapters I have been drawing attention to the way in which much contemporary management literature portrays the manager relatively unproblematically as a detached observer of organisational life, in which they can intervene for the good. Alongside this understanding of the role of the professional, rational manager, the idea of vision may appear to sit uncomfortably. However, in our exploration of the literature we have seen how there is still an attempt to claim evidence for the efficacy of visionary leadership. Indeed, there appears to be a similarity between the idea of a detached, rational scientist discovering the truth about an organisation's state, and the idea of a detached, individual leader who draws upon their insight based on a natural inner essence to discover how the unique path for an organisation will be realised. Although appealing separately to the rational mind or the religious imagination, both lay claim to a higher truth about the way things really are, or could be. Both arise from highly individualised, abstract ways of knowing that are disinterested in the complexity of everyday life. As a contemporary manifestation of what Charles Taylor calls 'expressivism', the idea of visionary and inspirational leadership is a foil to the rationalisation of management as a profession, encouraging employees to enlarge their sense of self through a commitment to the broader organisational mission conceived as quasi-religious revelation.

Against Individualism, Towards Emergence

I want to reprise the arguments I have been making against the trend to individualise the practice of management. As an alternative I have begun to raise questions about how helpful it is to think of managers as autonomous and rational individuals and how far they can really stand separate from the processes they intend to influence. I have been developing an argument that leaders, managers and consultants are severely constrained in how they can behave because of the strong patterning of power relationships into which they are acting. By drawing on an analogy from complex adaptive systems theory, which highlights the paradox of how on the one hand interaction between agents acting locally contributes to global patterning, and yet on the other the global patterning constrains how local agents are interacting, I am offering a critique of the idea that individuals are entirely free to choose what to do. More than this, I am calling into question the idea of a rational, autonomous self and offering instead the concept of a social self, one that arises in social interaction with other selves. What we can conceive of, how we understand ourselves and what is possible, arises out of the society, time and culture into which we are born. I think this is quite a disturbing idea from a contemporary perspective, since a lot of what we read and hear convinces us of our own separateness, our essential individuality, even to the extent of a famous British politician proclaiming that: 'And, you know, there's no such thing as society. There are individual men and women and there are families.'[1] It calls into question the idea that we can choose which management style we can adopt, we can surface our mental models or are capable of 'blue skies thinking' or 'thinking outside the box', or the other phrases that get used to denote an Archimedean point outside our interactions with others. If who we are and how we think of

---

1   Margaret Thatcher interview (23 September 1987), published in *Woman's Own* (31 October 1987).

ourselves has arisen in repeated social interaction with other selves, which in turn has been shaped by many centuries of human interaction, then there is no separating ourselves from the box we find ourselves in with others.

By drawing on Mead in Chapter 2 I have been putting forward the idea that mind, self and society all arise through communicative interaction with others. In a continuous, co-created process both consciousness and self-consciousness arise. No one, no matter how powerful, can impose meaning on others. Instead meaning emerges from the continuous iteration of gesture and response between engaged people. This interaction produces social patterning which is both regular and fluid at the same time. Our capacity to locate ourselves within social regularities and respond to them is possible, Mead argues, because humans have a unique ability to take themselves as an object to themselves. The spontaneous self continuously encounters an internalised and generalised other: self and other arise in a paradoxical melding.

To assume a profoundly social understanding of the interactions between self and others also offers a significant challenge to the idea of 'vision', which is considered in the dominant managerial discourse to be something that a leader 'has' or can be taught. My understanding of the social nature of self makes me want better to understand the idea of vision as a social phenomenon rather than as 'a unique creation of nature, issuing from its womb suddenly and inexplicably as Athene sprang from the head of Zeus' (Elias, 1939/1991: 56) and used as a justification for paying individual leaders exceptional rewards. Clearly there is something to the idea that people look for some kind of emotional fulfilment in their work above and beyond turning up each day simply to earn money. And organisations in the public and not-for-profit sectors, which often have more explicit moral commits to public service or to social justice do attract many employees who are motivated by ideals. I am interested to uncover the process of vision–creation more fully, particularly as my experience of visionary leadership has taught me that it can create problematic behaviour in organisations, which I will set out below.

Narrative – Utopian Strategy, Repressive Behaviour

I was asked to carry out some research for a chief executive of an organisation into how other organisations in their market sector undertook strategy, and I interviewed a senior manager from a similar very large organisation. He told me that a new chief executive had recently started and had spent six months listening to the staff in the organisation and had then decided it was time to come up with a new vision. The previous strategy and ways of working were deemed to have failed because they were insufficiently ambitious. The new vision needed to be more stretching and exciting. So the new chief executive committed with staff to transform the organisation so that it became dynamic and 'fit for the twenty-first century'. In committing to such a transformation the new chief executive and his colleagues decided that there was no way they were going to achieve this target if they did not also change themselves. They needed to be, in the words of Gandhi, the change they wanted to see.

So alongside the many working groups that they had set up in order to 'realise' the new vision, they also decided that they needed a 'culture change agenda', by which they meant a programme of work and reflection on their day-to-day working practices which would need to change radically if they were going to reach their new ambitious targets. My respondent told me that he was concerned that they had begun to get bogged down in working groups: staff were beginning to complain that they had no time to do their day-to-day work because of the extra commitment to changing themselves, and changing everything about the way the organisation ran. Some working groups had begun to produce new rules for the ways that colleagues should interact with each other: for example, there was a set of 'best practice' rules for running meetings efficiently which were posted up in meeting rooms. Whenever colleagues met together they were to appoint a keeper of the rules whose job involved showing yellow or red cards when they felt that any rules had been infringed. They had started to police their meetings.

Reflections on the Idea of Changing Human Nature

I pointed out in the previous chapters that most approaches to management are underpinned by systems theories, which imagine the organisation as an idealised whole with a boundary, which in turn is made up of parts. Systems theories assume that organisations can be redesigned and altered in a way that brings about 'whole' organisational change, and/or put forward the idea that organisations can choose a 'direction' by locating themselves within a bigger whole, society. Within this paradigm, individual staff members can also be conceived as being parts of a whole organisation, and sometimes values and belief systems can be understood as 'parts' of the whole individual. This encourages the idea of alignment: if I can realign my beliefs by redesigning them, and my colleagues can too, then our team can reorient within the department, the department within the organisation and so on, until transformation is complete. Vision is understood by contemporary management theory as being a means for achieving alignment, of generating the cult of conformity that so enthused Collins and Porras that I mentioned in Chapter 1.

What is interesting for me in the narrative above is the way in which social processes involving symbolic and imaginative projections get taken up literally and instrumentally by leaders in organisations as though they can be directly realised. Vision in this and many instances becomes an instrument of management so that particular leaders can reorient the organisation according to their own view of the world, no matter how achievable or otherwise. This is of course their prerogative. But in appealing to a unifying vision this particular leader is also making a very powerful intervention in their organisation which I understand also to be about covering over dissent. The appeal to morality is also an appeal to obedience. Understanding vision as a rule to be followed then leads to creating more and more rules until staff were trying to change their very natures. The moral tone of the exercise then began to cover over and occlude the necessary opportunities for dissent, struggle and sense-making so that day-to-day work began to suffer. In Foucault's terms (1979) it becomes a form of disciplinary power. What interested Foucault is the way in which forms of organising inevitably produce disciplinary techniques, and not just from those who are in positions of power. Borrowing from Jeremy Bentham's idea of the Panopticon, an observation platform where prison guards could see but not be seen, which would lead prisoners to start supervising their own behaviour rather than being forced to do so by prison guards, Foucault developed the idea that modernity has encouraged us to discipline ourselves and each other more and more. I think this narrative gives a good example of what Foucault meant by panopticism as employees took up the chief executive's ideas quite literally and began to discipline each other.

Vision statements might be necessary utopian generalisations which sustain followers or employees in the work that they commit to. But in being generalisations they are not necessarily adequate to inform how we might go on together in particular circumstances. This is at least partly because generalisations always need interpretation as particular circumstances present themselves. The process of interpretation, who gets involved, how they are involved, is constitutive of how that generalisation is then worked with. The moment that we think that we can take an idealisation, make plans around it and implement it without making constant reference to the objects of our plans, in their particular contexts, they are more likely to experience becoming an adjunct to the plans rather than the cause of them. Making reference to the objects of our intentions is likely to mean more than just engaging them in episodic consultations about highly abstract strategic generalisations, but taking seriously the experience of encountering and responding to them in the daily process of work. Vision is ultimately realised in an emergent way, which is an idea I derive from Hannah Arendt whom I mentioned earlier, and to whom I am now returning.

Disposing of the Future as Though it Were the Present

Hannah Arendt was intrigued by the power of collective purpose-making, since most of her life's work was a reflection on social processes of exercising power and authority, leading to her seminal work on *The Origins of Totalitarianism* (1979). She regarded herself more as political theorist than as a philosopher, and as such she would probably have been alive to the intersection of power and politics in organisations to which I have already drawn attention in this book. In reflecting on the way that humans come together to achieve things in *The Human Condition* (1958) Arendt divides human activity into three modes of being; labour, work and action. Starting with the last of these, action; action is a means of expressing individuality and self in concert with other beings involved in action. Action allows us to begin something new. Because everyone is acting with their own intentions, together and alone, we cannot be certain of the outcome since we are acting into a web of pre-existing relationships. And because of the vagaries of the human heart, we also cannot be certain that we will be tomorrow who we are today. As a hedge against uncertainty, then, Arendt describes the importance of making and keeping promises in the face of the unpredictability that afflicts human life. Collective promises have added power:

> *The sovereignty of a body of people bound and kept together, not by an identical will which somehow magically inspires them all, but by an agreed purpose for which alone the promises are valid and binding, shows itself quite clearly in its unquestioned superiority over those who are completely free, unbound by any promises and unkept by any purpose. This superiority derives from the capacity to dispose of the future as though it were the present, that is, the enormous and truly miraculous enlargement of the very dimension in which power can be effective.*
>
> *(1958: 245)*

The importance of a collective process which brings people together to make promises to work for a world without poverty and injustice, which an organisation in the not-for-profit sector might do, or perhaps to be a leading innovator in IT, is a force to be reckoned with, since it creates an enlarged sense of purpose that unites people in a common course of action and solidarity. A sense of excitement and group purpose arise at the same time – the individual and the collective interpenetrate as we imagine our enhanced power to achieve things together. It can feel like an island of certainty in a sea of unpredictability and assumes a realisable future. However, it is also important to consider the other more limited characteristics of this collective purpose-making that Arendt draws attention to:

> We mentioned before the power generated when people gather together and 'act in concert', which disappears the moment they depart. The force that keeps them together, as distinguished from the space of appearances in which they gather and the power which keeps this public space in existence is the force of mutual promise. Sovereignty, which is always spurious if claimed by an isolated single entity, be it the individual entity of the person or the collective entity of a nation, assumes, in the case of many men mutually bound by promises, a certain limited reality. The sovereignty resides in the resulting, limited independence from the incalculability of the future, and its limits are the same as those inherent in the faculty itself of making and keeping promises.
>
> (Ibid.: 244/5)

Arendt is clear that the collective promise making, though powerful, exists in a 'space of appearances' which takes on 'a certain limited reality'. Arendt wishes to remind us that the 'limited independence' we can achieve by engaging in a collective act of promise-making is an act of freedom, the only alternative to domination over ourselves and others. There is a danger, however, to this exercise:

> The moment promises lose their character as isolated islands of certainty in an ocean of uncertainty, that is, when this faculty is misused to cover the whole ground of the future and to map out a path secured in all directions, they lose their binding power and the whole exercise becomes self-defeating.
>
> (Ibid.: 244)

I think Arendt seems to be suggesting that collective promise-making is an insufficient exercise on its own. She considers it to be a partial, temporary phenomenon which sustains only as long as people come together, and only as long as the process does not pretend to map out a path in all directions. To understand this collective process otherwise could be committing staff in organisations to the 'self-defeating' exercise that Arendt warns against, if we think that our idealisations can be directly realised. If collective promise-making can be an act of freedom it also brings with it dangers for curtailing that freedom, ours and other people's.

I would argue that Arendt is pointing to something very similar to the historian of science Steve Shapin whom I quoted above. The venture capitalists who are thinking of funding entrepreneurial scientists are looking for a moral commitment from them, a promise, if only temporary, of creating a better world together. The science of the ideas on their own is not enough. But the venture capitalists are hard headed enough to realise that excitement and promises of transformation are insufficient on their own to guarantee profit.

Taking up this idea that we can over-depend on our promises of a better future Arendt developed an interest in how totalitarian regimes such as Stalinism and Nazism arise, and how it is that individuals, and sometimes whole societies, seem to suspend their ability to discriminate right from wrong. According to Richard Bernstein (1996), the contemporary pragmatic philosopher, Arendt was drawn to Kant's (1790/2008) *Critique of Judgement* since in this treatise he (Kant) describes a form of reflective judgement that does not subsume particulars under a universal principle or general rule. What this enables us to do is to respond to the unexpected and the unprecedented without trying to accommodate it to an inappropriate rule, or to assume that whole areas of human experience, even human nature, can be transformed. In developing her own ideas after Kant, Arendt developed the proposition that thinking and judging were tantamount to political acts, and allow us to behave like gadflies in the way that Socrates did:

> [A]t these moments, thinking ceases to be a marginal affair in political matters. When everyone is swept away unthinkingly by what everyone else does and believes in, those who think are drawn out of hiding because their refusal to join is conspicuous and thereby becomes a form of action. The purging element in thinking ... is political by implication ... [and] has a liberating effect on another faculty, the faculty of judgement,

which one may call, with some justification, the most political of man's
mental abilities.

                                                            (Arendt, 1971a: 445–446)

The collective disposal of the future as though it were the present is a
paradoxical phenomenon that enables us to have an enlarged sense of purpose,
but at the same time can convince us that wholesale transformation is possible,
both of ourselves and of what we plan to undertake together. I realise that
what I am suggesting here is provocative, that the comparison between the
phenomena that Arendt was trying to understand, some of which lead to the
production of totalitarian regimes, is a similar phenomenon to a visioning
exercise in organisations. Many people in organisations might find this a difficult
comparison since there is widespread contemporary belief, almost a cult of
positivity to which I have alluded before, that managers and staff work in a way
that is oriented to the good. I believe that Arendt's cautions about the dangers that
accompany collective promise-making must be remembered, however, if we are
to avoid some of the behaviour of staff in the organisation which I noted above.
Here the process of visioning resulted in staff generating more and more ways
of policing each other's behaviour as a way of attempting to transform human
nature itself to the extent of distracting from their day-to-day work. The rules
they had begun to set themselves in an illusory project of self transformation.

Moral Visions and Consensus – Politics and the Mediation of Power Relations

In the first chapter I made the claim that managerialism, the privileging of
management over other forms of organisational control, had become the
dominant ideology in public and private sectors alike (Clarke and Newman,
1997). As managers take up the language of managerialism they often lay
claim to the high moral ground for a project of transformation at the same
time as claiming greater organisational effectiveness. Commenting on the
way that mangerialism has infused the public sector, Clarke and Newman
note that narratives of organisational survival are closely tied to narratives of
transformation:

> *This more expansive view of change is carried through narratives which*
> *centre on organisational (and social) transformation. Here change is*
> *viewed as not merely necessary because of the pressure of external forces,*
> *but as a progressive force for transformation and the development of a*

new order. The key metaphors are 'reinventions' of the old and 'visions'
of the new.

(Clarke and Newman, 1997: 42)

Whilst appealing to social and organisational transformation it is sometimes the case that managers deny that what they are doing is in any sense political; they are simply interested in what works. A thread of this discussion is taken up by Giddens in his book entitled *The Third Way* (1998) where he makes the claim, recycled by the previous British Prime Minister, that the old left/right antagonisms are dead, and that there is now a liberal consensus about trying to find out pragmatic and rational solutions to society's problems based on what Giddens calls 'dialogic democracy'.

In the public sector in particular, the transformational project can be portrayed by managers and leaders both as an organisational and a moral necessity, and they go on to make the claim that they have the particular competence to bring about the necessary change. On the one hand it is difficult to dissent from this because of the promise of social transformation that managers often make (who would be against improving the lot of disenfranchised communities, or healthier patients, or children who are protected from harm?), on the other it is hard to oppose because of the promise of greater organisational effectiveness and accountability which is often made at the same time. The project of transformation is propositional, and is at the same time often described as a participative and consensus-building project. Visioning is about moving ourselves towards a new reality to which we all aspire, whilst having nothing to say about how we might get there. This makes visioning exercises and the excitement that they generate very hard to gainsay, or to express doubts, reservations and alternatives.

In much contemporary management literature there is a big emphasis on developing a shared corporate culture, of trying to manipulate employee behaviour so that it conforms to organisational values, and generally being invasive of what Habermas (1985) referred to as the 'life world' of employees. Some business gurus, such as Collins and Porras, are quite explicit that if you don't share the company ideology (their word) then you should be ejected. This, too, I would argue is a kind of totalitarianism which tries to develop the organisation into a cult and works to prevent negotiation, discussion and argument, the sharing of different points of view. It is a form of violence since in Arendt's terms it seeks to undermine the exercise of politics.

In her work *On Violence* (1970), Arendt reflects on the interconnection between power and violence. When human beings gather together to act in concert to do something new then power arises, but so does the potentiality for violence. Violence can be justifiable but it can never be legitimate, since it is the exercise of power through politics that restrains the destructive tendencies of violence. Violence unconstrained by power exercised through politics consumes its own children as we have seen in the Terror of the French Revolution and in totalitarian states. However, power and violence are not just different, she argues, they are opposites. Violence brings about the destruction of power and becomes more manifest when power is in jeopardy.

What are the consequences for Arendt's thinking on power and violence for organisational life? One of the central themes for me in organisations is the exercise of power, which occurs in the everyday politics of working together. We negotiate, we discuss, we are polite and impolite to each other, we reveal and conceal, we pull rank, we delegate, we take decisions alone and we ask others for their points of view. This, for Arendt, is the proper exercise of power in public space and leads to the greatest of human civilising achievements. When the daily political process breaks down, however, and there is no longer a potential for negotiating how we might go on together, then we can experience this as violence.

Second Narrative

I have been working with a group of senior middle managers in a higher education establishment where the Principal has developed what she considers a 'strong vision' for the institution which relies upon it being publically perceived as being very entrepreneurial. In the spirit of the times it is understood to be a good thing to be business-oriented, and the institution has been attracting a lot of notice for the claims that it has been making. There is a good deal of both excitement and opposition to the idealised claim to be entrepreneurial from different groups within the institution, depending on the length of time they have spent in the organisation, their professional background or their values. So, for example, some of the teachers in the organisation have moved from business to a teaching career and do not have the same idealised understanding of what it means to be entrepreneurial as the Principal and some of her colleagues seem to.

The visioning and strategy-making process has spawned a whole set of organisation-wide initiatives, however, which are aimed at 'realising the vision'. These range from something called 'small steps for change' where departments are invited to send a 'champion' to a regular meeting to explain how they have made small steps towards being more entrepreneurial, through to 'challenge meetings' where senior managers are invited to give an account of why they have or haven't become more entrepreneurial to a star chamber of other senior managers. The challenge meetings have indeed been very challenging with incidents of senior managers shouting at more junior managers and demanding that they justify themselves. New initiatives are often followed up by quite peremptory e-mails demanding why the last directive has not been complied within the deadline specified.

The group I am working with are using the time we spend together as a reflective space to think about the difficulties of managing. One of the things they return to again and again is the time that it takes to respond to the endless new initiatives that the strategy process has thrown up. The managers present do not consider themselves 'against change', indeed they are committed to what they are doing, and are constantly making the necessary improvements and adjustments irrespective of the corporate strategy. Indeed, many of them would already consider themselves quite entrepreneurial. However, the anxiety that surrounds the strategy for everyone concerned has created an environment where it has become quite difficult to argue against what is being proposed, no matter how unworkable some of the suggestions. The managers I am working with have a variety of responses: some just keep their heads down and hope that senior management scrutiny will pass them by; others write long and patient e-mails explaining why what is being proposed is unworkable or even counterproductive. Other do their best to comply with what is being put forward even though this sometimes puts them in a position of having later to apologise to their teams if the initiative proves to be unimplementable.

There is agreement in the group that these proposals are hard to resist, and that it is difficult to speak out against them for fear of being labelled unco-operative or against change. There are a few brave souls who do, but these tend to be older, more experienced colleagues who are close to retirement or who feel that their position within the institution is powerful, despite their rank. Being able to speak out or not becomes a judgement about one's relative power in the organisation. There is another interesting phenomenon happening: there are one or two colleagues who used to be senior middle managers who have been promoted. While they would once complain about the way they themselves have been treated in managerial processes, now, in public at least, they appear to be speaking out in support of what is happening.

REFLECTIONS ON THE NARRATIVE

Strategy processes based on strong idealisations can evoke powerful feelings in groups of people, particularly when there is robust invitation to conform, either explicit or implicit. This creates a dynamic of inclusion and exclusion, a phenomenon I shall be exploring in more depth in the next chapter on values. In the narrative above there is an invitation to belong to an idealised cult of an entrepreneurial tomorrow which middle managers spend a lot of their time dealing with. It is clearly such a powerful dynamic that even those who were critical of it find themselves obliged to 'play the game' when they find themselves promoted. To find ways of openly opposing what is going on then requires a good deal of courage potentially to jeopardise one's stake in the game.

At the same time the public narrative about the higher institution's entrepreneurial claim is responded to in a variety of different ways, with some people sustaining it, some people publically opposing it, and some people more tacitly subverting it, at least as far as being able to get on with what they think is really important. In this sense, and in Mead's terms, the exact meaning of senior managers' gestures in the shape of a vision statement can only be understood in the many and varied responses of the people being gestured to. This has a dramatic effect on the way that strategies get taken up and interpreted, as I will explore in the next chapter and in Chapter 7 on strategy. I will return once more to the idea that global patterning arises simply and only from the interactions of people acting locally with others.

Concluding Thoughts on Vision

In the last 25 years that I have been involved with organisations the world has changed a lot, and to a large extent these organisations have changed with it. In the area of strategising, however, leaders and managers still seem to be relying heavily on outdated ways of understanding a complex world for orienting their staff. This involves conceiving of strategy as a process of identifying an idealised end point, the vision, then working back from there in logical steps. This implies a belief in a utopian but predictable future which can be realised if staff are motivated and enthused enough. These promises of transformation by managers and leaders invest a good degree of faith in rational management techniques to 'deliver' the end results, but also effectively cover over the exercise of power and the ideological nature of the proposition. The combination of high moral purpose rationally applied can sometimes get extended to believing that staff behaviour can also be transformed, in seeking some kind of alignment between the way staff work together and the goals set for the organisation. In this way managers commit to programmes of 'culture change', which can sometimes mean developing a process of mutual policing, bullying and recrimination which can proliferate so much as to get in the way of the work. What happens is the highly elaborate forms of mutual and self-disciplining techniques arise where it becomes impossible publically to dissent.

The idea of vision is ubiquitous, and is usually understood in highly individualised and abstract terms. It is a revelation of an idealised future that individual leaders can make on the basis of their unique ability to articulate an inchoate 'truth', allowing an organisation to fulfil its true nature. It is a means by which leaders can appeal to their employees' need for psychological fulfilment in the workplace. However, it is also often framed as an invitation to conform, or worse to join a cult mediated by the powerful threat of exclusion. In Chapter 7 on strategy I will be exploring some of the reasons why I think that dissent and deviance are important for novelty to arise in organisations, particularly those that make an explicit commitment to innovation. Compelling employees to conform and at the same time inviting them to innovate places them in a frustrating double bind.

By drawing on Taylor and Arendt, I have made alternative claims for the visioning process: that it is a necessary and powerful way for groups of staff to exercise freedom together, of imagining a new future, but that it is a temporary and partial process which cannot map out all aspects of knowing how to take the next steps. As generalisations, such statements only take us so far in knowing how to act. Rather, it is incumbent upon staff in organisations continuously to look for ways to discuss, argue over, rework and functionalise these idealisations. I am arguing that change is not something which can be just designed and prescribed by senior managers in an idealised strategy process, but is happening every day in every department and unit in the organisation. Being open to what the organisation is already becoming allows for the possibility of the practical implications of a visioning process to emerge. The dangers of not being open implies that we already know what's best for the organisation irrespective of the variety of work environments where staff are already largely doing their best to make things work. It then has the potential

for bullying and even violence, where by violence I take Arendt's definition of
the prevention of the necessary daily struggles over power.

In my own view calling attention to the ambivalence of vision as a tool of
management has particular, but not exclusive implications for the public and
not-for-profit sectors, where the vision is often conceived on behalf of others,
the objects of the organisation's attention, 'a hospital which delivers the best
care for patients' for example, or 'a school where every pupil fulfils their full
potential'. I once met a senior manager for an international Non-Governmental
Organisation (NGO) who asked his colleagues how the needs of the villagers he
was working with fitted with his organisational vision and mission. I wonder
whether it would be more helpful to ask the question the other way round: how
his organisational vision and mission could be realised through the particular
needs of the villagers he encounters. Rather than understanding them as grand
statements of intent that presuppose action, he might, alternatively, think of
them as made up of a patchwork of myriad numbers of particular people's
needs manifested in particular contexts, as understood by Blake:

> He who would do good to another must do it in Minute Particulars.
> General Good is the plea of the scoundrel, hypocrite, and flatterer:
> For Art and Science cannot exist but in minutely organized Particulars.
> William Blake, Jerusalem, (1815, Chapter 3, plate 55 l.60)

The general impetus to do good informs the work of public organisations
and not-for-profits in the first place but needs replenishing through the daily
contact between staff and particular others. The effect of these encounters is to
help staff functionalise what are often very abstract and idealised intentions.

In my experience staff in most organisations are restive for success; they
are concerned to know that they are doing well while doing good (Moss Kanter
and Summers, 1987). But as I work with not-for-profit organisations I find a
greater confusion amongst staff about the political nature of what it is that
they are doing. This arises partly as a consequence of the interpenetration of
public, private and not-for-profit sectors, where one is just as likely to find
staff with a commercial background working in not-for-profits and the public
sector, as those who committed to not-for-profit work from the beginning.
This is not to argue that staff in the private sectors are somehow de-politicised,
since I would consider any enterprise that involves human interaction to be a
political activity. Rather, what I am pointing to is the particular nature of not-
for-profit work, where what one is undertaking is dependent on the views and

aspirations of those one is trying to help. The product, if we can use this word here, is relational and cannot be conceived and disposed of as separate from the beneficiaries that staff in not-for-profits aim to help. The conviction of the morality of what one is doing, however, and the belief in rational management cannot be enough.

I am not so naïve that I do not realise that this places an extra burden on both staff and managers. If staff in not-for-profits are not to be mere functionaries following what they consider to be simple rules in the furtherance of their work, they could be instead regard themselves as researchers interested in the data that informs the what and the how of their mission. The vision and mission would not then become a blanket and bureaucratised response to injustice or public service, but a detailed and emergent patchwork quilt of particular responses.

Implications for Managers and Leaders

Visionary language has become so ubiquitous that it has also become banal, especially when vision statements are expressed simply as a utopian reversal of our current predicaments and difficulties. The leaders I most enjoy working with, and the ones I consider visionary, are the ones who spend least time articulating idealised end states, but who take the work of their employees seriously and in doing so help them to recognise themselves in what they are doing and discover new meaning in it. It seems to me that good leaders and managers are more committed to insight rather than vision, the continuous opening up of the possibilities of the here and now. Excitement is generated not with an appeal to what we might achieve together at some future point, but rather an intensified realisation of what we are achieving together, as we discover each other, and ourselves, anew.

References

Argyris, C. (1990) *Overcoming Organizational Defensives: Facilitating Organizational Learning*, Needham Heights: Alleyn and Bacon.

Alvesson, M. and Sveningsson, S. (2003) Managers doing leadership: The extra-ordinarization of the mundane, *Human Relations*, 56(12): 1435–1459.

Arendt, H. (1958) *The Human Condition*, Chicago: University of Chicago Press.

——. 1970. *On Violence*, New York: Harvest.

—— (1971a) Thinking and moral considerations: A lecture, *Social Research*, 38(3): 417–446.

—— (1971b) *The Life of the Mind*, New York: Harcourt.

—— (1979) *The Origins of Totalitarianism*, New York: Harvest/Harcourt, Brace, Jovanowich.

Bennis, W. and Nanus, B. (1986) *Leaders: The Strategies for Taking Charge*, New York: Harper Businesss.

Bernstein, R. (1996) *Hannah Arendt and the Jewish Question*, Cambridge: Polity Press.

Block, P. (2000) *Flawless Consulting*, San Fransisco: Jossey Bass.

Clarke, J. and Newman, J. (1997) *The Managerial State*, London: Sage.

Clegg, S., Courpasson, D. and Phillips, N. (2006) *Power and Organisations*, London: Sage.

Collins, J. and Porras, J. (1991) Organizational vision and visionary organizations, *California Management Review*, 34: 30–82.

—— (2005) *Built to Last: Successful Habits of Visionary Companies*, New York: Random House.

Conger, J.A. and Kanungo, R. (1998) *Charismatic Leadership in Organizations*, London: Sage.

Elias, N. (1939/1991) *The Society of Individuals*, Oxford: Blackwell.

Foucault, M. (1979) *Discipline and Punish: The Birth of the Prison*, London: Penguin.

Giddens, A. (1993) *New Rules of Sociological Method*, Stanford: Stanford University Press.

Giddens, A. (1998) *The Third Way: Renewal of Social Democracy*, Oxford: Polity.

Habermas, J. (1985) *Theory of Communicative Action*, Boston: Beacon Press.

House, R. and Shamir, B. (1993) Towards the integration of transformational, charismatic and visionary theories, in Chemers, M. and Ayman, M. *Leadership Theory and Research: Perspectives and Directions*, San Diego: Academic Press.

Jackson, M. (2000) *Systems Approaches to Management*, New York: Kluwer Academic.

Jonas, H. (2001) *The Phenomenon of Life: Towards a Philosophical Biology*, Evanston: Northwestern University Press.

Kant, I. (1790/2008) *Critique of Judgement*, Oxford: Oxford University Press.

Kirkpatrick, S. and Locke, E. (1996) Direct and indirect effects of three core charismatic leadership components on performance and attitudes, *Journal of Applied Psychology*, 81: 36–51.

Kotter, J. (1990) *A Force for Change: How Leadership Differs from Management*, New York: Free Press.

Mead, G.H. (1934) *Mind, Self and Society from the Standpoint of a Social Behaviourist*, Chicago: University of Chicago Press.

Mintzberg, H., Ahlstrand B. and Lampel, J. (1998) *Strategy Safari: The Complete Guide Through the Wilds of Strategic Management*, Edinburgh: Pearson.

Moss Kanter, R. and Summers, D. (1987) Doing well while doing good: Dilemmas of performance management in nonprofit organisations and the need for a multi-constituency approach, in Powell, W. (ed.) *The Non-profit Sector: A Research Handbook*, New Haven: Yale University Press.

Schein, E. (1987) *Process Consultation Vol. 1: Its role in Organization Development. Process Consultation; Vol. 2: Lessons for Managers and Consultants*, Reading: Addison-Wesley.

Senge, P. (1990) *The Fifth Discipline: The Art and Practice of the Learning Organization*, London: Century.

——, Scharmer, C.O., Jaworski, J. and Flwoers, B.S. (2005) *Presence: Exploring Profound Change in People, Organisations and Society*, London: Nicholas Brealey Publishing.

Shamir, B., House, R. and Arthur, M. (1993) The motivational effects of charismatic leadership: A self-concept based theory, *Organization Science*, 4(4): 577–594.

Shapin, S. (2008) *The Scientific Life: a Moral History of a Late Modern Vocation*, Chicago: University of Chicago Press.

Stacey, R. (2007) *Strategic Management and Organisational Dynamics: The Challenge of Complexity*, 5th edition, London: Routledge.

Taylor, C. (1989) *Sources of the Self: The Making of Modern Identity*, Cambridge: Cambridge University Press.

—— (1991) *The Ethics Of Authenticity*, Cambridge: Harvard University Press.

—— (2007) *A Secular Age*, Cambridge: Belknap Harvard.

Willmott, H. (1993) Strength is ignorance, slavery is freedom: Managing culture in modern organizations, *Journal of Management Studies*, 30(4): 515–552.

—— (2003) Renewing strength: corporate culture revisited, *M@n@gement*, 6(3): 73–87.

Zaccaro, S.J. and Banks, D. (2001) Leadership, vision and organizational effectiveness in Zaccaro, S.J. and Klimoski, R.J. (eds) (2001) *The Nature of Organizational Leadership: Understanding the Performance Imperatives Confronting Today's Leaders*, London: Wiley.

6

Choosing Organisational Values, Changing Culture

Like vision, values figure centrally in the dominant managerialist discourse in recognition of the fact that work, and places of work, matter to us. The way that values usually get taken up in orthodox understandings of managing is as a means of clarifying and unifying purpose, and of aligning employee and organisational values. It is taken for granted that we should 'share values'. In the context of a strategy which involves acknowledging the mission, submitting to the vision and sharing values, managerialist texts seek the alignment that is thought to cascade from top to bottom in organisations as employees unite in a common purpose. In this chapter I will explore some of the literature that deals with values and explore how it assumes that they are a legitimate subject for managerial intervention which managers have the power to choose and change. This is based on a familiar contention that managers can assess values using objectively verifiable tools and techniques arising from idea of management as science. Moreover, I will argue that the dominant literature creates simplistic dualisms which suggest that sharing values is always good, while having differing values is potentially destructive or confusing. Instead I will be putting forward an alternative view that it is only through the exploration of difference, conflicting understandings of the good, that true novelty can arise. This is congruent with my previous claims that novelty arises not from homogeneity and stability, but from the exploration of difference.

Many discussions of values in the literature link together values and the idea of culture change, as we began to explore in the previous chapter. The central proposition is that organisations need to adapt to a fast-changing environment so that they can be better suited to succeed, and that organisational culture usually stands in the way of this necessary change. 'Culture' is here taken to mean the individual behaviour that contributes to the habituated daily interaction between employees. The appeal to values in organisations is directly consonant with some of the other management methods used by managers, which I have been discussing in previous chapters. These methods draw on ideas derived from systems theories which conceive of organisations as idealised wholes. Individuals are understood to be parts of these wholes, and in turn, values are sub-systems of individuals which can be reconfigured and lined up in a slightly different way which is more fitting to the imagined end state. If behaviour is guided by values, it is thought, then influencing people's values will bring about the required behaviour change, that is to say, the types of belief and behaviour that senior managers think is necessary for the organisation to adapt to a new environment.

This is another example of what I have been writing about in previous chapters where attempting to shape the employee's 'lifeworld', their hopes, desires and sense of identity, is considered to be the legitimate domain of management. In addition, the manufactured anxiety around the necessity of organisational change can develop in employees the need for feelings of safety which can result in their conforming to changes which are required of them. In reaction, some critical management theorists (du Gay, 2007; Casey, 1999, Willmott, 1993) are suspicious that this is another form of identity manipulation.

But is it fair to talk about the desire for values congruence as management 'manipulation'? It is sometimes the case that workers can be aware of, and can agree to, manipulative management approaches if they perceive that their own interests are being fulfilled at the same time. However, the idea of control through values is very much to the fore for organisations like the Chartered Institute of Personnel and Development (CIPD), who have a key role in helping organisations in all sectors develop human resources policies:

> *Successful organisations are characterised by strong values and a strong guiding vision that communicates what behaviour is appropriate and what is not. If these values are widely shared across the organisation and are reflected in the everyday actions of employees at all levels, both individually and collectively, then there is a strong culture.*[1]

The CIPD explicitly links values congruence with enhanced business performance, and describes the exercise as 'unlocking the black box'. What I take this to mean is that there is some secret source of currently unpredictable energy or wisdom in organisations, a code, like the black box flight recorder in passenger jets, which can be unlocked to reveal the necessary information which

---

1   http://www.cipd.co.uk/research/_visionandvalues.htm

will chart its course. As a result of the unlocking of the black box, employees will become more predictable and controllable. The corollary to this way of thinking is that it is no longer enough that potential employees are attracted to working in an organisation because of their own personal motivation to do so. They are also invited to open up their valuations for inspection and possible modification by managers, because to remain closed to this scrutiny, to remain a black box makes them too unpredictable.

As an alternative in this chapter I will suggest that values are not so easily subject to management manipulation as the dominant literature pretends. I will argue that they are instead a profoundly social and emergent phenomenon which inevitably draws us into negotiation and compromise with each other. Our values arise in intensely social situations where we are struggling to find a way of going on together. In the everyday our valuations will conflict with others' and we will be forced to choose between one course of action and another, between different interpretations of the good. This decision will always be mediated by power relations. Powerful invitations to submit to organisational values are a call to join a cult, as Collins and Porras (2005) make clear in their book which we discussed in Chapter 1, which can be understood as generating strong pressures for employees to belong and conform, rather than face exclusion. However, in many organisations it is my experience that there are often quite intense value conflicts taking place which have the potential for both creativity and destruction, which we will explore further below.

Culture and Values in the Literature

It is worth a small detour into the idea of organisational culture since it is much written about but nonetheless remains very amorphous as a concept. Alvesson (2002) notices the broad definitions used in the management literature to denote the term 'culture'. Despite the lack of a solid definition and the largely superficial way in which it is addressed, Alvesson defines culture as 'a frame of reference of beliefs, expressive symbols and values, by means of which individuals define their environment, express their feelings and make judgements' (2002: 5). He notes that the term is used both 'offensively' and 'defensively' in the literature. In the offensive formulation culture can be used as a tool or a guiding concept to achieve effectiveness. Defensively, organisational literature sees culture as an obstacle to economic rationality and effectiveness. Alvesson describes how culture is often collapsed into a dualism of good and bad cultures, where good cultures are linked to harmony, consensus, clarity and meaningfulness (2002: 44). Once again it is important to note the importance in the orthodox management literature of harmony, balance and homeostasis, as well as dualism.

In the dominant literature it is proposed that managers should assess the current culture of the organisation and use a variety of tools and frameworks to shift the way that it is currently shaped towards one which is more fitting to anticipated change. Conventionally this is can be expressed as wanting to move culture from being a vicious to a virtuous circle (Hampden-Turner, 1994), where the culture understood as system reinforces itself for the good. This will involve encouraging individuals to behave differently by appealing to their values. Most change programmes fail, it is claimed, because the thorny issue of organisational culture has not been adequately addressed. A typical example of this way of thinking is Cameron and Quinn's *Diagnosing and Changing Organizational Culture Based on the Competing Values Framework* (2006) which sets out some diagnostic tools and step-by-step guides to help managers change employees' mindsets and behaviours towards a desired state. The authors claim scientific validity for their competing values framework across different organisations and even across different countries, because of 'an underlying similarity of people at the deep psychological level of their cognitive processes', (2006: 33). The authors explicitly allude to Jung (1981) and his theory of personality archetypes upon which to base their framework. Archetypes also inform the ubiquitous Myers-Briggs Type Indicator (MBTI) assessment framework which is used diagnostically in many organisations. The idea of an archetype imprinted on the soul at birth was originally suggested by Plato.

Milton Rokeach, a cognitive psychologist, also understood values principally to be an individual attribute and divided them into two categories (1973), terminal and instrumental, based on the content of the values. Terminal values are end states of behaviour that individuals try to achieve (lifetime loyalty, true friendship), while instrumental values are those which guide behaviour towards those end states. A lot of organisational research has focused principally on Rokeach's definitions and has concentrated on instrumental values. Researchers drawing on Rokeach have tried to create typologies and use them to predict human behaviour and when values will conflict (Schwartz, 1992, 1996). Taken up in organisational theory, this has then become a way of identifying whether employees will stabilise the organisational mission because their values somehow conform to existing organisational values, or assist with innovation because they don't. Again we encounter the ways in which organisational literature attempts to yoke employee values to the organisational mission with the assumption that alignment of values is necessary for an organisation to succeed.

Previously (Mowles 2007, 2008) I have discussed the ways that different scholars understand values instrumentally. In the management journals both Sachs and Rühli (2005) on the one hand, and Dolan and Richley (2006) on the other discuss instrumental values. For the former scholars, the new environment for business at the beginning of the millennium implies a broader approach by managers in their strategic thinking towards understanding what stakeholders, as well as shareholders want. By offering incentives to managers to consider a broader constituency, Boards can change their managers' values. Sachs and Rühli seem to be suggesting that simple behavioural psychology can account for changing values, and that categories of people will change their values in accordance with a similar stimulus, incentives. Equally, Dolan and Richley generalise the phenomenon of values and consider them as a thing to be managed; first came management by instruction, they argue, then management by objectives and now it is time for management by values. In a mixture of complex adaptive systems thinking, chaos theory and pathetic fallacy, the authors describe organisations as 'complex living entities' where values act as a governing principle:

> For individuals, groups, organisations and society, value systems are the strange attractor that determines the general form of their behaviour.
>
> (2006: 236)

For Dolan and Richley it is for the manager to stand outside what is happening and control things for the good of the firm:

> Thus, today, effective managers should tap into peoples' values as a way of motivating them.
>
> (Ibid: 237)

Being a good manager is likened to tapping in to some mysterious energy source, which, once found, can be channelled for the good of the organisation.

Weber (1993) also approaches values from the perspective of cognitive psychology and enquires whether it is possible to prove an empirical link between personal values and moral reasoning. He combines Rokeach's (1968, 1973) four personal value orientations with Kohlberg's (1981, 1983) stages of moral development to produce a variety of grids showing the relationship between an individual's values and their ability to take certain kinds of decisions on moral grounds. The utility of this, Weber argues, is that managers could then better predict the likelihood of staff behaving in a particular kind of way, new staff could be recruited who would fit the culture of the recruiting organisation, and the information could assist firms to develop training courses to promote ethical decision-making and behaviour.

In the not-for-profit sector Pasteur and Scott-Villiers (2004) take a very explicit systems perspective, and, drawing on both Argyris (1982) and Senge (1990), assume values, attitudes and behaviours to be the last box in a series of nested boxes that make up an organisation and the people that work in it. An organisation is disaggregated into parts and whole. Managers and employees should use different 'lenses' to scrutinise what is going on in the different levels of the organisation in order to fully understand what is happening. Paying attention to one's attitudes and values allows one to 'close the gap', the disconnect between rhetoric and practice:

> ... learning requires ongoing honest reflection on the kinds of personal, organisational and institutional assumptions that underlie programme goals. It involves a deep questioning of personal attitudes and behaviours and whether they are congruent with espoused objectives. It also requires a broader reflection on whether the procedures, cultures, and relationships are supportive of the expressed goals.
>
> (Pasteur and Scott-Villiers, 2004: 196)

This way of thinking takes a very instrumental approach to value statements and represents them as tools of management which are thought to be directly realisable. It places a burden on the individual somehow to get their attitudes and behaviour in alignment with everyone else's and with the explicit policies of the organisation. It implies that some kind of synergy is possible if individuals are 'honest' enough in their enquiry, and their personal enquiry is deep enough. 'Closing the gap' between policy and practice is essentially a problem to be solved on our own; it becomes a matter of individual conscience and enquiry to effect a transition to what remains an idealisation. It neglects the fact that organisational value statements are idealisations, which by their very nature are unachievable in any direct manner.

Summary of the Dominant Discourse

In many of these theories outlined above, the concept of values is highly individualised: like Senge's mental models, values are cognitive attributes which can be isolated, intervened upon and changed in the interests of the firm. Addressing individual values is understood to be crucial to achieving anticipated changes in organisational culture which leads to increased performance, and they are a legitimate focus of managerial intervention. The literature implies that, by using the right validated tools often derived from typologies thought to be based on human universals, managers can assess organisational culture and employee values and intervene to change them. Either this or managers can appeal to their employees to scrutinise themselves and bring about the necessary alignment between current and ideal behaviours, informed by personal values: I am arguing here that this amounts to an invitation to join an organisational cult, and for employees to discipline themselves. The pervasive practices associated with discipline and self-discipline in the twentieth century is a theme which has been extensively taken up in the works of Michel Foucault (1980; 1991) as I mentioned in Chapter 5. He describes modern societies as being sites of 'perpetual penality' as we find more and more elaborate ways of disciplining and punishing each other and ourselves, not least through the ubiquitous use of performance targets and hierarchies of achievement which get used by governments of schools and hospitals in the public sector.

With the necessary alignment, the organisation is thought likely to make the necessary transition from current imperfection to more fitting state. In the charismatic leadership literature, the leader is thought to have a particularly important role to play in influencing employee values through who they are and what they do, and the gesture that they make to employees to align with the organisational mission. However, in an essay enquiring into just this claim, Brown and Trevino (2003) argue that despite the widespread assumption in the charismatic leadership literature, there is little evidence to show that leaders' values are internalised by those they lead.

It is a very common thing to find managers in organisations trying to think and work with values in just the way that the literature has described above, as a unifying phenomenon which orients employees towards a new future. However, managers' attempts to speak to values can often have unintended and conflictual outcomes, which will be explored in the following narrative.

Values Narrative

In one organisation I have been working with recently is a set of working procedures which they have brought together in one binder together with the organisation's value statements. The binder claims not just to offer methods for planning, reflecting and report writing, but also defines the 'behaviours and attitudes' that it expects employees to follow if they are to be true employees fulfilling the vision. It has been much talked about in the organisation and beyond, and during periods of quite dramatic organisational change, in particular a restructuring in response to previous economic crises, it has come to signify continuity. It has helped to stabilise some employees' sense of identification with what they are doing and the broader organisation in which they find themselves. Although reviews of the effectiveness of this set of procedures always conclude that somehow the values are not being lived up to, or the procedures are not being adequately followed, nonetheless significant numbers of staff recognise the binder and what it has come to stand for as a strong organisational symbol.

At the same time, however, there are newer members of staff recruited some years after the binder of procedures was introduced to undertake new functions in the restructured organisation who do not share the same affinity with the binder. For them it represents an older organisation of which they have little experience. Some of these staff feel that they represent a new order and are there to take the organisation forwards which involves newer ways of working. The binder does not help: it is not so relevant to them and simply gets in the way.

Rather than looking backwards towards the good old days, the newer senior managers have persuaded the directors' group that it would be forward thinking to be 'rebranded'. This involved employing a marketing agency and survey specialists to conduct profiling of the organisation's customers and of the organisation's employees to develop a more compelling brand image to generate greater brand recognition amongst the public and greater unity and commitment amongst staff.

The rebranding exercise affects the organisation top to bottom, from the way the company livery is presented on headed notepaper, to the way the notice boards are organised. Some senior advocates of the rebranding exercise start to exhort staff to 'live the brand': this can be used as a way of encouraging staff not to put notices in the wrong place on the notice board, or to run their meetings in a more businesslike way by making them timed and less discursive, or not to write reports which are too long.

This organisation, like many others, is currently facing cutbacks and retrenchment. The small unit responsible for being stewards of the planning binder are one of the first in the firing line. The act of trying to make the staff members in the planning unit redundant provokes both open and covert disagreement and conflict amongst staff about personal and organisational identity. There are at least two groups, those identifying with the older values, and those identifying with the rebranding exercise, who claim to speak for what the organisation 'really stands for'. Both appeal to organisational values.

Reflections on the Narrative

In the organisation described above, values are taken up by both the older and newer generations of employees as forms of social control, as an invitation to conform. However, and as I identified in the narrative in Chapter 5, employees are likely to experience multiple identifications which call out sometimes conflicting values in them when such invitations are made. This will depend upon whether employees also belong to a professional body, such as accountancy, which is informed by its own professional values, how long they have worked for their particular organisation and why they chose to work there in the first place, and what they commit to in their personal lives. In the organisation cited above and in the 'Second Narrative' section in Chapter 5, the appeal to values provokes not conformity but more or less open contestation over identity, about belonging and about valuations of the good. There is inevitably a struggle over who can best impose an interpretation of what it means to be fulfilling organisational values, or in this case living the brand. The appeal to values brings with it the promise of inclusion in the dominant group, or conversely, the threat of exclusion from it, a phenomenon which has been explored in separate ways by both G.H. Mead and Norbert Elias.

Inclusion and Exclusion from the Cult – Philosophical Interlude

George Herbert Mead developed a theory of cult values, as taken up in Griffin's book *The Emergence of Leadership* (2002), which is helpful for understanding the way that the dominant managerialist discourse on values, and in particular the way that Collins and Porras (2005) have been using the idea.

Mead became interested in how it was possible for the two opposing sides in the First World War to ascribe to themselves and their populations' noble motives, and yet be in deadly conflict. He was intrigued by the dynamic of nationalism that accompanied waging war. In two essays written in 1914 and 1923, Mead argued that when countries or institutions think of themselves as if they were wholes they then can start to ascribe to all the members of that idealised group values that are deemed universal and overriding norms. These values are an important part of who we are and where we come from, but ethical issues arise when the values of an idealised group become norms to which individuals must subscribe if they are not to be deemed sinful or selfish, that is, they become a cult which can exclude or include according to the level of adherence to values understood as norms. Mead is trying to treat the difficult but generative paradox between the inclusionary and exclusionary dynamic of the public discussion of values. He is also trying to discuss the difference between values and norms, which are both generalisations, and often two sides of the same coin. On the one hand values are an important part of our identities and help us to become who we are; on the other hand they set up powerful processes of inclusion and exclusion, which I will explore further below, and strong compulsion to belong.

The distinction that Mead is making here, between values and norms, is one that has been subsequently described by Hans Joas. For Joas (2000), norms are obligatory and constraining and describe the right: values, meanwhile, are imaginative idealisations and describe the good. Norms restrict action and provide evaluative criteria for judging what ought to be done, while values are compelling in a voluntary sense: we choose to be constrained by our values. They are paradoxical in the sense that they are voluntary compulsions, and imbue our lives with meaning and purpose. Both are by their very nature generalisations, and are likely to arise together when we discuss choices between different goods. Mead is putting forward the idea that valuations of the good when taken up as cult values become group norms according to which one will be included or excluded in the group.

Two examples of cult values that one might refer to in recent political life are when President Bush argued in favour of freedom and democracy in support of his 'war on terror'. He adduced the values of freedom and democracy in invading Iraq and Afghanistan: to oppose what he was doing was to place oneself at risk of being accused of being against freedom and democracy, and by inference, in support of terrorism. Equally, in the UK the Blair government has opened up the public sector to private investment in the name of 'reform', a theme which has been taken up again in a similar way by the current coalition government. It then becomes very hard to argue against what is tantamount to ideological action for fear of being portrayed as being 'against reform'. I am using the term ideological here in the sense that I explained it in Chapter 1 (see p. 14), when ways of talking and thinking about what we are undertaking are taken up in a way that attempts to prevent conflict arising, and to present interpretations of events as though there were no other alternatives. Mead drew attention to how values are taken up ideologically and powerfully to make opposition to what is going on undiscussable. There are any number of current political processes which we would recognise, in organisations and in society at large, where a value proposition is put forward as a strong bid to dominate discussion and debate. This is a similar dynamic to the one I discussed in the previous chapter on vision.

Similarly, the sociologist Norbert Elias was interested in the generalisable tendency of people to form groups and to include and exclude on the basis of membership of these groups. In group formation there is a strong appeal to the particular, often heroic characteristics and values of the group, and the denigration of those who do not share them. Because we are social animals, he argued, the threat of exclusion is very powerful and is a particularly effective form of social control.

Elias carried out a study of Winston Parva with his student John Scotson (1994). Winston Parva is a fictional name for a real village in Leicestershire, UK where there were three distinct communities. The study was provoked by Scotson, an ex-teacher, wanting to find out why the levels of young offending were particularly high in one part of a particular village. His research work became delayed, so by the time he came to undertake the work he found that the levels of crime across the village as a whole were relatively even: it was no longer possible to point to one community as being the major source of high crime statistics. However, in the village and in the district in general, the common perception was that most crime was caused by the inhabitants of one particular neighbourhood of the village. This phenomenon intrigued Scotson, and with Elias' help, he turned his research into a discussion of group formation and maintenance.

In Winston Parva there were rich professionals living in big houses, a poorer, established community and an equivalent 'outsider' community in terms of class to the established community who had more recently moved in from slums demolished in London. The established community aspired to be more like the group of professionals and richer residents, and in doing so were keen to distinguish themselves from the recent immigrants even though they were from a very similar socio-economic background. They talked themselves up, creating what Elias and Scotson called a heroic 'we' identity, at the same time as denigrating the incomers, or outsiders. They did so by means of gossip and stereotyping ascribing to the whole 'outsider' community characteristics of a small minority of more troublesome community members. What interested Elias was the dynamic of inclusion and exclusion that this set up, and the way in which, over time, the outsiders began to talk of themselves in self-denigrating ways. They had come to believe the derogatory things that were said of them, and to think of themselves as being 'lesser'. Established communities are also likely to try and police their own community members so that they do not undermine the social distinction which is being made between one community and another, and are likely to be just as hostile to 'treacherous' same community members as they are to outsiders. Elias and Scotson were pointing to same processes of inclusion and exclusion that Mead drew attention to in his discussion of cult values.

At the same time, Elias noted in the *Civilising Process* (1993/2000) how the evolution of longer and longer chains of interdependent people leads to the internalisation of social norms experienced as shame. The way that Stacey (2007) interprets the social functioning of norms, drawing on Elias, is as follows:

> *Norms, therefore, are constraints arising in social evolution that act to restrain the actions and even desires of interdependent individuals, so much so that the constraints become thematic patterns of individual identities.*

> *(2007: 345)*

The dynamic that both Elias and Stacey are pointing to is the way in which strong group identities are created in societies or communities, often based on heroic and idealised descriptions of the values of the group, the creation of a 'we' identity that may be expressed as a cult. When expressed as a cult, individuals are invited to lose themselves in an idealised group, to join the morally good. The appeal to values opens the potential for being either included or excluded on this basis, where the threat of exclusion may be experienced as both socially shaming and disempowering. Powerful appeals to join the in-group carry with them the potential of threats to identity and belonging.

This is similar to what happens in organisations when leaders make strong appeals to follow particular values: it is an appeal to join a heroic 'we' group. If employees are keen to continue with a particular company it is a very difficult invitation to turn down, as Collins and Porras (2005) previously have made clear. It might be helpful to explore the phenomenon of values a bit more thoroughly as a way of better understanding how they arise and what this might mean for the way we might work with values in organisations.

A Different Way of Thinking About Values

It is not surprising that management theory should be so preoccupied with values and their link with the imagination, since our ability to imagine a better future has long proved a spur to radical action, as we were exploring in the previous chapter. Joas (2000) makes the connection, drawing on the works of James (1902/1983) and Durkheim (1912/2001) between the origin of values and their relation to religious experience. Both philosophers draw attention the fact that religious experience involves a transcendence of self in some greater whole, and Durkheim in particular noted the group dynamic of religious belief, with belief a form of collective ecstasy. By coming together to experience the promise of salvation we can transcend the constraints of the situation in which we find ourselves. Since the dominant discourse in management is preoccupied with ideas of predictability and control, there is no surprise that human values should become another area of human experience which the managerialism might consider a legitimate object of management manipulation and moulding. People's values could be bent to the utility of the organisation.

There is a residual question for managers though, as to whether values are really open to rational intervention: is it possible for a manger to manipulate and redefine employee values? In *A Common Faith*, a reflection on religious experience, Dewey (1934) describes how our values arise not out of rational choice, but from our ability to use the imagination to reshape our experience to describe idealised ends:

> *The idealising imagination seizes upon the most precious things found in the climacteric moments of experience and projects them. We need no external criterion and guarantee of their goodness. They are had, they exist as good, and out of them we frame our ideal ends.*
>
> (Dewey, 1934: 48)

Through the power of imagination we are able to experience a wholeness of purpose from our fragmentary, frustrating and partial lives which we cannot ever realise, but which enlarges our sense of self. The idealised and whole self is a projection, according to Dewey, which does not exist any more than values themselves exist separate from human experience in some ethereal way. This process of idealisation is not something that can be willed or determined in any way 'a fact that helps explain, psychologically, why it has so generally been attributed to a supernatural source' (ibid.: 19).

It is not to the supernatural that Dewey himself looks, however, for the source of our values but to our everyday encounters with others. In a series of essays of reflections on the nature of values in an essay entitled 'Logic and judgement of practice' (1915) Dewey builds the argument that 'a judgement of value is simply a case of practical judgement, a judgement about the doing of something' (1915: 243). Values, then, do not reside in objects, or statements; these objects and statements provide the data for evaluation. He does not consider values to be subjective states of mind that equate to individual choosing or the fulfilment of desire; they are merely practical reflection upon action, 'a present act determining an act to be done, a present act taking place because the future act is uncertain and incomplete' (ibid: 246). Because there is latent uncertainty about the course of action to be taken, values imply both judgement and criticism arising out of reflection, an argument that Dewey takes up in *Experience and Nature* (1958). For Dewey the use of human intelligence, and ultimately the role of philosophy, is the permanent uncovering of and reflection upon value:

> It starts from actual situations of belief, conduct and appreciative perception which are characterised by immediate qualities of good and bad, and from the modes of critical judgement at any given time in all regions of value; these are its data, its subject-matter. These values, criticisms and critical methods, it subjects to further criticism as comprehensive and consistent as possible. The function is to regulate the further appreciation of goods and bads….
>
> *(1958: 403–404)*

In trying to promote the primacy of judgement, and of discussion about method, Dewey also tried to liberate values from the proscriptiveness of Kant, and a rule or model-based approach, to discriminating between the good and the bad, which is the weakness that I perceive in discussions around values in the management literature. Dewey did this in two ways. The first was to develop an emergent theory of values, challenging the relevance of past experience to the dilemmas of the present, and the second was to highlight the importance of mutual sympathy as a constituent part of giving value to action. In both, Dewey sets the practical judgements that are necessary in day-to-day life within a framework that takes more cognisance of the dynamic in which we find ourselves living with others.

To take emergent values first, Dewey leads, as usual, by idealising intelligent reflection on lived experience as a means to further values. In encouraging reflection Dewey is no different from Pasteur and Scott-Villiers (2004) above. However, the conclusions that he draws from the process of reflection are very different. The danger he perceives is that we lose our moral vitality if we try to apply rules that are irrelevant to the circumstances and thus deprive ourselves of the faculty of judgement. In the previous chapter I noted how this appeal to judgement, to critical thinking, was also made by Hannah Arendt (1971a, 1971b). Both are pointing to the dangers of being lost in idealised 'wholes', in pursuing a course of action simply because lots of other people are doing so and to believe that our 'whole' imaginings can be realised.

This is not to argue that we should not learn from experience, merely that we also have to weigh whether that particular experience applies in the situations which we encounter. There is no guarantee that the circumstances we come across in the future will be amenable to our previous ways of working we have used in the past. We are constantly asked to evaluate what is new about what we are experiencing. Dewey suggests that to presuppose a model for moral action irrespective of the situation, in which one finds oneself as did Kant, is to misunderstand scientific method, which is driven by formulas, or principles, rather than models. The distinction is that formulas and principles describe a way that conclusions have been reached rather than the conclusions themselves. For Dewey, exercising judgement is a vital act, a response to the contingency of the particular circumstances that one is having to deal with right here, right now.

The second thread of Dewey's argument concerns moral sympathy in the judgement of goods. He begins to argue that we cannot know how to exercise our valuations without taking into consideration the valuations of others in a highly socialised context. Dewey starts from the position that affection, or rather mutual affection, is at the bottom of values that influence behaviour. In an essay entitled 'Sensitivity and thoughtfulness' (1932/1998), Dewey sets out the argument that being appreciative of other people's points of view, of their valuations, is the best way of appreciating the full complexity of what one is dealing with. The 'expanded personality' (ibid.: 333) is able to fuse sympathy with other impulses to perform a more objective view of the people and events one is engaged with. In these situations we are not just applying values as though they are rules, but broadening our own values with an appreciation of others' values. In the same way as I alluded to in the previous chapter on vision, Dewey is arguing that in following our own valuations and motivations it is important not to override those of other people unthinkingly. Although we cannot foresee the consequences of acting, nonetheless, by entering into a situation taking the attitude of the other is at least a way of complicating our first responses to things, contributing to what Dewey calls 'perplexity', which stops us in our tracks and forces us to ponder on things and turn them over in our minds.

Dewey appeals to rational but emergent judgement, a reappraisal of the particular circumstances that we find ourselves in, as a way of understanding afresh the values that we hold dear. To do otherwise would involve suspending our judgement and acting unthinkingly.

In comparison with the authors that I quoted earlier who regard reflection on values as a way of cutting through the difficulty of working with others, of simplifying the inevitable conflict by urging value congruence, Dewey is offering a radical alternative. Rather than simplifying our understanding of what we are doing he is inviting us to make the situation we are in more difficult by being more open to considering the attitudes of others. In doing so we are obliged to exercise judgement, which for Dewey combines intelligence and experience, as well as intelligent reflection on that experience. He is inviting us to be alive to the complexity of the situations we find ourselves in, trying to organise with others, rather than encouraging us, as it seems to me most modern management methods do, to overpower, or manipulate others for 'the good of the organisation'.

Returning to Values in Organisations

In the course of this chapter I have drawn a distinction between the ways that the orthodox literature takes up values in the context of culture change in organisations. Particularly in the visionary leadership discourse, but not just here, identifying and changing employee values are thought to be key to facilitating organisational change from the current lack of fit to the environment, to a more desired state where the organisation will flourish. Organisational change requires culture change, which in turn demands a focus on values. Ideally, the orthodox literature aspires to values congruence, to 'sharing values'. And values are often taken up as cult, a powerful invitation to join an exclusive group with a heroic 'we' identity that can achieve the new tomorrow. In organisational cults, values are treated as norms, rules which proscribe behaviour, and thus attempt to close down contestation and difference. They are a form of what the management theorist Edgar Schein (1999) has termed 'coercive persuasion'.

Schein developed his thinking about coercive persuasion after working with released prisoners of the Korean War who had undergone what we would now term 'brainwashing'. He realised the similarities between what had happened to American prisoners of war who had been indoctrinated into thinking communist states had been misrepresented in the West and that they, the prisoners, were criminals, and organisational change programmes. Both involved processes of destabilisation and reorientation to a new way of thinking, both were about persuading people to adopt new behaviours without completely unravelling their sense of self; both were interested in the power of the social on the individual as individuals look to their peers to adopt a new understanding of themselves. Schein realised that new social standards must be socially and personally reinforced.

The attempt to align values is based very much on the concept of organisation, and even the individual, understood as system and that the role of management is to intervene to realign and control. Schein is very explicit about the way that systems thinking has affected his work in organisations. So just as the organisation can be disaggregated into parts and whole, so too can the individual: values are something an individual 'has' and they can be identified, isolated and rearranged. Lining up the values 'in' an individual with those 'in' an organisation is thought to be a legitimate activity, particularly for senior managers and visionary leaders. Here the emphasis is placed on the importance of unity and consistency above the idea of value pluralism: values are taken up explicitly as a form of social control. They are also a form of Platonism, according to whom, after Berlin (2003), all genuine questions must have one true answer, there must be a dependable path towards the true answer, and that each truth, when discovered, must be compatible with each other and form a perfect whole. The compatibility of truths in the whole produces the perfect moral life. But for Berlin the pursuit of moral wholeness and compatibility entails giving up one's humanity, the inevitability of choosing what is good in any situation, and is a dangerous illusion.

In trying to explore a different understanding of values I have made a distinction between values and norms, the former being primarily idealisations which we freely choose, and the latter being constraining rules. In arguing that they are distinct I am not suggesting that they are separate since the good and the right usually arise together. I have argued instead that values and norms, as generalisations, require an interpretation of what they might mean in practice and are mediated by power relations. Far from bringing about alignment when value propositions are articulated by senior managers they often provoke strong feelings in employees which will bring about a struggle over identity, belonging, interpretations of the good and even resistance. Our valuations are multiple, often conflicting and arise in social situations where we are asked to make choices. They evoke strong feelings in us because they speak to our idealising imagination and they are not rationally chosen. If they are not rationally chosen this automatically problematises the idea that they can be rationally rearranged to suit the good of the organisation. Invitations to 'align' one's values with the highly abstract values of the organisation are likely to be met with a variety of responses since they are also attempts to shape identity.

The Importance of Difference

I mentioned at the start of the chapter the way in which the idea of sharing values is taken up in the dominant literature as being unproblematically a good thing, with the concomitant conclusion that differences in values will have a negative impact on organisational performance. I think there are at least two good reasons for taking a sceptical view of the idea that unity and conformity are good for organisations, particularly if there is an intention that this will produce innovation, novelty and organisational fluidity.

In Chapter 2 I made an analogy between complex adaptive systems theory and the non-linear interactions that take place between humans in organisations, drawing on the work of Stacey, Griffin and Shaw (2000) and Stacey (2007). To recap, complex adaptive systems are computer-based models which demonstrate self-organisation and emergence as a result of small differences arising between interacting agents. Although the model is constrained by the algorithmic parameters set in advance by the programmers, and algorithms themselves have an if-then causality, the model nonetheless exhibits the ability to evolve by itself arising from the micro-diversity of the interacting agents. It is both the non-average nature of the interactions and the different types of agents that shape novel patterns emerging in the system. System change arises from diversity, not from sameness. The point I am making when we return to thinking about organisations is that there seems to be an assumption in the dominant managerial discourse that staff in organisations can choose to do novel things, particularly if they unify their efforts and align with the vision and values of senior managers. The conclusion that one could draw from insights from the complexity sciences is quite the reverse, that it is in the exploration of stability and instability, sameness and difference that novelty will emerge. Far from leading to novelty, the suppression of difference is likely to lead to stuck and potentially destructive patterns of organising to emerge.

I want to dwell on this point because I think it is very important, and because it goes against the grain of most literature on values and the cult of positivity and alignment which predominate in management thinking. If we draw on insights from the complexity sciences, and from the work of the pragmatic philosophers I have been quoting above, novelty and innovation arise not from conformity and unity, but from the engagement with difference. In organisational terms this might mean being open to critique, diverse points of view, struggle and contestation, rather than trying to cover it over or inviting people to 'believe in' the values of the organisation. This is not to imply that just anything goes, since in any organisation, with its particular history and context, there will be traditions, ways of thinking and acting which help frame the conversation about what we think our values mean.

Second, exhortations to align values are likely to provoke a variety of reactions from employees, not all of them consensual, if we accept Mead's theory of gesture and response, how meaning arises not just from our intended meaning but people's reactions to our gestures. Groups of workers will find opportunities to put forward their own interpretations of their organisational identities which will differ from what senior managers intend. On the basis of their recognition of the contradictions and tensions that arise from attempts to impose values or 'culture', workers will sometimes resist politically, a phenomenon which has been studied by a number of scholars writing about organisations (Meyerson and Scully, 1995; Thomas and Davies, 2005). Equally the political scientist James C. Scott (1990) has noted how overt attempts to dominate, to impose one way of understanding the social often provoke covert resistance from those who feel they are being dominated. This does not always find expression publicly, as resisters use what Scott refers to as 'hidden transcripts', discussed only amongst themselves and away from those they think are trying to dominate them. In extreme circumstances those being dominated may privately imagine an alternative idealised future, one that is often the reverse of the one being put forward. The organisational equivalent of what Scott is pointing to are the jokes that circulate round organisations in times of upheaval, the discussions round the coffee machine and the small acts of rebellion where workers profess one thing but actually carry out something quite different. Occasionally, as the narrative quoted in the paragraphs above shows, alternative and conflicting value propositions break out openly in organisations.

Exhortations to staff to align their values are problematic if they close down opportunities for discussion, negotiation and difference both because they have the potential for dampening down the emergence of spontaneity and novelty, and because they may provoke the very opposite of what they intend. In Hannah Arendt's (1970) terms closing down the opportunity for difference to be explored potentially excludes the practice of political engagement, which is for Arendt the proper exercise of power. Scott has noted in *Domination and the Arts of Resistance* (1992) how people who feel dominated are likely to use the ideology espoused by those imposing a form of order as a weapon against them, in Shakespeare's terms to hoist them with their own petard, and it is just this dynamic that I explore in the next organisational narrative on values.

It is also the case that the higher the values to which people aspire, values such as bravery, humility, loyalty the less open to utility and manipulation they become. The higher values cannot be grasped or manipulated by an effort of will – the more fiercely we may grasp after them, the more elusive they become.

Working With Values – a Narrative

I am working with some teachers in a school. The behaviour of students in this school is no better and no worse than many other inner city schools, but there has been a rumbling of discontent particularly amongst the more articulate middle-class parents about turbulence in class. A new head has been appointed who has come in with a new vision for the school. It is breathtakingly ambitious, involves huge amounts of change and is set out on the basis that this vision will be 'shared and owned' by staff and governors.

One of the first things to tackle, then, in creating 'a new culture' towards realising this vision is the behaviour of students in school. There has been an implication, articulated gently by teachers at some staff meetings, that developing a good behaviour policy would not just be about working with the students about their behaviour, but would also involve working with teachers to ensure that they implemented the policy coherently and consistently. Some teachers were clear that not all of their colleagues adhered to the behaviour code as rigorously as they might. Some teachers think the existing behaviour policy is perfectly clear but just needs careful follow through: others think processes for 'behaviour management' are inadequate and need a complete overhaul.

One of the teachers I am supporting has been tasked with developing and introducing the new behaviour policy. The method the new head has suggested to him is that he go and visit other schools where they have developed 'best practice' in behaviour management, then he brings back some of these models for discussion in school with teachers and students. Once this has been done we would write a behaviour policy for this school together. The person I am supporting in this task is convinced, perhaps because of the way the Head has presented the task to him, perhaps on his own account, that one of the essential things to do is to set out a clear value base for the behaviour policy. Once the values are clear, he argues, then the policy, and the way students and teachers take it up, will be clear also. He gives me lots of examples of student behaviour in and around school which he says gives him evidence that the values in school are not clear. If they were clear, everyone would know how to behave. We would all be sharing the same values so there would be alignment between what the Head wants to achieve and everyone's efforts.

In a group of colleagues we begin to discuss the subject of values and how we might come to understand them.

Reflections on Values in the Narrative

The example taken from a school is very typical of the ways in which values are taken up in many change programmes despite the fact that in this sector schools often promote the idea that they value the diversity of the ethnic and religious backgrounds from which their students are drawn. Schools do need a degree of control so that they can function, and this legitimate concern may contribute to the tendency to take up values as a way of bringing about behaviour conformity. There may be a fear that to promote values pluralism or a negotiation of values would imply some kind of regime where anything goes. You can see why managers in schools would take a particular interest in both values and norms, where insufficient discipline in schools could lead to learning being seriously compromised.

In schools we are dealing with a community of people which comprises newly forming personalities who, in order to shape their very growing, will want to challenge the rules of the community in which they are obliged to belong. They will do this for a whole spectrum of reasons: because they are curious, because they push in order to experience being pushed back, because they are inexperienced in how to deal with rules, perhaps because there are very few rules at home, or even values at home about breaking other rules. Taking up values as though they were rules that everyone must understand and comply with, risks creating a cult around them that covers over the very power relations with which students are invited to conform, and this may become the pivot of rebellion.

What would it mean practically to involve young people in the creation of values and rules of a community to which they are obliged to belong until they are 16? After that point they are in school voluntarily, which changes the whole power dynamic between them and their teachers. Perhaps the word 'power' is a starting point, and any more open discussion of values and rules would involve finding ways of drawing attention to the power dynamic which defines the relationship between people in communities. Teachers, as people principally responsible for running schools, have a responsibility to define the rules and explain the values that underpin them. However, they also have to find ways of engaging others in this defining process in a continuous way so that school community members will experience, not just learn about, what is being talked about. So, for example, the word 'respect' features a lot in many organisations' values statements, and a number of rules will follow to try and create an environment where people practise respect towards each other. But respect will be experienced by young people in the way that the rules are applied. If rules are applied in a peremptory and high-handed fashion, or perhaps unthinkingly in ways which take no account of the specific context of the person being dealt with on the one hand there will be talk about respect, but on the other teachers could be treating young people in disrespectful ways.

What would constitute consistency in the application of rules? All communities have to come to understand that actions have consequences and we are right to look for fairness of treatment. But our understanding of 'fairness' is also conditioned by our particular circumstances and the particular context in which we find ourselves acting with others. Unthinking application of the rules despite the context will sometimes also feel 'unfair' and rigid to us. So, it is important for young people to experience the consistent application of rules, but also in a way that continuously engages them in the process of being ruled that leaves the opportunity for them to experience respect. In an asymmetrical power relationship, we need to find ways to engage them in relationships which increase their autonomy and their sense of belonging. This will occasionally involve encouraging discussion about the rules and what we mean by what we say. It is important to have values but we may also have values about being able to discuss values: this is what we might mean by being interested in people's continuing education. We can educate ourselves and others by experiencing the continuous opening up of possibilities. We can be explicit and admit to having legitimate power over others, but also to involve those others in the continuous legitimisation of that power.

Coming to understand values as social and emergent phenomena, and not as rules to be applied in a process of idealised conformity, allows us more scope to explore what we mean by what we say. This seems to be particularly important in schools, which are places of learning, but also in all organisations, and particularly those which have values of service to others. It is not just our organisation's vision and values that should compel us when we take up our tasks with the people we set out to help, but their particular needs expressed in a particular way, in a particular context. We will be required to negotiate with them, to problematise the situation we find ourselves in together.

Concluding Thoughts on Values – Implications for Managers

In much contemporary management theory there is a great deal of emphasis on the identification, assessment and manipulation of values 'for the good of the organisation'. This may be in recognition of the fact that, according to Taylor (1989), we live in a 'flattened world' where discussions of efficiency and effectiveness are unlikely on their own to motivate employees. From the perspective of humanistic psychology, which has also significantly influenced managerialism, organisations are sites for the fulfilment of human potential which creates legitimate space for the discussion of values. However, in the dominant discourse self actualisation is only likely to be encouraged if it coincides with the needs of the organisation as interpreted by senior managers. In many instances these become exercises in what Edgar Schein (1999) has called 'coercive persuasion', where attempts are made publically to socialise employees into new ways of thinking and behaving. Managerialism treats values instrumentally, as a means to organisational ends, and the organisational ends that are intended are conformity and alignment. It is thought that managers can design organisational culture by aligning employee values with wider strategic intentions of changing organisations from one state to another. This is broadly based on thinking that understands human beings as atomised individuals who 'have' values, which they can rationally choose and/or change, or that are open to modification by managers. As usual such thinking, when expressed in management theory is often buttressed by empirical studies that 'prove' that value manipulation is both possible and productive.

As an alternative I have put the case that values are impervious to intentional manipulation since they are not rationally chosen, but arise in intense moments of imagined wholeness. They are pre-cognitive and orient us daily in our world without our necessarily being consciously aware of them except retrospectively. In John Dewey's (1934) terms they afford a feeling of an enlarged sense of self. They are a profoundly social phenomenon which emerge on a daily basis as we interact with others, and are likely to provoke both conflict and compromise. Grander statements of collective values, what G.H. Mead (1914, 1923) called 'cult values', such as appeals to nationalism, or resilience in the face of adversity, are an important part of who we are, but also have the potential for inclusion and exclusion. While offering opportunities to become part of an undertaking larger than the individual, they also create the potential for anxiety and shame that arises from fear of exclusion. This is more or less explicitly acknowledged in some management literature, such as Collins and Porras (2005), who recommend excluding on the basis of a failure to submit to a 'cult like culture'.

The charge I have made against this kind of thinking is that it amounts to a kind of totalitarianism, confusing values with norms and has a powerful manipulative potential. However, when managers appeal to values in the workplace they are likely to call out a variety of different responses from those in the organisation, from compliance, to rebellion, to outward conformity but more hidden subversion. Invitations to actualise higher values for the good of the company cannot be willed into practice by employees, any more than each of us can know whether we will be brave in a situation of danger, or will be humble when heaped with praise.

Another difficulty of the appeal to cult values is that they are, by their very nature, generalisations, which are insufficiently detailed for us to know how to go on together. Only through negotiation over a particular example in a particular context can we discover what it would mean to work co-operatively according to the expressed values. This implies not alignment and conformity, but the openness to explore difference and the plurality of value positions which are likely to be evoked by any given situation. The ability to do this in the workplace is constrained by relationships of power.

What, then, are the implications for managers? Throughout this book I have been making an argument, drawing on insights from the complexity sciences and from other intellectual disciplines, that despite the claims of much management literature, managers are not in control of what is happening in their organisations, and that the changes that they make are likely to have both unexpected and unwanted consequences. Because the appeal to values will provoke a variety of responses from employees, the quest for final alignment of values towards metaphysical whole change can thus never be achieved. What is important about the discussion of values in organisations, however, is the opportunity it affords for the discovery of similarity and difference – it allows for the continuous uncovering and intensification of understanding what it is that people are trying to do together. This arises not by an appeal to some idealised, mystical whole, but from within the process of mutual enquiry itself. The potential for transformation is self-generated.

Discussing values in organisations is both inevitable and necessary, but needs to be undertaken with some circumspection because of the enormous potential for creating what the philosopher Richard Bernstein calls 'a false *we*' (1991: 51). Perhaps one way into the discussion is acknowledging the importance of having values about discussing values and looking for opportunities to find hope in the everyday process of communicating and struggling with each other.

References

Alvesson, M. (2002) *Understanding Organizational Culture*, London: Sage.

Arendt, H. (1970) *On Violence*, New York: Harvest.

—— (1971a) Thinking and moral considerations: A lecture, *Social Research*, 38(3): 417–446.

——(1971b) *The Life of the Mind*, New York: Harcourt.

Argyris, C. (1982) *Reasoning, Learning and Action: Individual and Organisational*, San Francisco: Jossey Bass.

Berlin, I. (2003) *The Crooked Timber of Humanity: Chapters in the History of Ideas*, London: Pimlico.

Bernstein, R.J. (1991) *The New Constellation; The Ethical Horizons of Modernity/ Postmodernity*, Cambridge: Polity Press.

Brown, M. and Trevino, L. (2003) Is values-based leadership ethical leadership?, in Steiner, D., Skarlicki, D. and Gilliland, S. (eds) *Emerging Perspectives on Values in Organizations (Research in Social Issues in Management)*, Charlotte, NC: Information Age Press.

Cameron, S. and Quinn, R. (2006) *Diagnosing and Changing Organizational Culture Based on the Competing Values Framework*, London: Jossey Bass.

Casey, C. (1999) 'Come join our family': Discipline and integration in corporate organizational culture, *Human Relations*, 52(2): 155–178.

Clarke, J. and Newman, J. (1997) *The Managerial State*, London: Sage.

Collins, J. and Porras, J. (2005) *Built to Last: Successful Habits of Visionary Companies*, New York: Random House.

Dewey, J. (1915) Logic and judgement of practice, in Hickman, L.A. and Alexander, T.M. (eds) (1998) *The Essential Dewey: Vol 2, Ethics, Logic, Psychology*, Indianapolis: Indiana University Press.

—— (1932) Sensitivity and thoughtfulness, in Hickman, L.A. and Alexander, T.M. (eds) (1998) *The Essential Dewey: Vol 2, Ethics, Logic, Psychology*, Indianapolis: Indiana University Press.

Dewey, J. (1934) *A Common Faith*, New Haven, CT: Yale University Press.

—— (1958) *Experience and Nature*, New York: Dover Publications.

Dolan, S.L. and Richley, B.A. (2006) Management by values (MBV): A new philosophy for a new economic order. *Handbook of Business Strategy*, 2006: 235–238.

DuGay, P. (2007) *Organizing Identity*, London: Sage.

Durkheim, E. (1912/2001) *The Elementary Forms of Religious Life*, Oxford: Oxford University Press.

Elias, N. (1939/1991) *The Society of Individuals*, Oxford: Blackwell.

—— (1939/2000) *The Civilising Process*, Oxford: Blackwell.

—— and Scotson, J. (1994) *The Established and the Outsiders*, London: Sage.

Foucault, M. (Rabinow, P. (ed.)) (1980) *Power/Knowledge: Selected Interviews and Other Writings*, New York: Pantheon.

Foucault, M. (1991) *Discipline and Punish: The Birth of the Prison*, London: Penguin Books.

Griffin, D. (2002) *The Emergence of Leadership: Linking Self-Organisation and Ethics*, London: Routledge.

Hampden-Turner, C. (1994) *Corporate Culture: How to Generate Organisational Strength and Lasting Commercial Advantage*, London: Piatkus.

James, W. (1902/1983) *The Varieties of Religious Experience*, London: Penguin.

Joas, H. (2000) *The Genesis of Values*, Cambridge: Polity Press.

Jung, C.G. (1981) *The Archetypes and The Collective Unconscious, Collected Works 1934–1954*, 9:(2nd edition), Princeton, NJ: Bollingen.

Kohlberg, L. (1981) *Essays in Moral Development: The Philosophy of Moral Development*, vol. 1, New York: Harper and Row.

—— (1983) *Essays in Moral Development: The Psychology of Moral Development* vol. 2, New York: Harper and Row.

Maturana, H. and Varela, F. (1975) *Autopoietic Systems: A Characterisation of the Living Organisation*, Biology Laboratory Research Report, 9(4), University of Illinois.

Mead, G.H. (1914) The psychological bases of internationalism, *Survey*, 23: 604–607.

—— (1923) Scientific method and the moral Sciences, *International Journal of Ethics*, 33: 229–247.

Meyerson, D. and Scully, M. (1995) Tempered radicalism and the politics of ambivalence and change, *Organization Science*, 6(5): 585–600.

Mowles, C. (2007) Promises of transformation: Just how different are international development NGOs?, *Journal of International Development*, 19(3): 401–411.

—— (2008) Values in international development organisations: Negotiating non-negotiables, *Development in Practice*, 18(1): 5–16.

Pasteur, K. and Scott-Villiers, P. (2004) Minding the gap through organisational learning, in Groves, L. and Hinton, R. (eds) *Inclusive Aid: Changing Power and Relationships in International Development*, London: Earthscan.

Rokeach, M. (1968) *Beliefs, Attitudes and Values*, San Fransisco: Jossey Bass.

——. (1973) *The Nature of Human Values*, Free Press: New York.

Sachs, S. and Rühli, E. (2005) Changing managers' values towards a broader stakeholder orientation', *Corporate Governance*, 5(2): 89–98.

Schein, E. (1999) Empowerment, coercive persuasion and organizational learning: do they connect?, *The Learning Organization*, 6(4): 163–172.

Schwartz, S.H. (1992) Universals in the content and structure of values: Theoretical advances and empirical tests in 20 countries, in Zanna. M. (ed.) *Advances in Experimental Social Psychology*, 25: 1–65.

—— (1996) Values priorities and behaviour: Applying a theory of integrative value systems, in Seligman, C., Olson, J. and Zanna, M. (eds) *The Psychology of Values*, London: Routledge.

Scott, J.C. (1990) *Domination and the Arts of Resistance: Hidden Transcripts*, London and New Haven, CT: Yale University Press.

Senge, P. (1990) *The Fifth Discipline; The Art and Practice of the Learning Organization*, London: Century.

——, Schwarmer C., Jaworski, J. and Flowers, B. (2005) *Presence: Exploring Profound Change in People, Organizations and Society*, London: Nicholas Brealey Publishing.

Sengel, P. (1990) *The Fifth Discipline: The Art and Practice of the Learning Organization*, London: Century.

Stacey, R. (2007) *Strategic Management and Organisational Dynamics: The Challenge of Complexity*, 5th edition, London: Routledge.

——, Griffin, D. and Shaw, P. (2000) *Complexity and Management: Fad or Radical Challenge to Systems Thinking?*, London: Routledge.

Taylor, C. (1989) *Sources of the Self: The Making of Modern Identity*, Cambridge: Cambridge University Press.

Thomas, R. and Davies, A. (2005) What have the feminists done for us? Feminist theory and organizational resistance, *Organization*, 12(5): 711–740.

Van Rekom, J., van Riel, C. and Wierenga, B. (2006) A methodology for assessing organizational core values, *Journal of Management Studies*, 43(2): 175–201.

Weber, J. (1993) Exploring the relationship between personal values and moral reasoning, *Human Relations*, 46(4): 435–463.

Willmott, H. (1993) Strength is ignorance; slavery is freedom: Managing culture in modern organizations, *Journal of Management Studies*, 30(4): 515–552.

7

Choosing the Future

In the course of this book I have been making the case that orthodox management theory is based largely on a realist understanding of the world and puts forward the idea of management as science. That is, by reflecting on a reality 'out there' managers can use rational techniques and tools to approximate that reality and steer, shape or guide their organisation more closely to fit with it. This is thought possible because of the presumed objectivity of managers and consultants who can step outside the organisation they are observing, understood as a system, then step back inside to make the necessary changes. Drawing on analogies from natural science methods and borrowing from their vocabulary, orthodox management literature describes managers observing, analysing, calculating, diagnosing and intervening in an organisation to facilitate a shift towards a more optimal state of functioning. Managers can draw on various recipes for success, best practice rules, and frameworks and two-by-two grids, which support them in identifying which state their organisation is currently in, and to which state they should aspire. The rationalist underpinnings of the dominant discourse on management is maintained at the same time as supporting the seemingly contradictory idea that an organisation is itself a self-regulating system and is constantly evolving to a closer fit with its environment of its own accord. This appeal to rationality and science, sometimes termed 'evidence-based practice', is often accompanied on the other hand with an appeal to the metaphysical: the values, ideals and potential for employees finding spiritual fulfilment in their work. Today's organisation is the locus of the competing and co-operating demands of both church and corporation.

Nowhere is this kind of thinking more manifest than in the domain of strategy, which is commonly understood to be a form of planning whereby managers engage in discussion of the what and the how of organisational becoming. The activity of strategy-making is described as a systematic attempt on the part of managers to shape the future in a coherent way (Araujo and Easton, 1996): they are choosing their organisational future. It also assumes a process of continuous improvement towards some kind of ideal. However, strategy literature is also a confusing and diverse domain with a very broad range of views which are just as prolific as the literature on leadership. Hundreds of books, articles and training courses have been produced as a support to managers because it is in the domain of strategy that the promise of managerialism is most put to the test. A coherent strategy is supposed to make the organisation more effective, efficient and perhaps profitable. Moreover, in the dominant discourse special abilities are attributed to managers as being the actors best equipped to undertake this exercise. We have begun to explore previously how this idea of a powerful, rational, choosing manager is tied up with late twentieth-century conceptions of the autonomous 'buffered' self realising themselves through the expression of an 'inner' truth. As Taylor argues, to be free in modern times is understood to render the individual fully disengaged from natural and social worlds, and therefore free to treat these worlds instrumentally to rearrange them to better suit the welfare of himself and others (1995: 7). However, in making such claims the strategy literature raises questions about causality, agency and how we think the future arises out of the present. It also raises questions about how we could know that the strategy we are choosing is optimal, all of which we will explore more thoroughly in this chapter.

Despite the fact that the literature on strategic planning has diminished significantly during the last decade (Whittington and Cailluet, 2008), perhaps denoting a recognition that this is another area of management which may never produce a stable body of knowledge, nonetheless it is something that managers in most organisations do routinely. I will explore what managers in organisations find themselves doing when they undertake strategy later in this chapter, but first it might be useful to set out how the literature on strategy has evolved over time, on this occasion taking up two critical perspectives, that of Haridimos Tsoukas and Ralph Stacey.

How Theories of Strategy Have Evolved

Tsoukas (2004) approaches strategy from the perspective of epistemology, which he means in the double sense of how knowledge is generated in organisations and how researchers know what they know about how knowledge is generated in organisation. He separates different schools of strategy into those offering 'outcome' explanations and those outlining 'process' explanations. In the first category are two sub-schools, standard equilibrium (SE) models and structural–functionalist (SF) models. Both outcome sub-categories are based on covering law explanations, that is to say they draw on natural science methods to make statistical associations between important variables. The strategist is like the scientist, concerned to identify regularities and to be able to use them to intervene in the natural world. Tsoukas claims that covering law models have been far and away the most influential in the field of strategic management, and outcome strategies, based in classical economics, have very little interest in what happens inside the firm.

SE models as the name suggests restrict themselves to the study of systems which are in states of rest, since they assume that it is impossible to obtain knowledge about systems which are unstable. According to Tsoukas, economists have a world view informed by Newtonian physics which implies that it is possible to isolate a system from its environment and at the same time assumes that the firm is the basic unit of study. As an isolated atom, without history and specificity, it will behave in an invariant way over time, as will other firms in the same market. Strategy theorists like Michael Porter (1980) consider the firm to be a black box, and are much more concerned with the way that it responds to its environment, the opportunities and threats of the market. SF models take into account a far wider variety of systems and draw on a Darwinian theory of natural selection to enquire into the way in which different structural arrangements are a response to different situational circumstances: they nonetheless make the same atomistic assumptions about firms.

For process explanations, covering law models are too crude and coarse grained since they do not give sufficient explanation of how variables influence each other: they do not explain the mechanisms beneath the causal story and may therefore lead to spurious explanations. For this reason they are more concerned to open up the black box of the firm and to enquire into decision-making processes and thus restore a sense of history to a particular firm. Tsoukas credits Chandler (1990, 1992) with being one of the first scholars to introduce the more holistic and historical models looking at the complex interactions between structure, strategy and environment. Process approaches to strategy have been credited with informing more recent game theoretical approaches to strategy (Tirole, 1988) which are capable of modelling more complex dynamic interactions over time. For Tsouskas, game theoretical explanations still have some of the same difficulties that economistic theories do: they assume that the basic unit of the game is the firm, and that these units are all uniform. Additionally, the game is broken down into a series of static sub-games where it is impossible to model the decision-maker as being able to co-ordinate their decisions over time. Each iteration of the game rules out path dependency of the current status quo and simply leads to a new game where the future is all important.

Tsoukas appraises both outcome and process schools of strategy and argues that more than 40 years of strategy research has led to enormous theoretical pluralism. However, drawing on Mintzberg, Ahlstrand and Lampel's taxonomy of strategy schools (1998), he argues that the planning and cognitive schools have predominated. These cannot offer context or time sensitive advice and assume that past action informs future strategy. As I mentioned in the opening paragraphs of this chapter, the planning and cognitive schools of strategy assume a realist understanding of the world where strategy is discovered rather than invented. What most schools of strategy lack, he argues, is a theory of creative action to account for the processes of dynamic change over time. Though still inadequate, the two theories of action which he perceives in current research traditions in organisations he terms 'representationalist' and 'enactvist'.

Representationalists view the world as given and assume a Descartian position that thinking is the only form of knowing we can trust. So, according to Tsoukas:

> *Actors, on this view, are deductive reasoners: from an abstract set of generally valid premises and from a particular set of current observations, they deduce conclusions which they proceed to implement.*
> *(2004: 361)*

In contemplating a real world we analyse and deduce a course of action, which we then go on to put into action: thinking precedes action since it is the most reliable approach. To explain enactivism, Touskas draws on philosophers Richard Rorty (1991) and Ludwig Wittgenstein (1958) to argue that the mind does not passively contemplate an existing world, but by actively engaging with it forms meanings and beliefs which are socialised as practices. Social practices and meanings form and are formed by each other. Rather than assuming that thought precedes action, therefore, enactivism assumes that the relationship is the other way round, that doing comes before thinking.

According to Tsoukas, strategy research has become more and more critical of representationalist approaches so that strategy is now broadly understood as a social process the outcome of which should be a novel one. It is not a question of discovering the future but of inventing it through active participation, discussion and imagination. However, despite the fact that concepts of strategy formation have been complexified, Tsoukas argues, this has not been accompanied by a matching complexification of theories of strategy formulation where representationalist grids and frameworks still persist as tools for managers to generate their strategy (Johnson and Scholes, 1997). Process explanations are better at explaining the complex interaction between thought and action as they unfold over time but lack the generality of outcome explanations. This can lead to process theorists borrowing concepts and heuristics which do not do justice to the complexity they are describing.

In conclusion Tsoukas argues that the concepts used in representationalist theories give an inadequate account of complex strategy processes and are unnecessarily reductionist. Process theorists still have a tendency to argue for the importance of context, agency and history in strategy development, but then produce familiar grids and frameworks for formulating strategy. In other words, for Tsoukas process theories are still under-theorised since they do not offer an account of the mechanisms which interweave intention, action and causality to explain how novelty arises. What most theories are still lacking, according to him, is a coherent theory of creative action, how it is that the future emerges from current actions, activities and planning.

Meanwhile Stacey considers strategy-making from the perspective of insights drawn from the complexity sciences (Stacey, Griffin and Shaw, 2000; Stacey, 2007, 2010). In his account the development of theories of strategy-making has been a history of problematising the idea of scientific rationality over time, taking increasing account of uncertainty in decision-making. Similar to Tsoukas, Stacey's own typology makes a distinction between content and process-based theories. Content research is concerned with *what* strategic positions led to optimal performance and focuses on the interaction between an organisation and its environment. Meanwhile process theories address *how* organisations achieve effective interaction between groups of people as well as competitive positions in the environment on the other. Stacey notes how the process school has gradually opened the context school up to critique, both from a macro- and a micro-perspective.

For Stacey macro-process theories (Chakravarthy and Doz, 1992) are less concerned with the role of organisational actors and what they do to make strategy. He argues that when macro-theorists write about strategy they double the process: what he means by this is that consciously designed administrative systems and decision-making techniques are thought to predict, shape and implement strategy, all of which are themselves processes. The process, understood as system, is then used to design another system. The micro-process strategy school (Whittington, 2002, Jarzabkowski, 2003; Samra-Fredericks, 2003) do have a theory of individual action, which they call practice, but separate strategy-making into levels so that individual practice draws on organisational practices, which are understood in the same way as the macro-process school. Practice is described very much within the conventional understanding of an organisation as a nested system.

Stacey mounts a critique of both macro- and micro-schools of process strategy theory, those dealing with strategy at the level of whole populations of organisations, and those dealing with what takes place within organisations, arguing that they are both adherents of systems thinking. Both are concerned to design a better functioning and idealised whole and ascribe to managers greater powers of agency than Stacey believes the literature demonstrating the broadly poor outcomes of strategic planning would warrant. In earlier chapters we have begun to explore how systems theories draw on analogies with the natural sciences and assume that a manager can step outside the system to optimise the design. In this sense they still privilege rational calculation and managerial choosing. Stacey argues that both micro- and macro-schools have a deliberate view of process, that is one that still assumes that the individual, cognising subject is in control of the processes of organisational life which aims to bring the organisation to a stable state of functioning optimally fitting its environment.

So while Tsoukas offers a critique of most schools of strategy for lacking a dynamic concept of creative action which gives an adequate account of the complexity they claim to represent, Stacey (2010) argues similarly that the theories of causality espoused by both process and content schools of strategy give an insufficient account for the emergence of novelty and the prevalence of radical uncertainty in organisations and their environments. This is because they are rooted in natural science methods which are predicated instead on certainty and predictability. Stacey develops a taxonomy of three main theories of causality which he considers are espoused by the dominant schools of strategy.

Efficient cause exemplified by content models of strategy, is concerned with movement over time from one stable state to another and change which is predictable. The future is understood to be a repetition of the past, and law-like generalisations are used to achieve an optimal fit for the organisation with its environment. This way of understanding strategy most closely approximates to generalisations based on Newtonian science.

Formative cause describes the movement over time towards a mature form which is already enfolded from the beginning, and is realised in the interaction between the parts and the whole. Although there may be small variations in form because of context and history, the state to which the system is unfolding is recognisable and pre-given. This theory of causality draws heavily on Kant's notion of the development of organisms which he writes about in the section entitled the *Critique of Teleological Judgement* in *The Critique of Judgement* (1790/1978). He was provoked by what he considered to be the inadequacy of Newton's efficient cause of mechanics, what we might term if-then causality, for explaining organic phenomena in nature.

Kant argued that an organism is a system of whole and parts which manifests both 'regressive' and 'progressive' causality: the whole is the product of the parts, but the parts in turn rely upon the whole for their own proper functioning and existence. While efficient cause enables us to explain progressive causality we can only appreciate regressive causality if we were to accept antecedent intelligent design of the parts, a priori. Kant insists that we have no justification for adopting a 'constitutive concept' for actual design, that is, this is no proof of the existence of God, merely that it is useful to think of parts of nature as if they had been designed as a useful mechanism for forming hypotheses. Nonetheless, the interaction of parts and whole for Kant demonstrates the way that organisms are always moving towards a mature form of themselves which is already pre-given. This Kantian idea is quite clearly taken up in contemporary organisation theory when organisations are thought of as 'living, breathing, wholes' which tend towards more mature forms of themselves.

Rationalist cause assumes goals chosen by reasoning autonomous actors who make choices within the bounds of ethical universal principles. These rational choices include selecting the rules by which the parts of the whole interact and the mechanisms through which employees can participate and become motivated. There is an assumption that managers can choose to innovate: novelty, then, is predictable and arises from the purposive activities of designing managers. Both formative and rationalist theories of causality can be found together in process theories of strategy at the same time, as we have been mentioning throughout the book. On the one hand it is thought possible for a rational, autonomous manager objectively to observe the organisation and design improvements to it, and at the same time and on the other hand they are part of the system being designed. A manager can shape the conditions which enfold the future for employees thought to be part of the system.

Stacey goes on to argue that even when scholars draw on the complexity sciences for explanations of how strategising is affected by non-linear processes, he claims that they often still try to draw them into a paradigm of predictability and control, particularly of formative causality. For example, Wheatley (1992), Lewin and Regine (2000) and Brown and Eisenhardt (1998) all take up the idea of the simple rules in their work which is derived from the boids simulation experiment undertaken by Reynolds (1987). In this computer simulation Reynolds programmed moving agents he called boids to mimic the flocking behaviour of birds. The flocking simulation produced complex patterning simply by the boids interacting with other local agents according to a few simple rules: there was no overall blueprint or plan for the whole flock. According to Stacey, Wheatley, Lewin and Regine and Brown and Esienhardt all replace the computer programmer with a manager or group of managers when drawing on the example of the boids experiment, who are encouraged to design simple rules for their employees to follow. These rules are then thought to enfold the kinds of self-organising behaviour of employees which is beneficial to organisational development.

Stacey describes a fourth causality, which he terms 'transformative causality'. By transformative causality Stacey (2010) draws on the Nobel prize-winning chemist Ilya Prigogine (1997) to talk about the way that ensembles of entities spontaneously self-organise in a way that is unpredictable. For Prigogine the future for ensembles is under permanent reconstruction because of the way in which instabilities, fluctuations and break symmetries allow for new order to emerge from disorder. I will explore the idea of transformative causality of populations of agents further below following the narrative of organisational strategy as a way of setting out a different concept of how the future emerges from the present.

Summary of the Two Critical Reviews of Strategy-Making

Both Tsoukas and Stacey describe the way in which the theoretical domain of organisational strategy theory has become more complex and diverse over time. Amongst scholars at least, this has gradually undermined the idea of the organisation as a reified object behaving according to discoverable rules in a population of other objects, using Newtonian physics. Latterly strategy theory has taken a much greater interest in what happens inside an organisation between employees who are formulating the strategy, and admit enactivist theories which claim that managers can both discover and create the world through interpretation and imagination. Some process theories of strategy pay attention to time, context and the qualitative assessment of practice between employees. However, despite the theoretical diversification of the field, Tsoukas claims that the planning and design schools of strategy still overwhelmingly predominate amongst contemporary organisations, most of whom still undertake strategic planning of one sort or another. He argues that they offer inadequate theories of creative action. Stacey too claims that many contemporary theories of strategy, even those which draw on analogies from the complexity sciences, are underpinned by what he terms rational and formative causality. That is, they provide explanations of the way that the future arises out of the present based on the idea of managerial choosing or, and sometimes at the same time, the organisation emerging from an archetype which is already enfolded, and which will arise from the interaction between parts and whole, or between different wholes. Most cannot account adequately for the emergence of genuine novel and uncertainty.

Given that the literature on strategic planning is so diverse and at the same time so inconclusive about the efficacy of doing it, what is it that managers in organisations think they are doing when they strategise? How might we understand the process of strategy making from if we are continuing to think of organisations arising from the complex interplay of intentions and actions, which we have started to explore in previous chapters?

The following narrative may give some insight into what kind of thinking prevails in discussions about strategy as well as the ways in which dominant ways of understanding the making of strategy have come to dominate. It will also pay attention to what people are doing as they make strategy together to try and give examples of the theories I have been developing in this book.

Narrative on Strategy

I was contacted by a senior manager in an organisation who had been given the task of co-ordinating the next round of strategic planning, given that the current strategy was due to expire in the next 18 months. She invited me to accompany her and her colleagues in a series of discussions over the coming period as a means of helping them reflect on the process of strategising as they tried to create the next strategic plan. The agreement I brokered about my role was that I would help them reflect on the way that they had been working so that I might support them to take the next steps in what they were doing.

When I joined the first discussion it became clear that managers in the organisation were determined this time to undertake the strategy exercise differently from their previous attempt. The last five-year plan was perceived as having been imposed by a small group of senior managers, some of whom were still present, and called for wholesale structural changes in the organisation and new methods of managing which might broadly be termed managerialist. The roles and responsibilities of managers at the centre were enhanced, and the targets were set for the different business units throughout the organisation, considered to be 'stretch targets'.

A mid-five-year assessment of progress concluded that in most areas, employees had only partially fulfilled their targets. In this first round of discussions, then, one of the primary topics was the necessity or otherwise of what the chief executive had previously called 'step changes', by which he meant deliberate, designed steps towards a radical change in ways of working which he thought were necessary to 'increase performance'. As this particular meeting progressed, the chief executive's senior colleagues seemed to be putting their boss on notice in a non-threatening way that they would resist further radical structural changes which to date had brought about far more work than had been anticipated, and had resulted in lots of pressure for managers throughout the organisation. Most of these changes had not had time to work through. In what appeared to be a face-saving formula, the chief executive and a small coterie of colleagues accepted these criticisms, at the same time as arguing that the previous strategy, and the way it had come about, had been necessary.

Between the first and second meetings of the top team, as an antidote to what they saw as making strategy from the top, managers involved as many people as possible in thinking about the organisation and its achievements; and a wide variety of employees began to participate in discussions about what had and had not gone well during the last strategy period. These workshops were very lively and sometimes difficult, and people who had been involved in them had asked when they might take part in something similar again in the future. I joined a number of these discussions where managers from elsewhere in the organisation discussed the extent to which they felt their work had been recognised, enhanced or hindered by the previous strategy. The discussions continued over a number of months.

Subsequently, my contractor had put together several drafts of the strategy, which was a synthesis of the workshops. This synthesis had been subjected to further discussions by the senior team when they had argued over what was and was not a priority, what they should and should not put their energies into. The Board had seen a later draft and professed themselves satisfied with the outcome. However, the more revised the draft became, the less my contractor could interest her senior colleagues in what she was doing. She found this very frustrating since her task was not complete until they could all 'buy in' to what the strategic plan was proposing. She needed to dot the 'i's and cross the 't's. Somehow they had lost their energy, and were now concentrating on other things as though the job were already done.

I was invited to a final discussion of the senior management team to discuss how the strategy might be completed, launched and then implemented. Two strong themes of discussion emerged in the morning. The first involved senior colleagues continuing to interpret what they thought was in the strategy document, and as a consequence jockey for position in the struggle over resources; they did this in both a co-operative and a competitive way, arguing for their position, but not arguing at the expense of other colleagues. Some of the senior managers whom my contractor had considered uninterested in finalising the document thought they had lost out in the struggle over resources and became reanimated once they realised that continued participation may recover their position. Thereafter, group members discussed how they might 'play' the strategy with the variety of groups for whom it would have significance: the Board, the employees, the population of other organisations amongst which this organisation functioned. They anticipated the reactions, both hostile and favourable, and began to think about how they might respond.

Reflections on the Narrative – Strategy, Politics and Power

There are a number of observations that I would like to make about the way that strategic planning was undertaken in this organisation over two iterations of planning. I will do so as a way of testing the possibility of making some generalisations about what happens between people when strategy gets developed, and to unpick some of the assumptions that they might be making about what they are doing.

First, the strategy process which preceded my intervention had all the hallmarks of current managerial thinking with its future orientation and a lack of acknowledgement of the past. To plan strategically had come to mean considering what a small group of managers wanted to achieve in highly idealised ways, and then to work backwards from there in logical steps. This particular organisation adopted a method which was made popular by the American management theorist Russell Ackoff (1999), with an approach he termed 'idealised design'. Through a process called visioning which we explored in Chapter 5, employees are invited to imagine an idealised end state which they are encouraged to believe they can achieve if only they are motivated enough. Although it is important to try and predict future constraints to what we might like to do in the form of global trends, this does not necessarily involve paying much attention to prior experience, indeed this experience is thought to be an impediment to the kind of radical change that is considered necessary to sustain the organisation. The reference point is what the organisation 'ought' to be doing rather than what it 'is' doing. In orthodox strategy literature there is a good deal of anxiety about and fetishisation of the requirement for change, which can sometimes justify strategic proposals which bear little relation to the kinds of work that staff in the organisation might have been undertaking previously. Indeed it can shut out a critical appraisal of what staff in the organisation have been doing in favour of what has come to be called 'blue skies thinking'.

What highly idealised and abstract methods often leave out in their account, however, is the intensely political process that takes place in groups, particularly over resource distribution and recognition. I drew attention to these political processes in Chapter 2. In the narrative above, the political engagement involved debating the methods of strategic planning. The first discussion I attended in the renewal of the strategic plan was an attempt to subvert a particular understanding of managerial authority which had been previously exercised by the Chief Executive Officer (CEO) and an immediate coterie of colleagues in the last formulation of the strategic plan.

Where it is usual in the dominant literature of Organisational Development (OD) to think of 'task' and 'process' as separate phases, from this narrative it is possible to see how task and process are intertwined. As the managers in the room began to engage with questions about method, so the relationship between this particular group of managers changed, and with it the task they were undertaking. In the previous formulation of strategy the task, idealised design, had also allowed certain conversations to take place and prohibited others. During the second iteration the broader group of managers was able to voice their scepticism about previous methods, and in doing so, they tilted the balance of power away from the CEO, and they were thus able much more directly to influence the outcome. Similarly, in this second round of discussions to which I was party the valorisation of participation as a method of engagement of staff lead to its own particular difficulties later on.

Third, one way of thinking about the strategic planning process, and perhaps the plan itself, are as what G.H. Mead (1938) referred to as 'social objects', which we explored in Chapter 3 (see p. 74). In other words, they are generalised tendencies of groups of people to act in particular ways: because many organisations develop strategic plans so many other organisations will do the same and the reiterated process produces certain expectations about how it should be undertaken. Contemporary strategic planning exercises are perpetuated because they have a history, they have become a tradition in organisational life. However, the exact characteristics of the particular social object, this planning exercise that I describe in the narrative above, will depend on how the participants in the meeting, including me, interact together. One of the things to draw attention to, then is the struggle over power that ensued between the participating managers. In the process of struggle this particular group were evolving and changing their methods as they tried to make sense of what they were doing. There was both continuity and change in the way they were planning together.

Fourth, engaging in the strategic planning process clearly evoked strong feelings in those who were participating as they negotiated over the way it would be conducted. But it also provoked feelings of boredom. The broader group of managers seem to have found it difficult to recognise themselves in the earlier strategic plan and moved to reassert a different way of organising the next round. This degree of engagement proved difficult to sustain, however, because the negotiation over the document was clearly more enlivening than the subsequent writing of the document. As the plan went through its various revisions my contractor found it harder and harder to maintain her colleagues' interest in what she was doing. Stacey (2007) has speculated that groups of managers engage in strategic planning in order to reduce their anxiety about uncertainty, since there is no stable body of evidence to suggest that the exercise of strategic planning is very successful at predicting change into the future.

Meanwhile Alvesson (2002) writes about the identity-sustaining nature of much managerial and leadership activity. This particular group, by participating in the social object of the strategic planning exercise, were also sustaining their identities as a group of senior managers doing what such a group is expected to do. This can be both anxiety-provoking and identity threatening. Would they be able to come up with something that would be recognised by each other, and by their wider stakeholders, as valuable? One way of interpreting their lack of engagement later was that they were no longer experiencing the anxiety that they felt before the exercise. Perhaps the main point of strategic planning is the taking part.

How might I locate these observations about what people are doing when they undertake strategy together in a broader discourse? How far could I answer the complaint from Tsoukas that most theories of strategy lacked a coherent theory of creative action, and Stacey's claim that the dominant discourse cannot account for the degree of uncertainty in organisations and give a coherent theory of how novelty arises? In what follows I will draw on theories from both the natural and the social sciences as a way of exploring the predictable unpredictability of strategy-making in organisations, and also as an attempt to investigate what Stacey might mean by 'transformative causality' continuing the discussion we started on this topic in Chapter 3.

In Search of a Creative Theory of Action that Accounts for Uncertainty

There is a pronounced queasiness on the part of scholars who would like management to be a science to turn to the social sciences for insight for fear of being thought relativistic or insufficiently rigorous. In defining themselves in opposition to what they see as less certain and precise methods they can sometimes take up quite extreme positions and claim that they are completely separate from the social situations they seek to research. They inhabit a Platonic world where something is either true or false, it is substantiated by 'evidence' or it is not: if the methods are not replicable and generalisable then they are not scientific methods. The way that time, context, relationships of power and values condition what it is possible to say and do are inadmissible variables. Such arguments are cloaked in the rhetoric of high science, where scientific method is derived mostly from the discipline of physics, which seeks timeless covering law explanations. Equally, social scientists can sometimes take up a polarised view against what they see as the shortcomings of positivism, such as the sociologist Bent Flyvbjerg (2001) who has argued that natural sciences can have nothing to say about the social, precisely for the reasons set out above, that they exclude themes of time, power, values and interdependence.

What is striking about some scholars from either natural scientific or social scientific backgrounds is how much they can find in common to say about complex social phenomena, but from very different premises. So some researchers, who would strongly consider themselves natural scientists are nonetheless developing their thinking in ways that challenge some of the usual certainties of their own tradition: that the truth is 'out there' to be discovered and that it is possible to be unchanged by the phenomenon one is observing, or that the phenomenon itself is unchanging.

NATURAL SCIENCE AND UNCERTAINTY

Take for example, two social scientists, Peter Allen from Cranfield and Peter Hedström from Oxford University, who make no secret of the fact that they cleave to a natural scientific position. If a phenomenon cannot be described mathematically, they claim, then science can have nothing substantive to say about it. And yet, in modelling complex social processes mathematically they come to some very similar conclusions to scholars working in a more clearly social scientific tradition which is more sceptical of categorical truth claims. What they begin to converge on is a science of uncertainty, where time, diversity and interpretation are key to understanding complex social phenomena.

Peter Allen (1998) has developed a variety of different computer models to pose questions about optimal strategy development for a fishing fleet wishing to maximise fish catches while not unsustainably depleting global fish stocks. In order to demonstrate his initial premise, that the conceptual framework of traditional science based on mechanical and equilibrium models are inadequate for describing human processes, he gradually makes his models more and more complex. Most modelling, he argues, is based on three assumptions: that microscopic events occur at an average rate, that individuals are of a given type and have a normal distribution around the average type, and that the system moves towards equilibrium. He develops his models through four stages of complexification from the initial equilibrium model, which contains the three assumptions above. Next at stage two he develops non-linear dynamical models, which contain the first two assumptions, but which are not assumed to move towards equilibrium. At stage three, self-organising systems, the model assumes average individuals but does not average microscopic events, nor does it assume the system will move towards equilibrium. Finally, in a model he terms evolutionary complex systems, neither the individuals nor the micro-interactions are assumed to be average, nor does the system move towards equilibrium.

Allen reminds us that these models are based on very strong assumptions, and still abstract from a much more complex reality, but nonetheless makes the case that his fourth and most complex model is able to tell us things that we could not know about current reality and future possibilities than we could learn from more reductive models. For example, he begins to problematise our current understandings about the need for an 'optimal' strategy. Indeed he suggests that there is no single optimal strategy for long. Rather, what the fourth model demonstrates is a series of particular moments in an unending imperfect learning process as different diverse players adapt to each other, and to the environment in which they find themselves acting. Time becomes an important factor in reading from the model, since what looks like a good strategy now may not become so after a number of iterations where everyone is adapting to what everyone else is doing. The patterning of interaction between agents, and the agents and their environment, is key to understanding what it is that is emerging:

> ... the landscape of possible advantage itself is produced by the actors in interaction, and that the detailed history of the exploration process itself affects the outcome. Paradoxically, uncertainty is therefore inevitable, and we must face this. Long term success is not just about improving performance with respect to the external of a complex society. The 'payoff' of any action for an individual cannot be stated in absolute terms because it depends on what other individuals are doing. Strategies are interdependent ... Innovation and change occur because of diversity, non-average individuals with their bizarre initiatives, and whenever this leads to an exploration into an area where positive feedback outweighs negative, then growth will occur. Value is assigned afterwards.
>
> (Allen, 1998: 157)

The future, Allen argues, is not contained in the present, and strategy is not a 'problem' to be solved: there are a variety of possible choices and each choice will lead to its own consequences, its own strengths and weaknesses and it own successes and failures. Very little of this can be known beforehand

and we will never be in a position to have enough information for a perfect understanding of what we are doing and what we need to be doing.

Meanwhile Peter Hedström describes himself as an analytical sociologist. That is he has, by his own definition, very little patience with theoretical sociology because it seems to him too 'imprecise'. He metes out particular criticism for one of the sociologists I have quoted in this book, Pierre Bourdieu, for offering explanations of social phenomena that mystify as much as they explain (Hedström, 2005: 4). Instead he has tried to explain social phenomena by simulating them mathematically using computer generated models like Peter Allen. In so doing he is careful to outline the limitations of the particular approach he is taking. Although he feels that his approach offers helpful explanations of how social phenomena arise, he counsels against using them as empirical predictions, or as literal statements about empirical reality. Like Allen's models, Hedstrom's interacting agents are diverse and are programmed with a varied combination of desires, beliefs and opportunities (DBO) which affects their interactions with local others.

One computer model was developed to help explain patterns of unemployment among young people in different districts of metropolitan Stockholm, and the simulation was run thousands of times to observe what happens. From this experiment Hedström draws some interesting conclusions:

1. *There is no necessary proportionality between the size of a cause and the size of its effect.*

2. *The structure of the social interaction is of considerable importance in its own right for the social outcomes that emerge.*

3. *The effect a given action has on the social can be highly contingent upon the structural configuration in which the actor is embedded.*

4. *Aggregate patterns say very little about the micro-level processes that brought them about.*

(2005: 99).

Hedström intends these observations to be taken together, rather than separately, but in analysing the interaction of agents within a network he concludes that small variables can make a big difference to outcomes. While in one situation the actions of X might lead to Y, in another context where the power relationship between X and the network of agents they are related to are slightly different, an entirely different outcome is possible even if the same actions are pursued. Moreover, Hedström also admits that other factors, outside the field of scrutiny, can also have a big impact on outcomes between interactions. Social patterning arises in unpredictable ways even if we can identify many of the important factors, and in addition to this there are other factors that we cannot identify which may also influence the outcome. So rather than being linear and predictable, he concludes that the relationship between the individual and the social, the individual agent and multiple agents, is 'complex and precarious' where 'large scale social phenomena that are observed may simply be due to an uncommon combination of common events and circumstances' (ibid.: 100).

Summary of Complex Mathematical Modelling

The threads of Allen's argument that I find most interesting are that he has introduced uncertainty, paradox, time and values as integral to our understanding of complex human experience. These would not usually be considered part of the discourse of conventional natural science methods. Moreover, Allen knocks a big hole in the idea of finding an optimal fit between a strategy and an anticipated environment and lends credence to Tsoukas' description of enactivist strategy-making. Strategy development in Allen's fishing model has no beginning, middle or end but is a continuous imperfect learning process where the process of exploration and the interaction between the agents affects emergent collective activity. One might argue that the global pattern, what we might term strategy, is emerging from the many, many strategies pursued by each of the separate agents, some of which will be deviant and eccentric in terms of existing norms.

Again, drawing on Hedström, we can see that in a situation of many interacting heterogeneous agents the model demonstrates uncertainty and unpredictability which can only be made sense of retrospectively. So differences in original starting positions or contexts, differences in relationships between agents, the connectedness or otherwise of actors in their particular environment all create a situation where a large effort can produce a small result, or a small intervention could bring about a profound change.

> In order to explain social outcomes, we must focus not only on the properties of the actors, but also on the way in which the actors interact and influence one another.
>
> (2005: 87).

In both models the fine-grained detail of interactions between locally interacting diverse agents helps to describe how it is that global patterns are forming, which would not be deducible from paying attention to the global patterns alone. The global patterns arise out of the many, many interactions alone and are not evolving to some pre-reflected archetype or ideal even though they have been programmed with clear deterministic parameters which follow an if-then causality. The patterning that arises is self-influencing, which leads to further patterning of mutually adapting agents.

SOCIAL SCIENCE AND UNCERTAINTY

Both Allen and Hedström acknowledge the shortcomings of developing computer models as a way of having something to say about human experience. They are precise and generalisable, but they are at the same time abstract and built on some strong assumptions. Neither would claim that a human would ever behave like a programmed agent in a computer model. Nonetheless, I want to argue that some of their observations about uncertainty, the importance of time, paradox, interpretation and the mutually-adaptive behaviour of humans can also be found in the work of the very theoretical sociologist, Pierre Bourdieu, that Hedström in particular has reserved such criticism.

Previously we have explored some of Norbert Elias' theories about how the interplay of many, many intentions of longer and longer chains of interdependent people bring about social and psychological effects and trends which no one has planned. These 'blind social forces' constantly amaze and frustrate us:

> *Again and again, therefore, people stand before the outcome of their own actions like the apprentice magician before the spirits he has conjured up and which, once at large, are no longer in his power. They look with astonishment at the convolutions and formations of the historical flow which they themselves constitute but do not control.*
>
> *(Elias, 1991: 62)*

Similarly Bourdieu reflected on how it is that we experience continuity and change in our social interactions with others by offering his own definition of *habitus*, a term also used by Elias. In developing his definition of practice, Bourdieu focuses on the micro-interactions between social actors in a way that reconciles the local and the global and explains the paradoxical relation between individuals and the societies which they form, and which form them. He describes this paradoxical relationship thus:

> *In short, the habitus, the product of history, produces individual and*
> *collective practices, and hence history, in accordance with the schemes*
> *engendered by history. The system of dispositions – a past which*
> *survives in the present and tends to perpetuate itself into the future by*
> *making itself present in practices structured according to its principles,*
> *an internal law relaying the continuous exercise of the law of external*
> *necessities (irreducible to immediate conjunctural constraints) – is the*
> *principle of continuity and regularity which objectivism discerns in the*
> *social world without being able to give them a rational basis.*
>
> *(Bourdieu, 1977: 82)*

For Bourdieu the individual's 'cognitive and motivating structures' cannot stand outside the objective structures of history which have formed an individual, and yet is also not reducible to them. The subject is not some free-floating essence, but arises out of objective conditions which shape them. And yet the subject still contributes to these objectifying structures through the creative improvisation with others. We are social products of our cultural and contextual history but this does not prevent us from acting spontaneously in our interactions with others. Our dispositions to behave, think and act in particular ways are embodied: we are not necessarily conscious of them since we are mostly absorbed in the game we are playing with others. There are some obvious parallels here with Mead's ideas of the generalised other, gesture and response that we investigated in Chapter 2.

Drawing on his field work analysing the rituals of the Kabyle people in Algeria, Bourdieu concluded that practical judgement occurs with improvisation on and around the *habitus*:

> *... only a virtuoso with perfect command of his 'art of living' can play*
> *on all the resources inherent in the ambiguities and uncertainties of*
> *behaviour and situation in order to produce the actions appropriate to*
> *each case, to do that of which people will say 'There was nothing else to*
> *be done', and do it the right way.*
>
> *(Bourdieu, 1977: 8)*

Social practice for Bourdieu is 'the art of the necessary improvisation', the iterative patterning of mutual adaptation within the constraints of the *habitus*, which I am claiming as a theory of emergence, when unplanned emergent novelty grounded in paradox arises between social actors. For Bourdieu, as for Mead, this improvisation is never something one can get on top of and master. We become aware of it only through reflexivity, after the event, and is not reducible to if-then causality:

> *This paradoxical logic is that of all practice, or rather of all practical sense. Caught up in 'the matter in hand', totally present in the present and in the practical functions that it finds there in the form of objective potentialities they contain; it can only discover them by enacting them, unfolding them in time.*
>
> *(Bourdieu, 1990: 92)*

Bourdieu suggests that practice, or the equivalent for Mead would be the cycle of gesture and response, are temporally bound. We cannot be aware of how we will respond until after we have responded, which in turn informs the next response in an endless chain of interactions. It is impossible to identify the genesis in terms of which gesture led to which response. To respond to others is to make evaluative judgements which we are not conscious of in the moment, although they will be informed by past judgements and the *habitus* in which we find ourselves. Although absolutely any response is impossible, what the actual response will be is unpredictable, even to ourselves. But the making of such judgements, the exercise of value-creation, is what makes us human since it is part of the formation of mind and self-consciousness. Causality becomes a matter of inter-subjective interpretation.[1]

I am bringing in Bourdieu's theory of *habitus* to make a parallel with the mathematical models of Allen and Hedström, arguing that it offers a similar interpretation of how individuals are constantly adapting to others in local interaction, within a broader population we call society. Individual activity is possible and intelligible because it is informed by a previous history of activity, while it in turn influences what is currently happening, which we will later interpret as history. Yet further interaction may lead us to reinterpret our history, and so on, and so on. Individual activity is constrained and informed by the activity of others, but there are sufficient ambiguities and possibilities to allow for spontaneous improvisation locally. So how might Bourdieu understand the purposive activity of strategy-making?

As a radical social activist and academic, Bourdieu was not that concerned with management or organisations. However, he did undertake an empirical

---

1   This argument about the inter-subjectivity of interpretation also undercuts the idea of 'mental models', Senge (1990), which suggests that human interaction unfolds from the basis of the intentions of individuals stored in 'inner' mental models.

study of the French housing sector, which prompted him to reflect on what he considered to be the narrow and reductive understanding of strategy development put forward by many economists. Classical economics, Bourdieu argues, is not concerned with reality, but rather with a more or less desirable ideal based on mathematical formalisation. It conceives of '... agents as pure consciousness without history, capable of determining their ends freely and instantaneously, and acting in complete awareness of what they do' (2005: 220). As an alternative, Bourdieu thought that strategy arose from the improvisational interactions between managers within the firm, mediated by power relationships as they move to maximise their social capital with each other. Additionally, organisations are adapting and adjusting to each other within a particular economic sector:

> *The field of forces is also a field of struggles, a socially constructed field of action in which agents equipped with different resources confront each other in order to gain access to exchange and to preserve or transform the currently prevailing relation of force ... Far from being faced with a weightless, constraint-free world in which to develop their strategies at leisure, they are oriented by the constraints and possibilities built into their position and by the representation they are able to form of that position and the position of their competitors as a function of the information at their disposal and their cognitive structures.*
>
> *(2005: 199–200)*

Bourdieu's understanding of strategy development is multiply complex: within the constraints of the *habitus* managers vie with each other, both co-operating to develop the company but competing to assert their understanding over those of others. In the context of this co-operative competition they have to make the best sense they can of their position vis-à-vis other companies in their domain, which will both constrain and enable their ability to act. As they do so they are, to a large degree, totally absorbed in the game they are playing. This is a very different understanding to most management theory, Bourdieu argues, where there is a tendency to overestimate the extent to which conscious strategies play a role in business.

I would argue that Bourdieu's representation of the competing and co-operating process between managers engaged in the game is very similar to the narrative I set out above about the consultancy I undertook with a group of managers.

Bringing Together the Natural and Social Sciences in Understanding Uncertainty

I began this chapter by pointing out how dominant ways of understanding strategy are based on the idea of the rationalist manager, or managers, choosing the future for the organisation. In doing so, they often borrow from the vocabulary of natural science methods, which imply linear cause and effect, and predictability. Next, in reviewing the strategy literature from the perspective of two critics of managerial orthodoxy, it became clear that despite the fact that the field of strategy theory has both diversified and complexified, still rationalist and instrumental theories predominate. Even theories which admit to the possibility of the future being enacted by managers still lack what Tsoukas calls a creative theory of action, or from Stacey's viewpoint, can adequately account for uncertainty and what he terms transformative causality. Transformative causality is neither already enfolded in the organisation understood as system, nor does it arise solely from the rational acts of managers, which would imply god-like percipience on their part, nor does it occur simply by collecting data, extrapolating from it and projecting the past forwards. Transformative causality, after Prigogine, is an inherent property of ensembles of diverse interacting agents.

By turning to some social scientists who consider themselves firmly in the natural science tradition, working with mathematically formalised representations of complex social phenomena, I set out to demonstrate that the sciences of uncertainty offer some explanations about how it is that novelty and change emerge. Novelty emerges through the local interactions of populations of agents. The insights that we gain from considering these mathematical models is that time, and the history of interactions is one of the key determinants in understanding what is going on, as is the quality of the relationship between the interacting agents. There is no overall blueprint or plan, but the future, in Prigogine's terms, is under perpetual construction arising from the disruptions, asymmetries and bifurcations that arise from the interactions within the population. The population is not evolving towards a state of equilibrium, or an optimal state, but develops through the mutually adaptive behaviour of agents in the population who sometimes behave in a deviant or eccentric manner.

In bringing in Bourdieu, a theoretical sociologist, I was making the claim that his theory of *habitus* similarly offers an explanation of continuity and change arising from individuals adapting to each other locally, informed by history and the nature of their relationship. Bourdieu also stresses the importance of time, paradox and asymmetries and the inherent amibiguities and uncertainties of social interaction. He also offers a critique of a rational theory of strategy, and argues instead that it emerges from the relationship of power between interacting managers, who themselves must form a view of their organisation's possibilities within a broader population of organisations.

Bourdieu's ideas have many similarities with his colleague and friend Norbert Elias, whose theories we have explored earlier in this book: longer and longer chains of interdependent people form dynamic figurations of co-operation and competition, which have probabilistic but not totally predictable tendencies, and which can sometimes cause surprising outcomes of which no one is in overall control. We are all caught up in long-term, historically formed social processes which inform our sense of self and what it is possible to think and do.

Reconsidering the Narrative

In the narrative in this chapter I explored the way in which a group of senior managers engaged together in making strategy. One of the things that I was drawing attention to was the way in which fluctuations in the relationships of power between them fundamentally reshaped they way they were working: all kinds of consequences followed from their reflection upon the assumptions they had brought to the last episode of strategy. Although strategy-making is thought to be a very future-oriented activity, nonetheless novelty and continuity were evolving in the present moment as they struggled over what they thought they were doing together. They were both co-operating and competing over what Mead called the 'life process' of the group. Although the CEO was clearly an influential person in the group of managers, even he was constrained by the reactions of his colleagues and their interpretation of the playing out of the last strategy.

By analogy I am making a comparison with those sociologists working from a natural science and a social science perspective whom I have explored above. I am claiming that whatever it says in an organisational strategy document, no matter how abstract and idealised, the exact way strategy will play out in any organisation can never be predicted and will depend upon the relationships of power between the protagonists in the environments in which they find themselves acting. The evolution of the strategy will be constrained but not determined by the history of interactions between the protagonists and others they involve as they interact locally. What managers deem to be the success or otherwise of the strategy over time will be their interpretation of the sum of these many, many interactions as people have struggled together to make meaning of what it is they think they are doing together. This is highly unlikely to turn out the way that any strategy document has predicted.

Concluding Thoughts and Implications for Managers

Although it seems to be more widely accepted that the future is unpredictable and that things never work out the way that we intend, nonetheless managers in organisations still spend a lot of time undertaking strategy. To call something 'strategic' is to endow it with considerable significance and meaning and to lift it out of the ordinary. Many groups of managers I work with often bemoan the fact that they are unable to work 'more strategically'. When talking about working or acting strategically they are mostly doing so using dominant methods based on assumptions of predictability and control, and linear cause and effect. They also rely heavily on abstractions and idealisations, where constraints, imperfections and ambiguities are tidied away. A strategy, if it is to have cachet, needs to be 'clear' and demonstrate that a group of senior managers has chosen the future. What would they be doing if they weren't so doing? We have explored previously how these methods are perpetuated socially, and are also linked to how contemporary managers sustain their identities as professionals, irrespective of how successful the methods are, and no matter how weak the evidence base is for using them. Strategic planning still provokes a lot of anxiety and strong feelings in staff and is a powerful social object. It is not an easy thing to offer a critique of strategising or to point out its limitations without evoking powerful reactions.

More often than not when I work with groups of managers reviewing their previous strategy, which can sometimes be an occasion for much rueful reflection on 'lack of success', they can then leap to the conclusion that this time they really need to get their strategies right. The perceived failure of past strategies provokes the reaction that they should be doing what they have been doing more comprehensively. They think that deriving lessons from the past will help them predict a better future. By doing so they trying to optimise, to produce a strategy of best fit for a set of circumstances which they cannot foresee. So, while I would not in any way argue that it is a waste of time to reflect on the past, nonetheless, in the light of the work of the sociologists considered in this chapter and their thoughts on the inherent unpredictability of the future, it is clearly insufficient to do so. Nor do future possibilities necessarily lie in the present, although the choices made in the present will have a significant bearing on what evolves. Previous choices, the nature of the organisation, the domain in which it operates will all have an effect on the kind of strategy that is conceivable or possible.

What actually evolves, as far as we can ever fully understand it, will be as a result of the way that strategies get taken up locally, including among the group of managers who conceived the strategy in the first place. So reflexively paying attention to the way that managers are working together as they undertake strategy, or any other kind of managerial activity, is constitutive of what transpires, as I have illustrated in my narrative. This then calls for a different focus for managers engaged in strategy-making since it turns conventional prescriptions on their head. In the end, strategy-making is at best a probabilistic activity where retrospective sense-making is at least as important as future-oriented planning. Moreover, paying attention to how the group is working in the moment, trying to think about how they are thinking and working together, will significantly affect what eventually transpires as 'strategy'. Strategy is not just about creating an idealised future, but involves paying attention to how we are reconstructing the future in the present as we reinterpret the past.

Turning conventional prescriptions for strategy-making on their head will have significant implications for what a group of managers pays attention to as they are making strategy. So rather than thinking that the most important thing for them to be doing is to identify a niche, or to agree a vision, they would instead spend time in exploration of similarities and differences, how they come to understand who they are and what they are becoming, and how this process shapes what they understand strategy to be. A greater toleration and exploration of the inevitable conflicting interpretations of how people understand what is going on, and their roles, could lead to significantly different outcomes. In Allen's models it is difference that makes the big difference. Complex models evolve over time because of the small differences that amplify in population-wide patterns. This is a direct challenge to the notion that organisations function optimally if managers all agree and somehow align their views.

Accepting that strategies will always be inherently fallible will also shape what it is possible to do for managers as they manage staff to implement a strategy, a topic I will deal with in the next chapter. If the future is unpredictable, how possible is it to manage staff against pre-reflected targets?

References

Ackoff, R.L. (1999) *Ackoff's Best: His Classic Writings on Management*, New York: Wiley.

Allen, P. (1998) Evolving complexity in social science, in Altman, G. and Koch, W.A. (1998) *Systems: New Paradigms for the Human Sciences*, Berlin: Walter de Gruyter.

Alvesson, M. (2002) *Understanding Organizational Culture*, London: Sage.

Araujo, L. and Easton, G. (1996) Strategy: Where is the pattern?, *Organization*, 3: 361–383.

Brown, S.L. and Eisenhardt, K. (1998) *Competing on the Edge: Strategy as Structured Chaos*, Boston, MA: Harvard University Press.

Bourdieu, P. (1977) *Outline of a Theory of Practice*, Cambridge: Cambridge University Press.

—— (1990) *The Logic of Practice,* Cambridge: Polity Press.

—— (1991) *Language and Symbolic Power*, Cambridge: Polity Press.

—— (2005) *The Social Structures of the Economy*, Cambridge: Polity Press.

Chakravarthy, B.S. and Doz, Y. (1992) Strategy process research: Focusing on corporate self-renewal, *Strategic Management Journal*, 13(Special Issue): 5–15.

Chandler, A, (1990) *Strategy and Structure*, Cambridge MA: MIT Press.

Chandler, A. (1992) Organizational capabilities and the economic history of the industrial enterprise, *Journal of Economic Perspectives*, 6: 79–100.

Elias, N. (1939/1991) *The Society of Individuals,* Oxford: Blackwell.

Flyvbjerg, B. (2001) *Making Social Science Matter: Why Social Inquiry Fails and How It Can Succeed Again*, Cambridge: Cambridge University Press.

Hedström, P. (2005) *Dissecting the Social: On the Principles of Analytical Socio*logy, Cambridge: Cambridge University Press.

Jarzabkowski, P. (2003) Strategic practices: An activity theory perspective on continuity and change, *Journal of Management Studies*, 40(1): 23–55.

Johnson, G. and Scholes, K. (1997) *Exploring Corporate Strategy*, 4th edition, London: Prentice Hall.

Kant, I. (1790/1978) *The Critique of Judgement*, Oxford: Oxford University Press.

Knight, K. (ed.) (1998) *The MacIntyre Reader,* Cambridge: Polity Press.

Lewin, R. and Regine, B. (2000) *The Soul at Work*, London: Orion Business Books.

Mead, G.H. (1938) *The Philosophy of the Act,* Chicago: University of Chicago.

Mintzberg, H., Ahlstrand B. and Lampel, J. (1998) *Strategy Safari: The Complete Guide Through the Wilds of Strategic Management*, Edinburgh: Pearson.

Porter, M.E. (1980) *Competitive Strategy*, New York: The Free Press.

Prigogine, I. (1997) *The End of Certainty: Time, Chaos and the New Laws of Nature*, New York: The Free Press.

Reynolds, C.W. (1987) Flocks, herds and schools: A distributed behaviour model, Proceedings of Siggraph '87, *Computer Graphics*, Anaheim, CA, 21(4): 25–34.

Rorty, R. (1991) *Objectivity, Relativism and Truth,* Cambridge: Cambridge University Press.

Samra-Fredericks, D. (2003) Strategising as lived experience and strategists' everyday efforts to shape strategic direction, *Journal of Management Studies*, 40(1): 141–174.

Scott, J.C. (1998) *Seeing Like a State: How Certain Schemes to Improve the Human Condition Have Failed*, New Haven: Yale University Press.

Senge, P. (1990) *The Fifth Discipline: The Art and Practice of the Learning Organisation*, London: Transworld.

Stacey, R. (2007) *Strategic Management and Organisational Dynamics: The Challenge of Complexity*, 5th edition, London: Routledge.

—— (2010) *Complexity and Organizational Reality: Uncertainty and the Need to Rethink Management After the Collapse of Investment Capitalism*, London: Routledge.

——, Griffin, D. and Shaw, P. (2000) *Complexity and Management: Fad or Radical Challenge to Systems Thinking?*, London: Routledge.

Taylor, C. (1995) *Philosophical Arguments*, Cambridge MA: Harvard University Press.

Tirole, J. (1988) *The Theory of Industrial Organization,* Cambridge MA:, MIT Press.

Tsoukas, H. (2004) *Complex Knowledge: Studies in Organizational Epistemology*, Oxford: Oxford University Press.

Wheatley, M.J. (1992) *Leadership and the New Science: Learning about Organization from an Orderly Universe*, San Francisco, Berret-Koehler.

Whittington, R. (2002) Practice perspectives on strategy: Unifying and developing a field, *Academy of Management Conference Proceedings*, Denver, August 2002.

—— and Cailluet, L. (2008) The crafts of strategy, *Long Range Planning*, 41: 241–247.

Wittgenstein, L. (1958) *Philosophical Investigations*, Oxford: Blackwell.

8

Performance Management and Targets – Control, Resistance and Improvisation

> *Whatever the strains, stresses and disorder that are occurring 'backstage', the 'frontstage' impression is still upbeat, a tale of rationality and order, progress and achievement.*
> (Paton, Managing and Measuring Social Enterprises, 2003: 29)

Reprise of Chapter 7

In the previous chapter I reviewed some of the conceptual assumptions of the dominant ways of understanding strategy and claimed that they were based on ideas of predictability and control, or alternatively on the idea that it is possible to identify a 'niche' in a given reality. I drew on two critics of the dominant view, who have described the process of diversification that has taken place in the field of strategic theory over time, but who nonetheless claim that the practice of strategy-making is still dominated by methods which imply enormous powers of foresight on the part of managers, or imply that the future is already enfolded in the present. Both Stacey and Tsoukas suggest that the dominant theories of strategy imply inadequate theories of action and causality. As an alternative I explored what Stacey (Stacey, Griffin and Shaw, 2000; Stacey 2007, 2010) has called transformative causality. By transformative causality he means that novelty emerges solely as a result of what diverse highly socialised agents in a population are doing in their local interactions with each other. Exactly what emerges cannot be explained by disaggregating the 'whole' into parts, nor can it be predicted by extrapolating from the past, nor is there a need for recourse to more metaphysical explanations of how change arises, such as the idea of some hidden order in the universe which can be revealed to those with unique or esoteric insight.

I drew on other scholars who have set out their own thinking along similar lines, either by designing agent-based computer models to simulate complex social phenomena, or by developing sociological theories to explain them. I argued that these attempts to understand complex social patterning were developing a more systematic approach to uncertainty, from both a natural science and a social science perspective. They shared a number of things in common: they took an interest in fine grained micro-interaction because they argue that large population-wide patterns emerge from small differences; they suggest that time, context and the structure of that interaction are central to explaining what is emerging; and they pointed to the importance of ambiguity and the paradoxical inter-relationship of the local and the global. Both these traditions investigating uncertainty offer a critique of many mainstream theoretical approaches to complex phenomena, arguing that they are insufficiently process- or mechanism-oriented. In other words they do not give an adequate account of how agents constantly adapt to each other within a population of agents. They focus instead on understanding individual agents in depth assuming that knowledge of parts can be extrapolated to the whole, or they study the complex phenomenon as though it were at rest, or best understood in a state of equilibrium.

There are obvious difficulties with the direct translation of agent-based modelling undertaken in a laboratory to organisational life, and with the ambiguity of some sociological theory. However, I am suggesting that these investigations into uncertainty produce explanations which are more congruent with my own experience of organisational life than theories based on predictability and control. I have tried to give examples throughout the book of how idealised, abstract theories based on linear cause and effect are often disrupted by the interplay of intentions of actors in any particular organisational drama. However, it is important to point out that I am not claiming that undertaking strategy is a waste of time, nor am I claiming that there is no point in planning. What I am suggesting is that strategising and planning are much more provisional activities than we normally take them to be, no matter how much we are open to being flexible with our plans. I am also claiming that strategy is enacted as managers engage with each other and their different interpretations of what they take reality to be. Strategy emerges between people as they co-operate and compete in complex responsive ways.

Implications for Planning and Performance Management

This insight is different from the widely accepted nostrum that plans can simply be adjusted to negative and positive feedback to a new state of equilibrium. Many strategy and planning activities in organisations are undertaken based on ideas of alignment, or realignment: so individual workplans are assumed to fit within departmental workplans, which should fit within organisational workplans towards an idea of optimal functioning. I understand the more systematic studies of non-linear phenomena to suggest that there is no such thing as optimal functioning. Rather, we are always working with imperfect information in an imperfect way, experimenting and improvising as our actions and intentions interweave with those of others. Moreover, novelty arises from sometimes bizarre and eccentric behaviour which we might take to be an improvisational response to the constraints of a particular situation, rather than through conforming to a pre-reflected plan. Not all of these improvisational actions will be successful, but we can only ascribe value, to estimate what we think has been successful, in retrospect. If the future is radically unpredictable it cannot be immediately obvious what a successful strategy or course of action would be in advance of acting.

Additionally, I have been arguing throughout the book for a different way of understanding how we are absorbed in the game of organisational and social life. We find ourselves competing and co-operating with others which in no way sustains the idea that we are following rational strategies that we work out in advance of acting. Our *habitus*, our feel for the game, is an embodied often unconscious response to the situations in which we find ourselves caught up, often struggling to control our own affective engagement which, according to Elias (1939/2000), is operating blindly. We are capable at the same time of taking a 'detour via detachment' which allows us to a limited extent to notice the game we are playing, and this can enable us to play more skilfully to our own advantage, or to the advantage of the group to which we belong. This is very different from saying that we are able to work out a game plan in advance of playing, however, and will know what a good strategy is in advance of participating. As the boxer Mike Tyson once observed; 'everyone has a plan until they get hit'.

I think these insights have profound implications for strategy-making, as I have described in the previous chapter, but also for the idea of performance management. Performance management is a term which is used to describe the panoply of management interventions, from the activities of boards of

directors through to the senior management team and managers throughout
the organisation to develop and supervise the work. Employees in most
organisations have appraisals at least annually where they are evaluated and/
or rewarded against pre-reflected targets. Successful appraisal can bring about
advancement in the organisation and sometimes greater reward. But in the
light of the previous discussion about the problems posed by trying to predict
a radically unpredictable future, exactly what is it that we are rewarding? I
will demonstrate below that the dominant understanding of performance
management, as taken up in organisations for the individuals who work in
them, rests on exactly the same paradigm of predictability and control that
we have been critiquing throughout this book. If novelty emerges not from
conformity with a fixed strategy but from improvisation and possibly deviant
behaviour, what are the consequences for managing employee performance
against standards which are set in advance?

The following section reviews the literature on performance management
particularly as it is understood in the context of managing and supervising
individual employees. As with other topics covered in this book, the performance
management literature is prolific and touches a number of different domains:
knowledge management, evaluation, management information systems
and broader human resource development concerns. In this chapter we will
confine our discussion to the implication of performance management for the
management of people and what they do in their day-to-day work.

The Performance Management Literature

The performance management literature explores the case that systematic
managerial intervention with employees and the way they do their jobs makes
a difference to overall organisational performance. According to the Chartered
Institute of Personnel and Development (CIPD) in the UK:

> *The overall purpose of performance management is to contribute to the
> achievement of high performance by the organisation and its people.
> 'High performance' means reaching and exceeding stretching targets
> for the delivery of productivity, quality, customer service, growth,
> profits and shareholder value.*
>
> *(Armstrong and Baron, 2005)*

To a greater or lesser degree the idea turns on questions concerning how to secure employee commitment and motivation. The concept of performance management is now widely taken up in organisations, and according to Kersely, Alpin and Forth et al. (2006) is used in two-thirds of all organisations with ten or more employees in the UK. It arises out of what Wood and Wall (2007) consider to be seminal arguments for management intervention to secure high worker involvement, such as Walton's 'high commitment management' (1985), and Lawler's 'high involvement management' (1986). That is, Walton and Lawler claim that higher employee commitment leads to lower turnover, a greater capacity for innovation and more flexible employees. For the quality of work movement, the securing of employee involvement was considered an end in itself and manifested itself in job enrichment, making jobs more interesting and diverse, and encouraging employee voices. If workers were fully involved, had high levels of discretion in their jobs and contributed to decision-making it was assumed that they would be highly intrinsically motivated. The role of managers in the performance management relationship was to mediate the extent of employee autonomy and development within the needs of the company. Over the last three decades, however, this understanding of performance management seems to have changed.

In tracing the evolution of how performance management is conceived, Wood and Hall claim that it has more recently been heavily influenced by resource-based views of the company (Barney, 1991, 1995) so that it is now much less committed to worker involvement. They make the case that performance management is currently much more concerned with job redesign, employee flexibility and extrinsic motivation of employees through performance-related pay. This more instrumentalist tone is typified by, for example, The Harvard Business Essentials volume *Performance Management* (2006). Good performance management is seen as a method of weeding out sub-optimal behaviour and punishing 'underperforming' employees, and makes no bones about the fact that 'slackers' should be sacked. The conceptual underpinnings of the Harvard approach is broadly realist in its assumptions, and restates the supposed logical connection between vision, mission, values and strategy that we have been setting out in this book as a taken for granted idea in the orthodox management texts. An organisation can be thought of as a whole, which can then be disaggregated into parts. The orientation of good performance management, then is to align the parts and whole. Through alignment comes greater coherence and focus:

Every company, every operating unit, and every employee needs goals
and plans for achieving them … The real power of these cascading
goals is their alignment with the purposes of the organisation. Every
employee in this arrangement should understand his or her goals, how
assigned activities advance the goals of the unit, and how the unit's
activities contribute to the strategic objective of the enterprise. Thus,
goal alignment focuses all the energy of the business on the things that
matter most.

(Ibid.: 2006: 5)

The volume is predicated on the idea of gap-closing and accountability.
The first idea suggests that it is possible to identify the ideal and then compare
and contrast current performance with this ideal and close the gap between the
two. The ideal can be logically derived from the vision and strategy. Meanwhile,
having committed to ideal targets, the subordinate is then held accountable
by the manager for meeting them. The idea that performance management
involves alignment and encouraging a positive orientation in employees (the
cult of positivity which we have explored in previous chapters) is widespread
in much contemporary performance management literature (Buytendijk, 2008;
Dresner, 2007).

In a similar systemic vein, de Waal (2007) encourages managers to adopt
strategic performance management. It is strategic because it underpins the
organisation's strategy and helps it achieve fitness to an ever-changing
environment. He understands strategic performance management to be a
natural development from previous management control and information
systems, which collect information mostly in quantitative terms to support
decision-making. It is more sophisticated than information systems and
control but is still predicated on managerial certainty through steering and
controlling the organisation towards continuous improvement, as though
what improvement might look like is known in advance. This is achieved by
formulating the mission, strategy and objectives of the organisation, translating
objectives to the various management levels of the company, measuring
these objectives using critical success factors (CSFs), key performance
indicators (KPIs), or a balanced score card (BSC), and then taking quick
corrective action based on regular reporting on indicator results. All employees
need to demonstrate performance-driven behaviour, which means for de Waal
goal-oriented behaviour. 'Individual responsibilities, targets and incentives
should be aligned with the strategic objectives of the organisation' (2007: 239).
He adduces research to show that nine performance management analysis

dimensions produce improved company performance, and that each of the dimensions is as important as the other.

De Waal bases his performance alignment model (PAM) on the idea of competencies, an idea derived from cognitive psychology. A competency is a category of ideal behaviour which an individual is thought to be able to acquire or demonstrate. He rehearses some criticisms of a competency approach raised by others, but leaves the matter unresolved as to whether they should or should not be used as the basis for a performance management approach. In one of his case studies he also points to some of the difficulties that have arisen as a result of introducing a performance management system: functional divisions set objectives which seemed to cut across those of other divisions and also facilitated a bunker mentality. Moreover, in the first instance objectives were set by top management at a very abstract level which did not make much sense to workers further down the hierarchy. However, over time, three to five years de Waal claims, the employees were able to 'own' the performance measures which made them feel 'empowered'. Empowerment in de Waal's terms is having the necessary information to do your job better and strive for continuous improvement. This is another example of the way that power often gets taken up in orthodox management texts, which I first pointed to in Chapter 2 on consultancy: as a commodity which managers can choose to use to good effect. It is important to note the circular nature of the discussion of power in de Waal's text, which verges on a double bind for the employees: workers can become empowered when they accept the dominance of the ideas to which they are subjected as being useful for their empowerment.

In as much as people and what they do day-to-day appear at all in de Waal's account, they do so in a highly individualised way with little recognition of the role of groups, political processes or power relationships in organisations. Performance management for de Waal is a largely unproblematic exercise. He mentions politics twice, once in the context of discussing politicians' influence over public sector performance management: difficulties with politicians can be resolved through negotiation. The second time he refers to power and politics is in relation to developing countries, which he describes as having powerful groups which impose and institutionalise social and economic norms. In developing countries employees are likely to have low 'self-efficacy', which means that they will attribute their own lack of effectiveness to external factors. De Waal does not make it clear why he thinks these two observations apply only to developing countries alone and why he does not understand his own role as being part of a powerful group, management consultants, who are busily imposing social and economic norms on other people. One way of understanding de Waal's treatment of power, is that he is mostly blind to it, and particularly the way he himself exercises power in taking up the mantle of performance management expert.

Not all performance management literature banishes employees and their development and motivation entirely from consideration. Purcell, Kinnie, Hutchinson et al. (2003) for example, are interested in the psychological contract between employees and their organisations and how to unlock the 'black box' of employee commitment. They are concerned with what is termed 'productive discretionary behaviour':

> *Discretionary behaviour refers to the choices that people make about how they carry out their work and the amount of effort, care, innovation and productive behaviour they display. It is the difference between people just doing a job and people doing a great job.*
>
> *(Ibid.: 2003)*

Following a study of 18 knowledge-intensive industries over a three-year study, the authors concluded that managerial intervention alone is unlikely to make employees perform better, since their engagement with the company is discretionary. Encouraging good performance turns on a negotiation over what is best for the company and what is best for the employee, which may not be coterminous. For Purcell, Kinnie, Hutchinson et al., a prescriptive list of best practice measures are unlikely to be successful. Meanwhile Snape and Redman (2010) anticipate that the current instrumental emphasis on job design will squeeze out employees' ability to respond flexibly in their jobs and diminishes what they term organisational citizenship behaviour. By citizenship behaviour they mean employees engaging in behaviours that support other colleagues to find better ways of working. Equally, in a more reflective account, Fletcher (2008) notes that many employees experience performance appraisal as disempowering, top-down and focused on ends rather than means and can be more ready to explore the shortcomings of performance management. For example, he is open to the idea that employees quickly learn how to assume or claim the competencies that the performance management interview is aimed at evaluating; 'it does not take much intelligence to "manufacture" convincing episodes showing how one demonstrated achievement orientation, interpersonal sensitivity, etc., the danger of synthetic evidence seems very real' (2008: 138). Moreover, he is also aware that when managing professional groups a manager cannot expect simple alignment between the values of the professional and the values of the organisation, given that any professional discipline will have its own values to which the professional may owe their own allegiance.

THE EVIDENCE FOR PERFORMANCE MANAGEMENT

So does a performance management approach indeed increase the performance of companies? Torrington, Hall and Taylor (2005) argue that the causal relationship between performance management approaches and company performance is contested. The studies which have attempted to establish a causal link have used a variety of different indicators and largely analyses to establish the link. These range from assessing the company's financial performance, to trying to gauge wastage and turnover, through to asking respondents what they think of performance management. In general, studies have used complex statistical analyses to establish a causal relationship and yet, according to Torrington, Hall and Taylor, the evidence is still inconclusive. Scholars such as Richardson and Thompson (1999) while suggesting something of a causal link, argue that: 'It is unlikely that merely adopting a specified set of HR policies is the high road to organisational success' (1999: 30). Equally Guest, Michie, Conway an Sheehan (2003) see the relationship between performance management of employees and company performance as very problematic, and raise questions about whether commitment and motivation can really be managed. In a review of 387 scholarly papers to explore the link between performance management as a tool of human resource management (HRM) and performance improvement Hyde, Boaden, Cortvriend et al. (2006) concluded: 'There is very little about *how* or *why* HRM is linked to performance.'

In the health sector Walburg, Bevan, Wilderspin et al. (2005) note the way in which outcome management, a discipline which seeks to improve the health outcomes for patients, has seen the application of business concepts of 'performance management' to health care, where previously it was concerned more with clinical outcomes alone. They argue that studies do not allow hard conclusions about the extent to which outcome management improves health care results, but do seem to indicate the regular feedback to health professionals helps them function better. Instead they make the case that in the health domain performance management is aimed primarily at the support of clinical practice. Meanwhile, as far as other not-for profit enterprises are concerned Paton (2003) notes the problematic nature of many performance management systems based on the wholesale and unreflected importation of concepts from the private sector. Instead he regards it as a promising sign if 'performance is accepted as multi-faceted, contested, contingent and provisional' (2003: 164).

Summary of the Literature

Overwhelmingly the performance management literature is realist and written from the perspective of managers, taking for granted the idea of cascading goals which are logically derivable from the organisation's strategic goals. The task of management, then, is to bring about alignment of the parts and the whole, the individual goals of employees and the goals set for the whole organisation, in order to achieve strategic intent, which is usually understood as a fit between the organisation and its environment. The role of managers is to design systems and 'create cultures' where optimum employee motivation and commitment can be achieved. In the chapter on values (Chapter 6), I pointed out how difficult it is to 'shape and design' organisational culture.

The literature is more or less open to the social and psychological implications of managing people, and equally, is more or less punitive in its intent. So the Harvard Business School appears to be in agreement with the authors of *Built to Last* (Collins and Porras, 2005): those that do not conform to the cult, the 'slackers', should be sacked. This implies that one can impel people to be motivated. Meanwhile, de Waal (2007) understands performance management simply as a technical and rational exercise of achieving maximum alignment through optimisation. The managerial task is to recruit the right employees with the right competences and to set and measure the right objectives. For de Waal, strategies often do not work in organisations because managers simply do not follow through to the level of the individual employee. Commonly, performance management is understood in these highly individualised terms, with little space given to the idea of ensemble performance. Equally, managers are assumed to be blessed with the ability to communicate effectively, create the right culture and instil the right values in staff, notions with which we have engaged critically in previous chapters. Employee 'empowerment' in these terms is being given the information that managers think is best for them to have to do their jobs, and then believing it.

Other scholars, from a minority but more critical position, are more aware of the difficulties inherent in performance management because the interest of employees and employers are not the same (Purcell, Kinnie, Hutchinson et al., 2003), or because of the ability of employees to game the system

(Fletcher, 2008), and because of the problematic nature of performance measures themselves. Scholars in the more critical tradition are concerned with themes of power, value conflict, and cultural and social variation which are often absent from the dominant discourse. They are more open to the idea that employees can experience performance management as something of an empty exercise, imposed from above, as merely a ritual to be endured, or as a construct which supports a managerialist discourse (Legge, 2001). Some scholars (Snape and Redman, 2010) note the change in focus of the performance management literature away from job enrichment and staff development for its own sake towards a more prescriptive emphasis on the needs of the organisation. The dangers of this shift are that it will inhibit the very 'citizenship behaviours' which managers would do well to encourage.

Even those scholars who consider performance management to be an unproblematic activity still acknowledge that it will need anything up to three to five years before it will show any results. Aggregate studies of the literature reveal that there is no one best way of working (Purcell, Kinnie, Hutchinson et al., 2003; Richardson and Thompson, 1999) that performance of the company also depends on stakeholders outside the company (Swart, Kinnie and Rabinowitz, 2007), and that there is a prevalence of fads and fashions which will not guarantee success. It is clear that despite the ambiguous and problematic nature of performance management and its link to company performance, the ideas have been widely taken up in the public and not-for-profit sector, presumably with the same mixed results. A number of scholars point to the importance of a manager's interaction with the people they manage, which can have a positive effect on the way those employees carry out their work. Beyond this minimal statement of the obvious, there is little we can point to in the form of a stable body of knowledge which would be helpful for a manager to know how they should interact with their employees and to what effect.

Complexity and the Implications for Performance Management

In previous chapters drawing on theories of complexity from a natural and social science perspective I have mounted a critique of what I have termed the dominant discourse of management literature. This latter assumes that managers and leaders have a special ability to design optimal change in their organisations by setting out a vision, instilling the necessary values in staff and shaping the organisational culture to suit the required outcome. Additionally, in Chapter 7 I made the case that there is no such thing as an optimal strategy, that innovation arises from deviant rather than from conformist behaviour, and that value can only be assigned retrospectively to novel approaches which may not have appeared to have value at the time. For me this immediately makes the task of performance management a lot more problematic, if performance is judged according to pre-reflected targets which are set in advance of employees undertaking the work. If the future is unknowable and we cannot know what an optimal strategy will be, how does it make sense to oblige employees to work to certain targets and outcomes?

I have encountered a frequent complaint from staff in organisations who feel that the annual encounter over the fulfilment of objectives is a lifeless and pointless exercise, an observation which the critical literature on performance management would support. Often their job has moved on and changed so much that the objectives are no longer relevant. Rather than focusing on what the worker is doing, the performance management conversation hinges on the question as to why previously set objectives have not been achieved.

In an environment where there is competition between companies, between not-for-profits for funds, or where there is a greater focus on how tax revenues are being translated into public services, managers in organisations are legitimately asking themselves how they can invite their employees to contribute to making a greater difference to the work that the organisation is attempting to do. It may also be the case that in very routine jobs it would make sense to set simple targets as a basis for talking about what an employee is doing. However, my assumption would be that there are fewer and fewer jobs which are merely routine, particularly considering the current rhetoric about economies needing autonomous 'knowledge workers' who are both highly skilled and highly adaptive. It seems to be hard to reconcile this admittedly idealised rhetoric about the needs of a twenty-first-century economy with the dominant way of thinking which frames 'good' management as based on assumptions of alignment with pre-determined objectives. At the same time that employees are encouraged to align and conform, they are also, and perhaps ironically, invited to be creative, innovative and autonomous. This seems to me to be a kind of double bind given that the idea of innovation and creativity suggests elements of surprise and the unexpected which management methods based in concepts of predictability and control seem intent on managing away. Performance management based on predicting the unpredictable can feel like tying ourselves up in knots.

Instead of trying to dig the same hole deeper, like de Waal, by assuming that strategies fail because of managers' inability to follow through in controlling the individual employee according to strict, logically-derived targets, I am going to pursue a different line of argument. This rejects the idea of an organisation as a collection of discrete individuals acting rationally according to targets they choose or are chosen for them, and understands it instead as an ensemble of actors absorbed in the game they are playing with others. Following on from arguments made in Chapter 7, I will make the case that employees are improvising creatively on a daily basis as they adapt to the intentions and actions of others, constrained by relationships of power. It is through this improvisation that the global patterning that we might refer to as strategy is realised, which we can only make sense of retrospectively. This releases the notion of performance from the straitjacket of predictability and restores some of the creative and spontaneous implications that we would normally associate with an artistic performance. The argument partially turns on a different understanding of time in human interaction.

Time, Improvisation, Local and Global

In Chapter 7, drawing on Mead and Bourdieu, we explored the way that agents in social interaction are obliged to adapt to each other informed by their history of interaction. I mentioned that this is what Bourdieu meant by this theory of *habitus*, our historically sedimented, embodied sense of how to act with others. But Bourdieu understands the logic of practice to be operating according to a different kind of logic and temporality to that of science. Natural science, he argues, attempts to derive predictive rules which are true at all times, and in all places: they aspire to being universal. The methods assume an if-then causality which reduces or eliminates variables including context and time. However, for Bourdieu, practice is probabilistic rather than predictive and is conditioned by the variables of both context and time: 'to reintroduce uncertainty is to reintroduce time …' (1990: 99). In other words, the two factors excluded by orthodox natural science in deriving universal rules about the natural world, context and time, have to be reconsidered if we want to have a more complete understanding of practice.

In setting out the importance of the role of time in his theory of action Bourdieu is drawing on a tradition of thought which originated with St Augustine (1998: 354–430) in Book X of the meditations. We live, argued St Augustine in the 'present of the past, present of the present and present of the future' (Book X, *Memory* and Book XI, *Time and Eternity*). That is to say, the meaning of an act takes place in the present and in the complex interplay of a reinterpreted history and an anticipated future which the act provokes. The meaning that we ascribe to our actions arises iteratively and cyclically as new events oblige us to reinterpret the past and reframe our expectations of the future. Equally, for Bourdieu, time is not a transcendent reality anterior to and independent of action: it shapes action and is shaped by it, which allows for completely different interpretations of action. In his reflections on the gift-giving traditions of the Kabyle people, Bourdieu observed that:

> *It is all a matter of style, which means in this case timing and choice of occasions; the same act – giving, giving in return, offering one's services, paying a visit, etc. – can have completely different meanings at different times, coming as it may at the right or wrong moment, opportunely or inopportunely.*
>
> *(1990: 105)*

What giving a particular gift 'means' is entirely dependent upon the cycle of giving and reciprocation in which it takes place: it cannot be interpreted context- and history-free. We can only negotiate the meaning of an action, Bourdieu is arguing, from within an interpretation of historical context. Practice for Bourdieu has its own logic which is inherent to the practice: there is no reference to a standard outside the practice itself, and the practice cannot be reduced to a set of rules which can be applied to another set of circumstances. We come to see ourselves, and others, anew as we constantly reinterpret and adapt to our improvisation of gesture and response, constrained and enabled by the relationships of power between us. The daily, improvisational performance of employees adapting to their circumstances and to each other operates according to its own very different logic to that of performance targets for employees, which are usually derived logically from a broader set of objectives set for organisations. In most schemes for performance management, employees are judged against criteria derived prior to action, separate from what they will find themselves obliged to do in situ.

Again making a parallel with arguments in the domain of natural science, Ilya Prigogine, the Nobel prize-winning physicist mentioned in the Chapter 7, also draws attention to the importance of time if we are to understand creativity and emergence. In his book *The End of Certainty* (1997) he asks the perennial question as to whether the future is given or whether it is under perpetual construction. Prigogine reaches for the second law of thermodynamics, entropy, to argue that in the natural world there is an arrow of time which is uni-directional. The second law of thermodynamics predicts that any isolated system will lose heat as it 'goes forward' over time. Time, then, becomes a significant factor in the calculation: in deterministic equations in physics the terms t and $-t$ can be used interchangeably, with the future equally determined, or undetermined as the past. In contradistinction to deterministic science where time, as Einstein once had it, is an 'illusion', Prigogine points to a number of natural processes where circumstances are far from equilibrium, like evolution, radioactive decay, the weather, where the processes are irreversible. There is then a present which is informed by the past, but the movement towards the future is probabilistic rather than predetermined and arises as a consequence of chance, small deviations and resonance between an ensemble of agents interacting together.

It seems to me that many performance management processes in organisations there is a similar belief in determinism which needs challenging: there is a presumption that we are in control of our bodies and our actions, and that what we do is a product of our conscious and rational application. We conceive of what we are going to do, and then we do it, or more likely in organisations, senior managers set objectives which are then fulfilled by employees. Performance management becomes a process of correcting employees' efforts towards the ideal and deterministic path that has already been rationally chosen.

Another way of understanding 'performance' would be to conceive of it as the necessary improvisation that employees will be obliged to enact as they take up generalised objectives in their particular context. As they try to act with intention they will find themselves behaving in particular ways, simply because of the way they have been acculturated, and will be obliged to respond to others in an improvisational give and take. In this situation, what the particular employee is trying to achieve is not the only thing going on, particularly if they are trying to achieve things with others who have their own objectives. A manager might be concerned not just with whether the employee has achieved 'results' but how they interacted with others in the process and what happened as a consequence. Outcomes of improvisation are likely to be probable, rather than certain. In soliciting from the employee what has happened as a result of them acting with intention, it may make what Bourdieu terms 'the necessary improvisation' that they have become involved with much more explicit. In taking up the challenge of meeting their objectives they may have come across more important things to be doing than what was presupposed. This could be more innovative and important than the set of objectives which was being followed.

Usually in contemporary organisations 'accountability' is taken quite narrowly to mean being held to account for fulfilling our pre-determined objectives. Another way of thinking about how we might hold each other to account could be to come to understand the word 'accountability' as the way in which employees give an account of what they have done and why, rather than describing in a more limited way whether they have hit a particular target or not. In the interaction between us we need to offer each other reasons why we have acted as we have. If managers tend towards taking a greater interest in means as well as ends, in the kinds of improvisations that have been necessary to do the work, then they will be following Prigogine's insights that the future is not inscribed in the present and sets of objectives only constitute a best guess at a particular point in time about what might be important to do in the future.

Power and Resistance in Organisations

I continue to be intrigued that according to scholars writing from a more realist perspective, any perceived failure of performance management is simply down to not following through to the logical conclusion. I am also interested in their blindness to the power of their own position as 'experts' on 'strategic performance management', that is to say if it is 'strategic' it is somehow much more important than mundane performance management (see de Waal, 2007 above). Somehow a realist and rationalist perspective covers over an ability to come to terms with performance management as a form of scrutiny and domination. Employees may resist and game the system because they feel so dominated.

Narrative

I was asked to facilitate an international conference for a multinational company and my facilitation was not going well, according to the managers who had contracted me. We had agreed an agenda comprising various workshops, but because one of the exercises we had agreed had taken longer than expected, and I had thought it important to let participants finish having their say, one exercise had taken the time allocated for another. The reason for things taking longer was that for many of the conference attendees English was not their first language and it sometimes took them a while for them to express themselves. In the competing priorities of what should take precedence, the agenda we had agreed before the event, or the situation that presented itself as a result of following said agenda, for me the choice was clear. It was far more important for participants to feel recognised and heard than it was to keep to time, which had only been a best guess anyway. From my point of view there was no problem about this, we would simply do fewer things more intensively. From the perspective of my contractor, we had agreed what we had agreed and there was to be no deviation. Anything less than this was unprofessional.

There followed a semi-public criticism of the way that I was doing my job by a senior manager in the conference as he expressed his anxiety that we would not be able to stick to the agenda, although at that stage of proceedings there was still plenty of time to achieve what we had committed to.

Throughout the next couple of days I was approached by four different people who had witnessed what had happened to me and came to tell me their own, similar stories of having been managed in the organisation, which all of them had understood as a form of bullying. There was something about the way they had experienced my public shaming which called out a resonance in them.

One manager, a senior figure in the organisation, had taken on a new role in the South African office. She had been set objectives before arriving, but in starting work in the office had been confronted with a team that was at war with itself. She spent the next weeks trying to sort out the high level of conflict between colleagues so that they could concentrate on what they were all supposed to be doing. This involved sacking some people, hiring others and beginning to work in a way that made the team more productive. It was not an easy job.

When it came to her annual appraisal her boss was only interested in whether she had fulfilled her objectives or not, and was singularly unimpressed by how she had spent her time. From her manager's perspective, he would be judged on whether he in his turn had fulfilled his objectives, one of which was to see that she had fulfilled hers. In the world of cascading, nested objectives, everyone found themselves bearing down on the next person in the line so that they might 'deliver their outcomes'.

Discussion of the Narrative

Clearly all of the managers in the narrative I describe had some degree of choice in how they responded to what they understood as the organisation's imperatives, as did I. However, it is easy to see how a particular understanding of professionalism and performance, that of delivering to the letter what has been agreed, when it becomes the only way of understanding, can be experienced as bullying and oppression. A particular view, with the attendant anxiety about this view prevailing as the only view, gave rise to feelings of shame and humiliation for me and my temporary colleagues.

A performance management process is a way of exercising control, a means of mediating what senior managers might think the organisation needs to achieve and what employees think is possible in their particular circumstances. Broadly, senior managers are paid to take a general view of what an organisation 'should' be doing, while employees are obliged to respond to this series of 'should's from their own contexts with a greater or lesser ability.

It is exactly this conflict between the universal and the contextual which the social anthropologist James C. Scott explored in *Seeing Like a State* (1998). The book is a reflection on what Scott calls 'high modernism', which is a faith he thinks is shared by a variety of engineers, planners, politicians, administrators and architects who envision wholesale rational engineering of social life in order to improve the human condition. For Scott it is a strong version of belief in scientific and technical progress associated with industrialisation in Western Europe and North America since the 1830s which wants to control nature, and human nature. High modernism is 'a particularly sweeping vision of how the benefits of technical and scientific progress might be applied – usually by the state – in every field of human activity' (1998: 91). This form of high modernism depends upon making simplifications, abstractions and generalisations from a rich background of complex activity. In the book Scott gives a number of examples, from cadastral map-making through to city planning and revolutionary politics, where the ideals of techno-rational science are pursued with muscular authoritarianism. Simplifications are required, Scott argues, in order for social realities to be legible to state regulators who sit at a distance. But more than this, the effect of creating abstractions and simplifications of complex social reality is to attempt to transform that social reality at the same time. The issuing of land title deeds, for example, describes a simplified form or reality but impacts upon that reality at the same time, changing the power relationships between people.

For Scott, adherents of the ideology of high modernism are imbued with hubris. For them the emphasis is always on the future since the past is something to be transcended. There is often a heavy reliance on visual images of heroic progress towards a transformed future, with progress objectified into a series of preconceived goals, largely material and quantifiable. Similarities with the theoretical underpinnings of Ackoff's (1999) idealised design method will not be lost on readers of the previous chapter on strategy. Moreover, Scott argues, high modernists are impatient with politics, since resistance and political contestation threatens to undermine techno-rational solutions for human improvement. In general, despite the often liberal inclinations of modernisers, the ends justify the means.

Scott argues, like Bourdieu, that social practices operate according to a different logic, given that they are largely inherited and shaped by social and family structure, values and power relations. In this sense it is not driven by rational scientific considerations, but rather the reasonable expectations of other human beings practising similarly. To understand how people interrelate is to become aware of the gap between general and situated knowledge. What guides local and specific action, according to Scott is the ancient Greek concept of *mētis*, or situated knowledge driven by gut feeling, sometimes 'cunning reason'. So a river pilot is able to guide boats on the basis of experience and judgement. This is learning by trial and error, a process of self-correcting approximations of a particular river in a particular location subject to different water levels and seasons. The parallel that he makes with language is that *mētis* is no more derivative of general rules than speech is of formal grammar. Scott makes a distinction between *mētis* and episteme, pure reason or mathematical knowledge, and *techne*, the practical application of pure knowledge, often organised analytically into small, logical steps. *Techne* is impersonal, universal and impervious to context. We are most reliant on *mētis*, Scott argues, when we undertake virtually any complex task involving many variables, particularly when those variables include not just the material environment but social interaction as well.

Previously in Chapter 3, I mentioned the work of Bent Flyvbjerg who had another way of understanding what employees are obliged to do at work, also drawing on an Aristotelian concept of *phronesis*. *Phronesis*, usually translated as practical reason, is the judgement that experienced people bring to bear on particular situations by asking the question: how does my rule of thumb become a particular way of working in this specific situation? Because *phronetic* judgement is particular and contextual, Aristotle argued, it could not be

thought of as being scientific according to the standards of science set out by
Plato. *Mētis*, 'cunning reason', and *phronesis* are two different ways of coming
at what Bourdieu meant by 'a feel for the game', our embodied and instinctive
feel for what we have to do in any particular social situation.

According to Scott, capitalist profit requires a combination of efficiency
and control, and this has led to the subordination, not to say the suppression of
mētis in many social contexts, including in the workplace. As an example, Scott
refers to the work of the early management theorist Frederick Taylor, whom I
mentioned in Chapter 1 who set about regulating the autonomous knowledge
of artisans into more suitable units of labour to increase factory productivity
from the factory-owner's perspective. Technical plans for the reordering of
social life depend upon what Scott terms 'thin simplifications' and by doing
so they are in danger of covering over the very elements which are essential to
their functioning: 'The more schematic, thin, and simplified the formal order,
the less resilient and the more vulnerable to disturbances outside its narrow
parameters' (Scott, 1998: 351).

Scott is not arguing against the application of technical knowledge based
in abstractions and generalisations for the improvement of human wellbeing.
Rather, he welcomes them and makes the case that there are few of us who would
prefer to return to times prior to the implementation of large-scale schemes for
human development. However, he is pointing to the danger of the inherent
authoritarianism of such schemes and the way that they are implemented which
can suppress the very conditions of their realisation. That is, people will need
to take up these generalisations locally, using their practical local knowledge in
mutually adaptive ways with others. What happens when people feel obliged
to comply with schemes of understanding which they feel does not square
with their experience or their values, as Scott explored in a previous volume
(1990), is that they resist. Their resistance may be overt, or covert: the more
aggressive the attempt to oblige people to conform to a particular scheme, the
richer the corresponding resistance. Scott draws the distinction between the
public transcript, which is the narrative of the dominant order and the 'hidden
transcript', those hidden narratives of resistance and rebellion which exist in
opposition to the governing regime.

Resistance in organisations takes place whenever changes are proposed
by managers, such as restructurings or reorganisations, or when schemes
of management such as performance management are carried out in a way
which attempts to cover over or control employees' 'necessary improvisation'.

Any grand plan or attempt to control is likely to provoke a variety of political stratagems by those about to be affected by them, as they struggle to gain some political or resource advantage from the process. People may not just be manoeuvring for personal gain, but may also be acting politically to protect the work which they consider to be valuable. While senior managers are attempting to 'see like a state', in broad, abstract and simplified terms, managers lower down the hierarchy are more likely to know the details of what happens and will form different judgements about what is and is not worth changing or preserving. There will be gossip, the shifting of alliances and groupings and subversion as employees collaborate and compete to affect the outcome. Political gaming and ploys, which rarely figure in orthodox accounts of management, are the norm rather than the exception, particularly in times of change but also when supervisory processes like performance management are taken up more or less vigorously. It is not that performance management works, rather it is made to work both by the supervising manager and the employee in the games that they get drawn into playing with each other.

Summary of the Argument So Far

I have pointed to the problematic nature of many theories of performance management which are written uncritically from the perspective of the manager and rest upon assumptions of predictability control. Despite the uncertainty in the research as to whether performance management processes make any difference to company performance, nonetheless companies persist with them and they have permeated the public and not-for-profit sectors. Beyond the obvious justification that one could make that it is always preferable for a manager to take an interest in the way the people they manage are working, one could be forgiven for thinking that performance management persists because it helps sustain the illusion that managers are acting rationally and are in control. Bourdieu was once asked in an interview why he thought there was such strong resistance to the idea that social practice arises from *habitus*, historically ingrained bodily dispositions to act in particular ways, rather than rational intent, and he concluded the following:

> *The answer is, I think, that it collides head on with the illusion of (intellectual) mastery of oneself that is so deeply ingrained in intellectuals.*
>
> *(Bourdieu and Wacquant, 1992: 132)*

Accepting the limitations of our ability to choose and predict is inherently identity-threatening. Moreover, with the setting of objectives for employees which are used as a reward or punishment the case for managerialism is sustained through the explicit manifestation of power relations. Perhaps the institutionalisation of performance management has less to do with 'driving up performance' and much more to do with the proliferation of apparatuses of surveillance and scrutiny which pervade many organisations and society in general.

In the preceding section I have tried to highlight the mismatch in thinking between the rational–technical assumptions of contemporary performance management, and the local, contingent and specific reality of social practices, which operate according to a different logic and privileges time and context. By drawing on Bourdieu and Scott I have tried to make the argument that performance management has three main weaknesses. It presumes an ability to choose an optimal organisational strategy and logically derive department and individual work objectives: I am making the case instead that the future is radically uncertain and cannot be predicted with a sufficient degree of accuracy. Second, these strategies are based on what Scott calls 'thin simplifications' which are in turn rendered into thin objectives which reduce often complex requirements into so-called measurable targets. When managers reduce complex realty in this way they are likely to cover over and even suppress the very contingent and context-specific social practices which help realise the strategies that are put forward. In order to fulfil any objectives workers will be obliged to improvise in their contexts with particular others and respond to the game they are obliged to play. They will of course also be obliged to take up their objectives, but this will be only one of the things that will be going on for them. And third, when aggressively pursued, schemes of performance management are likely to call out subversion, rebellion or gaming strategies from staff that Fletcher (2008) identifies in his book. Employees will pretend submission but practice subversion more or less openly.

In the narrative I described above I experienced exactly what Scott alluded to in *Domination and the Arts of Resistance* (1990), where employees sought me out to tell me their 'hidden transcripts'. When employees experience a particular way of managing to be oppressive, they will organise against it, seeking out allies, gossiping and telling stories, sharing what it is they are obliged to do to carry out their jobs effectively.

Performance Management in the Public Sector

In most organisations it has become axiomatic that in order 'to drive up' organisational performance, some kind of performance management process is needed. It would be a brave manager or consultant who attempted to claim that there is no evidential basis for thinking that performance management schemes make any difference to the efficacy of organisations, or to point out that, on the contrary, performance management can contribute to feelings of demoralisation and perhaps poor performance, in the workplace. I would argue further that the assumptions underpinning performance management have completely transformed organisations, particularly in the public sector, and by no means necessarily for the better. They have influenced the kinds of services that public sector organisations develop, the way these are talked about, and what we choose to value. It seems to me that the move to 'see like a state' is in danger of hollowing out a rich interpretation of what we consider to be civic goods, which I will explore further below by drawing on two critics of the prevalent way of thinking about performance and targets in the public sector.

In reviewing the way that managerialism evolved under New Labour in Britain (Clarke and Newman, 2000), Janet Newman makes the case that it was taken up as a much more technocratic discipline with a heavy emphasis on performance targets. The Prime Minister set up something he called a 'Delivery Unit' in 2001 under Professor Michael Barber, which was to try and 'deliver' his most important policy outcomes. This led to a proliferation of other delivery units such as the 'Reform Delivery Unit' and the 'National Safeguarding Delivery Unit', where the intention is to set clear targets for managers of public sector services and to ensure that they meet them. The 13 years of the Labour government has led to widespread target setting and performance management in all aspects of public service with the goal of service improvement. Additionally, there is a whole apparatus of inspection and audit and cadres of managers whose job it is to ensure that targets are met and policies complied with. It has become an edifice of scrutiny and control.

John Seddon has mounted a critique of target setting by government in his book *Systems Thinking in the Public Sector* (2008). Targets, he argues oblige managers in the public sector to pay attention to the wrong things, what politicians require rather than what local service users need and this leads to perverse consequences. Targets prevent staff from dealing with the variety of what they encounter by obliging them to serve inflexible and pre-determined rules which have been set by someone else sitting outside the situation that local staff and managers are dealing with. Targets and performance measures arise out of an ideology of control and a pessimistic assessment of public sector staff: that if civil servants are not standing over them with exacting standards then somehow they won't do their jobs properly. It has resulted in what he describes as an army of bureaucrats whose job it is to specify, inspect and report compliance on targets and measures which are driving public services away from what the public really wants and needs. In these ways this approach has contributed hugely to waste and cost.

He describes the difficulty he has had of getting many of his ideas accepted because setting targets has become axiomatic – to suggest that setting targets is the cause of many of the problems rather than the solution to the problems is to present oneself as being eccentric. Seddon points to the ways in which other ungrounded ideological obsessions, that consumer 'choice' is the best way to develop services, that it is always a cheaper option, that the private sector will always deliver a better deal for service users, have come to dominate decision-making and management in the public sector.

Seddon's heroes are W. Edwards Deming (2000), who developed statistical techniques for better managing manufacturing processes, and the Toyota boss T. Ohno (1988). Ohno, for example, was deeply sceptical of 'best practice' regarding it as a kind of rigid thinking importing alien ideas from elsewhere. The key to developing work for Ohno was from within the work itself. What Seddon takes from these two management thinkers is their attention to work flow, rather than rules, and their prioritising of method. Developing a patient and detailed understanding of what it is you are dealing with, rather than coming up with answers in advance ('how can we set up a one stop shop?') is the only grounded and evidence-based way of improving services, according to Seddon. He would like to replace all the targets and measures with a simple question to all managers in the public sector; 'What measures are you using to help you understand and improve the work?' There are no other prescriptions than that.

In general he is using the term 'systems thinking' in contexts where there is a factory-like process, such as processing benefits or matching people on the housing waiting list with vacant properties, where systematic approaches to mapping how the work flows through an organisation is extremely helpful to thinking about how to respond to that work. It is a kind of business process mapping.

Where I part company with Seddon is with his prescription that the public sector can best be improved with better systems thinking, particularly if he means that an organisation can be thought of as a system, rather than the patterning of the interactions of many, many people, as we have been exploring in this book. When organisations are thought of as systems it often leads to organisational development initiatives where employees are treated as though they are parts of systems, which we have been discussing in previous chapters. It would be possible to make the argument that the thinking Seddon is criticising is also driven by systems thinking, although perhaps he would say that it is not systemic enough.

Similarly in the domain of education a report written by Professor Richard Pring, formerly of Oxford and Exeter universities (Pring, Hayward, Hodgson et al., 2009) on the education of 14–19-year-olds in Britain entitled *Education for All* points to the way that managerialism has shaped education. The authors claim that the reductive focus of the performance regime seriously diminishes what education has come to mean:

> As the language of management and performance has advanced, so we have proportionately lost a language of education which recognises the intrinsic value of pursuing certain types of question, or trying to make sense of reality (physical, social, economic and moral), of seeking understanding, of exploring through literature and the arts what it means to be human....
>
> (Ibid.: 2009)

The authors of the report take issue with the British government's apparent single-minded approach to education as the engine of economic development and success, where there is a pronounced emphasis on developing skills to serve the economy. This includes a relentless focus on setting learning objectives in advance of teaching classes, and trying to measure whether the objectives have been fulfilled or not.

Instead, the authors set out their alternative understanding of what constitutes a good education. An educated 19-year-old, should, the authors argue, be more aware of those qualities and attainments which make them distinctively human and the ways in which those qualities might be enhanced. They should have experienced intellectual development, meaning that they have entered into the world of ideas. They should have a practical capability, understand the importance of community participation, and have developed some degree of moral seriousness. In addition, young people should be exposed to ideals which encourage them to aim high, at the same time as developing an awareness of self in their relations with others. In sum:

> *That, then is the educated 19 year old: one who has a sufficient grasp of those ideas and principles to enable him or her to manage life intelligently, who has the competence and skills to tackle practical tasks including those for employment, who has a sense of community and the disposition to make a contribution to it, who is morally serious in the sense that he or she cares about fairness and responsibility to others, who is inspired by what has been done by others and might be done by oneself, and who has a sense of a knowledge of self – confident and resilient in the face of difficulty.*
>
> (Ibid.: 2009)

The difficulty with the current emphasis on performance and management, the authors argue, is that it hollows out this broad definition of education and is based on a spurious idea that teaching is a science. X input brings about Y output. As an alternative the authors set out the idea that teaching is a practice where ends are not separate from means: 'The end or purpose should be shown or captured in the very act of teaching. Teaching is a transaction between the teacher and the learner, not the delivery of something to the learner.'

At the heart of this report is the idea that education is an improvisational practice between teacher and learner, the outcome of which cannot be fully anticipated or predicted. It is also concerned with the development of important but less tangible processes such as moral awareness, fairness and civic responsibility which are not measurable, only describable. The report points to the way that a particular management regime increases the importance of some aspects of education and reduces the value of others. This has important consequences for the way that we educate our children.

I have set out in brief what both Seddon and Pring and colleagues have to say about target-setting and performance management as a counterweight to the prevailing ideology that there is no alternative to the way we are preceding. Additionally I think what they are pointing to is the way that a performance management regime does not just 'drive up performance' but does so in a particular way which privileges some ways of knowing and diminishes others. It begins to amplify the ability of the centre to control and works against local autonomy and the very conditions of the realisation of improvement as local managers and workers spend all their time on compliance, or gaming the system. There have been a number of high profile cases in the public sector in the UK where a hospital, for example, has on the one hand been able to produce a high score in terms of compliance with targets, yet on the other hand has allowed clinical standards to decline in a way which has proved life-threatening to patients. This is testament to the way in which performance management processes are made to work with more or less subversion and actual compliance as well as a salutary reminder about what may get ignored.

Conclusions and Implications for Managers

In this chapter I have engaged with the concept of performance management, an idea which is widely taken up in organisations with the intention of increasing organisational performance. Broadly speaking, managers logically derive a set of objectives from a strategy, and set targets for departments, units and individuals who work in them. I have argued that these objectives and targets rest on thin simplifications and are likely to suppress the very conditions of their own realisation. It is not that targets work in organisations, but they are made to work by employees acting honestly and dishonestly, playing the game, subverting the game and presenting the work they are doing to the good. The idea of performance management rests on assumptions of predictability and control as well as a highly individualised understanding of the contribution of employees to strategy. This leads in turn to further individualisation with schemes such as performance-related pay, where employees are rewarded for fulfilling their individual targets. Such schemes seem to be predicated on the idea that organisations comprise atomised individuals who achieve what they are doing despite what others are doing or perhaps in competition with them. It ignores the daily ensemble improvisation that is organisational life.

If the future is radically uncertain and strategy-making is at best a probabilistic exercise, what then is the point of setting tight objectives for employees (often conceived in SMART terms – specific, measurable, achievable, realistic and time-bound)? Where previously I have argued in this book that my critique of taken for granted ways of planning, for example, does not necessarily mean to say that I am against making plans provided that managers have a more critical understanding of what they are doing. Here I am happy to say that I am unequivocally against setting employees targets as part of performance management. The more complex the job, the less sense it makes to set targets. Targets and objectives are just as likely to get in the way of what needs to be done, to hinder as much as to help.

A good manager will take an interest in the work of the employees for whom they are responsible. However, they will enquire into how these employees perform with others, in the broadest sense of the word 'performance', meaning an improvisation undertaken by a group of people. A performance review would be an opportunity for a manager to sit with those they are responsible for to make sense of what has been happening, and for the employee to give an account of what they have found themselves doing, the expected, the unexpected and the unwanted. The manager and the person being managed will not always agree on the value of what the employee has been doing and this too will need stating explicitly. What a team of people find themselves doing in order to get the work done is as likely to inform strategy as the strategy is to inform the work.

References

Ackoff, R.L. (1999) *Ackoff's Best: His Classic Writings on Management*, New York: Wiley.

Apffel Marglin, F. and Marglin, S. (eds) (1990) *Dominating Knowledge: Development, Culture and Resistance*, Oxford: Clarendon.

Aristotle (2004), *The Nichomachean Ethics*, London: Penguin Books.

Armstrong, M. and Baron, A. (2005) *Managing Performance: Performance Management in Action*, London: Chartered Institute of Personnel and Development.

Barney, J. (1991) Firm resources and sustained competitive advantage', *Journal of Management*, 17: 99–120.

Barney, J. (1995) Looking inside for competitive advantage, *Academy of Management Executive*, 9: 49–61.

Bourdieu, P. (1977) *Outline of a Theory of Practice*, Cambridge: Cambridge University Press.

—— (1990) *The Logic of Practice*, Cambridge: Polity Press.

—— (1991) *Language and Symbolic Power*, Cambridge: Polity Press.

—— and Wacquant, L. (1992) *An Invitation to Reflexive Sociology*, Chicago: University of Chicago Press.

Buytendijk, F. (2008) *Performance Leadership: The Next Practices to Motivate Your People, Align Stakeholders, and Lead Your Industry*, London: McGraw-Hill.

Clarke, J. and Newman, J. (2000) *The Managerial State: Power, Politics and Ideology in the Remaking of Social Welfare*, London: Sage.

Deming, W.E. (2000) *Out of the Crisis*, Cambridge, MA: The MIT Press.

De Waal, A. (2007) *Strategic Performance Management: A Managerial and Behavioural Approach*, London: Palgrave MacMillan.

Dresner, H. (2007) *The Performance Management Revolution: Business Results Through Insight*, London: Wiley.

Elias, N. (1939/2000) *The Civilising Process*, Oxford: Blackwell.

Fletcher, C. (2008) *Appraisal, Feedback and Development: Making Performance Review Work*, London: Routledge.

Flyvbjerg, B. (2001) *Making Social Science Matter: Why Social Enquiry Fails and How It Can Succeed Again*, Cambridge: Cambridge University Press.

Guest, D., Michie, J., Conway, N. and Sheehan, M. (2003) Human resource management and corporate performance in the UK, *British Journal of Industrial Relations*, 41(2): 291–314.

Hyde,P., Boaden, R., Cortvriend, P., Harris, C., Marchington, M., Pass, S., Sparrow, P. and Siebald, B. (2006) *Improving Health Through Human Resource Management: Mapping the Territory*, London: Chartered Institute of Personnel and Development.

Kerr, R. (2008) *International development and the new public management: Projects and logframes as discursive technologies of governance,* in Dar, S. and Cooke, B. (eds) *The New Development Management*, London: Zed Books.

Kersley, B., Alpin, C., Forth, J., Bryson, A., Bewley, H., Dix, G. and Oxenbridge, S. (2006) *Inside the Workplace: Findings from the 2004 Workplace Employment Relations Survey*, London: Routledge.

Lado, A. and Wilson, M. (1994) Human resource systems and sustained competitive advantage: A competency based perspective', *Academy of Management Review*, 19: 699–727.

Lawler, E.E. (1986) *High Involvement Management*, San Francisco, CA: Jossey-Bass.

Legge, K. (2001) Silver bullet or spent round? Assessing the meaning of the 'High Commitment Management/Performance Relationship', in John Storey (ed.) *Human Resource Management: A Critical Text,* London: Thomson Learning.

Makinson, J. (Chair) (2000) *Incentives For Change: Rewarding Performance in National Government Networks*, London: Public Services Productivity Panel, HM Treasury.

Marsden, D. (2007) Individual employee voice: renegotiation and performance management in public services, *The International Journal of Human Resource Management*, 18(7): 1263–1278.

Mead, G.H. (1932) *The Philosophy of the Present*, New York: Prometheus Books.

—— (1934) *Mind, Self and Society from the Standpoint of a Social Behaviourist*, Chicago: University of Chicago Press.

Ohno, T. (1988) *Toyota Production System: Beyond Large-scale Production*, Portland: Productivity Press.

Paton, R. (2003) *Managing and Measuring Social Enterprises*, London: Sage.

Purcell, J., Kinnie, K., Hutchinson, S., Rayton, B. and Swart, J. (2003) *Understanding the People and Performance Link: Unlocking the Black Box*, London: Chartered Institute of Personnel and Development.

Performance Management: Measure and Improve the Effectiveness of Your Employees, (2006), Harvard Business Essentials, Boston, MA: Harvard Business Press.

Prigogine, I. (1997) *The End of Certainty: Time, Chaos and the New Laws of Nature*, New York: The Free Press.

Pring, R., Hayward, G., Hodgson, A., Johnson, J., Keep, E., Oancea, A., Rees, G., Spours, K. and Wilde, S. (2009) *Education for All – The Future of Education and Training for 14–19-year-olds*, London: Routledge.

Richardson, R. and Thompson, M. (1999) *The Impact of People Management Practices on Business Performance: A Literature Review*, London: Chartered Institute of Personnel and Development.

Schuster, J.M. (1997) The performance of performance indicators in the Arts, *Non-Profit Management and Leadership*, 7(3): 253–269.

Scott, J.C. (1990) *Domination and the Arts of Resistance: Hidden Transcripts*, New Haven: Yale University Press.

—— (1998) *Seeing Like a State: How Certain Schemes to Improve the Human Condition Have Failed*, New Haven: Yale University Press.

Seddon, J. (2008) *Systems Thinking in the Public Sector: The Failure of the Reform Regime and a Manifesto for a Better Way*, Axminster: Triarchy Press.

Snape, E. and T. Redman (2010) HRM practices, organizational citizenship behaviour, and performance: A multi-level analysis, *Journal of Management Studies*, 47(7): 1219–1247.

Stacey, R. (2007) *Strategic Management and Organisational Dynamics: The Challenge of Complexity*, 5th edition, London: Routledge.

—— (2010) *Complexity and Organizational Reality: Uncertainty and the Need to Rethink Management After the Collapse of Investment Capitalism*, London: Routledge.

——, Griffin, D. and Shaw, P. (2000) *Complexity and Management: Fad or Radical Challenge to Systems Thinking?*, London: Routledge.

Swart, J., Kinnie, N. and Rabinowitz, J. (2007) *Managing Across Boundaries*, London: Chartered Institute of Personnel and Development.

Torrington, D., Hall, L. and Taylor, S. (2005) *Human Resource Management*, 6th edition, London: Pearson Education.

Walburg, J., Bevan, H., Wilderspin, J. and Lemmens, K. (eds) (2005) *Performance Management in Healthcare*, London: Routledge.

Walton, R.E. (1985) From 'control' to 'commitment' in the workplace, *Harvard Business Review*, 63: 77–84.

Wood S.J. and Wall, T.D. (2007) Work enrichment and employee voice in human resource management performance studies, *The International Journal of Human Resource Management*, 18(7): 1335–1372.

9

Rethinking Management Drawing on Radical Insights from the Complexity Sciences

Throughout this book I have been engaging with what I have been terming the dominant management ideology. By calling it dominant I am by no means implying that it is the only way that management gets written or spoken about, and nor am I claiming that I am the only one who has a contrary view. It is probably evident from the previous chapters that books and journal articles on leadership and management are legion, hugely diverse and often contradictory. Moreover, at times in this book I have been drawing on a number of other scholars who are also critical of the dominant discourse with whom I have a lot in common. In this the final chapter of this volume it behoves me to spell out again what I see as some of the common features of current management orthodoxy despite the diversity, as well as to identify the similarities and differences that I have with those with whom I share a critique. What is so 'radical' about what I am offering, taking up the body of ideas called complex responsive processes of relating developed by Stacey, Griffin and Shaw (2000) and how might insights from the complexity sciences, and from social scientists and philosophers who have taken an interest in complex social phenomena, help contemporary managers? If, as I have set out in the first chapter, I am determined not to provide tools and techniques for managers, consultants and leaders, then in what way is this book of any practical use?

The Claims of the Dominant Discourse

In this book I have argued that the claim of modern management theories and the managers who espouse them is that they offer access to a particular body of knowledge, and provide a particular set of skills and approaches which are uniquely helpful in controlling organisations. In making this claim a cadre of people calling themselves leaders, managers and consultants are also aspiring to recognition as a professional group. The claim of expertise is also an appeal for power, recognition and reward in society, and I think would be hard to make an argument against the view that all three have become immensely powerful figures in our society, and are often extremely well rewarded. Management vocabulary has come to pervade everyday language. The tropes of contemporary management discourse are everywhere present in our thoughts and conversations, as we speak of 'managing' our emotions, or our time, 'buying in' to particular schemes or changes, or 'adding value' to what we undertake with others, perhaps having a 'clear vision' of what we want to achieve.

This body of specialist knowledge to which managers lay claim is created by a vast army of academics working in business schools, who produce a large output of what I am terming realist literature: that is to say that it understands there to be a world 'out there' that we can come to know as objective, individual observers and which can be controlled towards specific ends which we can identify in advance. The discourses presuppose that thought precedes action: first the rational, calculating manager works out what is to be done, and they implement a plan in a way which unfolds largely according to intention. In broad terms, contemporary management, and the majority academic literature that underpins it, aspires to being modelled on the natural sciences, where the manager, consultant or leader is thought to be a detached observer of organisational reality who can use various 'lenses' to assess what is going on in organisations as a way of making suggestions for improvements for more ideal ways of working, which then systematically proceed according to linear cause and effect. If we implement an idea, we can anticipate most of the consequences. There is often a heavy emphasis on organisational 'improvement' generally towards a way of working of an ideal kind, the way an organisation 'should' be structured, or employees 'should' be working according to industry standards. Sometimes industry standards are known as best, or possibly just good practice and are thought to apply to all companies in the same domain.

Strong empirical claims are often made for the body of knowledge produced in the many books and articles produced by academics and management consultants and it is thought to be increasingly stable over time, more and more to be 'evidence-based', and is often offered as being 'effective' in creating 'successful' organisations. The heuristic of a system is widely used in many contemporary orthodox approaches to management, where the organisation is thought of as if it were a whole with a boundary which can be disaggregated into parts. In previous chapters I have argued that this kind of thinking is derived from the philosophy of Kant, in particular the *Critique of Judgement* (1790/1978), where he argued that one way of thinking about Nature is as a whole made up of parts, where parts and whole mutually interact to unfold a pre-determined end.

Given that systems theories inform the disciplines of medicine and engineering, with huge success in the last two centuries, there can be no surprise to find the vocabulary from both domains taken up extensively in contemporary management theory. An organisation might need a 'diagnosis' to be moved towards greater 'health', or alternatively it might need to be 're-engineered' for more optimal working within the organisation, or for a better fit with its environment. In the National Health Service (NHS) at the moment, for example, 'lean six sigma' (George, Maxey, Rowlands et al., 2007), is a statistical method developed to improve manufacturing at Motorola, which has become very popular as a way to approach the improvement of health services. The idea of greater alignment, or perhaps realignment, of parts and whole, figures prominently in the dominant management thinking. If it is possible that an organisation is a system to be re-engineered, then it follows that it is possible to produce 'tools', grids and frameworks for managers to use to adjust the system. Much research is carried out to demonstrate that particular, often famous, companies who have used these tools, or sets of ideas, have achieved significant and beneficial change, and this would be a reason for other managers to act similarly. This has led to the burgeoning literature recommending recipes for success, five steps to remember, eight ideas to apply, which are supposed to guarantee success because they are derived from 'the world's leading companies'. The tendency to offer prescriptions for managers, based on research, 'best practice', or what many managers take for granted because of what they have learned on their management courses, creates a trend in management publishing where it is expected that authors will produce further grids and frameworks. To do otherwise is deemed not to produce anything 'practical' for managers, especially by management book publishers. Grids and frameworks have in turn become industry standards against which new literature is compared so that the dynamic towards producing them becomes amplified.

Much of the thinking that underpins this approach is highly abstract, by which I mean that it abstracts away from the rich and complex background of what people are actually doing in organisations, to produce simplifications and categorisations. In conceiving of an organisation as a whole, and following the assumption that whole system change is possible, chosen by managers and leaders, orthodox systemic theories of management rely heavily on spatial metaphors to convey meaning. So, a group of managers, who are looking at the 'big picture' are thought to 'move' an organisation in a 'new direction'. Leaders will ask their senior colleagues where they want to 'get to', which 'niche' they want to fit into, how they want to 'position' the organisation. The strategies of top managers, the way that senior managers choose the future for their organisation, once they have been developed are then supposed to cascade down the organisation through different 'levels'. By setting targets, or benchmarking for success against other companies it is assumed that change is possible for the 'system as a whole'. Thinking strategically, which means abstracting from the daily detail in order to dispose of whole organisations, is thought possible because of managers' separation from the situation which they are observing. The role of the contemporary manager is to design and plan, and set the rules for others to follow. The strategy can be disaggregated into logical steps, or milestones, which in turn can be disaggregated further into specific workplans and objectives for workers. It is a manager's role to supervise employees, to manage their performance so that these targets are met and thus the milestones realised. Cascading objectives are often thought to be one of the keys to success. If they prove not to be, then this is because leaders and managers have not disaggregated enough, or have not followed through assiduously enough, or in some other way have lacked thoroughness or courage.

The rules that managers set are also assumed to govern the quality of interactions between people, if this is how we might think of organisational 'culture', as well as employees' values. So by setting out a new vision for an organisation, a leader, or a top team can invite their staff to behave in particular ways, and by encouraging them to believe in the new future for the organisation, get them to adopt a set of behaviours informed by 'appropriate' values which will make that future achievable. Good leaders have some immanent quality, a unique ability to envision the future of an organisation, because of qualities that they have as individuals. They are able, uniquely, to articulate something about their true nature, which is close to Nature itself, which will be uplifting and inspiring for employees because of its authenticity. Values are parts of the whole human being, so they can be intervened upon and realigned, just as the parts of the organisation can be realigned to create a different whole. They may also be useful in recruitment so that a manager can assess whether a potential employee sufficiently 'shares' the organisation's values, and will thus fit in. There is a great stress placed on unity, and politics and difference are phenomena to be 'managed' away. Some management theorists are prepared to propose creating an organisation which is run like a 'cult' – that is to say, talk of values and behaviours is continuous and explicit, and failure publicly to conform to the explicit rhetoric of the organisation as articulated by senior managers, could result in dismissal. This is the way that Collins and Porras (2005) write, whom I referenced in the first chapter of this book.

Summary of the Dominant Position

At the risk of overdrawing the case, in much management literature senior managers and leaders can choose a future for an organisation, which includes choosing the right culture and behaviour for its employees. They do this by applying technical skills to analyse and diagnose what the organisation needs in order to make it evolve to a new fit with its environment. The ideal future can be mapped out in advance because of some unique insight that leaders have, which is sometimes of an esoteric kind, and they can inspire and motivate their employees to achieve an often ambitious set of goals, which are logically disaggregated from the idealisation. Leaders are often people who can bring about organisational transformation, which separates them from ordinary managers who are merely transactional, because of particular kinds of creativity or novelty which they can 'unleash' in an organisation. If employees resist, it is because they are not sufficiently inspired and motivated, they do not believe enough, or do not have enough information, but usually if the leader can explain the reasons for the urgent need for change, political opposition can be overcome. Leaders may well appeal to employees' good selves in order to convince them of the need for change, in which case employees might surface their mental models of what they think is going on and then change them to fit the new reality. They align themselves to the new unity, including their values and behaviours. Occasionally managers have to help employees to review how far they are achieving the new vision and they will do this by helping them to 'close the gap' between what they think they are doing and what they are actually doing, between their espoused theories and their theories in use. What is important in urgent periods of change, which seem to occur more and more frequently in the rush to adapt to the highly complex modern world in which we are living, is to remain positive.

I have noted the way in which the majority management literature is both shaped by, and amplifies the dominant ideology in its turn. There is an expectation that a management book will offer 'practical' advice to managers and leaders, and by practical it is usually meant that an author will produce familiar grids, tools and frameworks to supplement existing ones, showing how they are now more relevant, accessible or dynamic than previous understandings. They will be produced to support the claim of more effective, successful or performance-enhancing formulae.

An Alternative Drawing on the Complexity Sciences

By drawing on the complexity sciences, and those philosophers and sociologists who have taken an interest in describing complex social reality, I have been making an alternative case that the future is radically uncertain; that novelty arises in self-organising, local interaction and the exploration of difference, even conflict; that we are highly social and political beings absorbed in the game we are playing with others; and that for all of the above reasons we should be paying attention to the way in which we find ourselves involved in daily interactions with others, rather than thinking that we bring about wholesale change simply by dealing in abstractions and simplifications.

A RADICALLY UNCERTAIN FUTURE ARISING FROM LOCAL INTERACTIONS

I have drawn both on the theory of complex adaptive systems and the work of the Nobel prize-winning chemist Ilya Prigogine (1997) to demonstrate the way in which some scientists from a natural science tradition have problematised the idea of linear cause and effect, and have called into the question the idea that the future is already enfolded in the present. Complex adaptive systems theory is usually demonstrated on multi-agent computer models simulating interactions between competing and co-operating bit strings, or agents. If the interacting agents are diverse, and if their behaviour is non-average, then radically unpredictable patterning can arise which is constrained by the parameters set for the system. Despite the fact that the agents are still being programmed, and are thus behaving according to deterministic instructions, the patterning which arises is irreducible to the set of algorithms programmed into the simulation. Complex adaptive systems are capable of demonstrating spontaneous novelty, where locally interacting agents are forming, and at the same time being formed by the global pattern they produce in a paradoxical way. I drew on the work of Peter Allen and the analytical sociologist Peter Hedström, both of whom build computer models simulating complex social phenomena, to show the way in which it is impossible to predict how the model with evolve over time. I will reprise this work further in the section on the importance of local interaction below.

Meanwhile, in extrapolating from laboratory experiments of chemical reactions which are far from equilibrium, Prigogine made two radical propositions about Nature which amounted to a significant break with the disciplines of the natural sciences. First, he argued for the importance of the notion of time, of the irreversibility of certain natural processes, when they are sufficiently complex and dynamic. Prigogine took issue with Einstein's assertion that 'for us convinced physicists, the distinction between the past, present and the future is an illusion, though a persistent one',[1] arguing that he could no longer believe in determinism in science. Rather than the future being a repetition of the past, he stated instead that the future is under perpetual construction in the present, where the possible is richer than the real. Prigogine explained that the reasons for the resistance to the idea that some natural processes are irreversible are ideological: it is an attempt, he says, to maintain a divine point of view of pure mathematical certainty. Instead he argues that no human measurements and no theoretical predictions can give initial starting conditions of systems to a sufficient degree of accuracy to warrant such a god's eye view of nature. Second, drawing on the work of the mathematician Poincarré, Prigogine argued that dynamical systems are non-integrable: that is to say that instabilities arise from groups of interacting particles. The more dynamic the system, the higher the chance of randomness and fluctuations in the population of particles owing to a phenomenon called resonance, where the motion of particles becomes amplified because of an intrinsic property of interaction. Approximating the interactions of ensembles of particles requires a very different statistical method, based on probability, than plotting individual particle trajectories, or extrapolating from the behaviour of individual entities to the population of particles as whole. What Prigogine is drawing attention to is the way that groups of interacting agents can behave unpredictably when the system is unstable in a way which is not reducible to disaggregation. If this were not the case then we would have no evolution, nor would we have highly unpredictable processes like the weather in nature. The richness and variety that we see all around us is due to complex, transformative dynamic which is intrinsic to matter itself.

---

1   Correspondence between Einstein and Michele Besso, quoted in Prigogine (1997: 165).

When the methods of science are adduced in what I have been calling the dominant discourse in management literature, it is often to the sciences of certainty and predictability to which scholars are making an appeal. A good deal of contemporary theorising about management tries to develop timeless rules and formulae which are intended to be applicable in all organisations because they are thought to mirror a truth about organisational life, or about human behaviour. In exploring briefly what I take to be some of the insights from complex adaptive systems theory and the work of Ilya Prigogine, I am pointing instead to the importance of the work of those scientists who are drawing on disciplines developed in the natural sciences but who nonetheless have done so to become interested instead in uncertainty, unpredictability and the radically evolutionary possibilities of ensembles of actors interacting together. Rather than turning on propositional logic of an if-then kind which shows linear cause and effect, systems which are far from equilibrium demonstrate a paradoxical ability to be both stable and unstable at the same time; interacting agents are forming a global pattern whilst they are being formed by it at the same time. A complex adaptive system evolves unpredictably as a result of the inter-patterning of agents which are interacting locally, provided that the agents are diverse and that their behaviour demonstrates variety. This occurs without any blueprint or plan, and without any overall controller of the process of interaction. The rules of interaction between agents are evolving at the same time as the global patterning they produce is evolving, so it is impossible to predict exactly how the system will develop. And in the evolution of a complex adaptive system time becomes an important determinant of what transpires, since the history of interactions shapes future possibilities.

In his most recent book on the importance of understanding insights from the complexity sciences for thinking about life in organisations, Stacey (2010) makes the following points about complex adaptive systems computer simulations:

> These models therefore produce evolutionary possibilities. They are all models which take on a life of their own, producing surprising, unexpected patterns which mean they cannot yield predictions of what will happen in the model, or in the phenomenon it is trying to model, but these models may help us to gain insight into the dynamics. Returning to organisational reality the implication is that even though we cannot predict what will emerge in the interplay of our intentions, we can understand more than we currently do about the dynamics

involved in such interplay. We can pay attention to the diversity of human behaviour.

(2010: 65)

In his work Stacey is putting forward two propositions. He is making the claim, which I explore and try and develop further in this book that we can draw on the complexity sciences as a helpful analogy for thinking about what happens in organisations. Just as much orthodox management literature either implicitly or explicitly draws appeals to the methods of the natural sciences to make claims about the efficacy of whatever is being recommended, so Stacey is pointing to an alternative source domain for thinking about organisational life which is also derived from another branch of the natural sciences. However, there are radical and different implications for taking up the complexity sciences, what Stacey calls the sciences of uncertainty, since to do so radically problematises the kinds of reductive and deterministic assertions which are made in many contemporary management books. Second, in this quotation I think that Stacey is demystifying the concept of transformation, a term widely taken up in realist management discourse and in doing so it calls into question the central role of leaders and managers as designers of change. Usually transformation is taken to mean a change process planned and executed by leaders and managers: it is a deliberate process designed to bring about predetermined ends undertaken by managers claiming a unique detachment from, and insight into organisational life. At the more metaphysical end of the management literature spectrum (Senge, Schwarmer, Flowers et al., 2005) this insight is thought to arise out of some kind of spiritual attunement with the universe. Instead of reaching for mysterious explanations of how change emerges, Stacey is pointing the way in which it occurs as a result of the many, many interactions of people acting locally with others, however well-conceived, planned and executed the project of transformation is. What actually transpires will be unpredictable, Stacey claims, and will be a combination of the expected, the unexpected and the unwanted, the result of what everyone is doing in their local interactions with others.

For me what Stacey is describing as transformative causality is an observation about ordinary, everyday life, but one which has very profound implications. What we take to be reality is sustained by what each of us is doing in our daily interactions with others, but which has the potential for both stability transformation of a radical kind at the same time. There can be no doubt that leaders and managers can have a profound effect on what transpires in organisations because of the power they have to influence what gets done, and how it gets done, which we will explore further below, but this is by no means the only factor which determines what occurs and what does not.

Another thing to notice about the way that Stacey takes up the complexity sciences, and the way that I am exploring them in this book, is as a resource domain for analogies with organisations. An analogy, then, brings to the fore comparisons and similarities between one thing and another. I am making no claim that organisations *are* complex adaptive systems, or systems on the edge of chaos. The shortcoming of assuming that organisations are complex adaptive systems is that there is still the presumption of a programmer, usually thought to be the manager, consultant or leader. When the complexity sciences are taken up as though they could be applied directly as some kind of a tool to organisations, scholars get drawn into modelling what they think is going on in organisations, which leads to problems about boundaries, assumptions and interpretations, but fails to relinquish the idea that managers can predict and control organisational dynamics. Here is a very typical example of what I am talking about. In a volume on complexity and leadership Russ Marion, an eminent scholar of complexity, says the following:

> *In complexity leadership* enabling leaders *work to catalyze the mechanisms by creating the conditions in which those mechanisms can thrive ... This is a different sort of role for leadership than is typically presented in the literature: enabling leaders allow things to occur over which they have relatively little direct control. They create the structures, rules, interactions, interdependencies, tension and culture in which complex mechanisms can thrive and unanticipated outcomes can occur – and they create mechanisms that weed out poorly adaptive outcomes.*
>
> (Uhl, Marion and Meindl, 2008: 11)

In his chapter on leadership Marion is calling for something he calls complexity leadership, which he claims to be a different form of leadership more suited to today's complex and highly interdependent world. Because events like the disaster following hurricane Katrina produce conditions which are highly turbulent, and which are too complex for a single leader to solve, it is important not to assume that top-down leadership will have all the answers. Instead the complexity leader will 'catalyse mechanisms' to encourage greater flexibility and creativity than a single leader can achieve working on their own. That is to say, they understand a mechanism to be something that helps to get inside the 'black box' of organisational interaction so that they can identify a process that produces a given outcome. Mechanisms for them are 'universally available, emergent patterns of behaviour that enable a dynamic mix of variables (agents) and causal chains'. In placing a leader in control of creating the conditions for mechanisms to thrive, Marion is claiming to turn the usual prescriptions for leadership on their head. However, in failing to recognise the radical implications of the complexity sciences, which I would take to mean that there is nowhere for a leader to stand to identify the said mechanisms, let alone control them in any way, it seems to me that he is simply producing more of the same prescriptions from the dominant discourse. If the future is radically uncertain, then there are no guarantees that what a leader does will bring about greater flexibility, a better fit with what is needed, or in any way produce a pre-determined outcome.

Marion is not alone in taking up the complexity sciences in an instrumental way, since drawing on complexity has become a common resource for writers who are reluctant to abandon the ideology that what leaders and managers should do is predict and control. They might be enjoined to set simple rules for their organisations so that they can be in harmony with simple truths about the universe (Wheatley, 1999), which are supposed produce creative and kinder conditions for working together than a cruel and deterministic Newtonian world. Otherwise managers are encouraged to 'embrace' complexity and emergence, to 'leverage' emergence in their organisations, perhaps even to push their organisations to 'surf' the edge of chaos and thus achieve dynamic and creative results (Pascale, 2007). Emergence is sometimes understood as something flexible and creative and is thought to be in contrast to approaches based on command and control: someone facilitating emergent organisational change will observe and intervene in processes to bring about successful and creative outcomes (Olson and Eoyang, 2001). This is very different from understanding emergence as a process which occurs as a result of what everyone is doing and not doing and has the potential for both stability and change, good and bad outcomes, depending on your point of view. Although a different vocabulary is being used here, the perceptive reader will be forgiven for wondering what the difference is between 'applying complexity' and applying any other form of prescription.

In making the argument that the complexity sciences cannot be directly 'applied' to organisations I am by no means trying to imply that there is nothing for managers to do beyond recognising that the discussion of uncertainty poses significant problems for the dominant way of thinking about management. It is not enough to point out that organisations are highly complex and unpredictable, although what I am intending to say in this chapter is going to fall a good way short of another set of prescriptions, grids and frameworks. I have attempted in this book also to turn to the social sciences to explore the similarities and differences between what I am taking from the complexity sciences and those philosophers and sociologists who have written about complex social phenomena. By bringing both traditions to bear on the subject, I think it is possible to shed more light on what it is we are talking about.

A Radically Uncertain Future – Finding Parallels in the Social Sciences

I have taken up a variety of sociologists and philosophers as a way of enquiring into paradoxical social processes of stability and change, particularly those such as the American pragmatists, Pierre Bourdieu, Norbert Elias and Hannah Arendt, because of their patient attention to the everyday processes of ordinary life. Each in their own way has thought about the 'mechanisms' that Marion writes about above, that is to say, they try to open up the 'black box' of interaction between people. I will try to point to what I see as some of the similarities between what these thinkers have written about social complexity and the sciences of uncertainty which I have written about above.

INVOLVEMENT, DETACHMENT AND GAME-PLAYING

Norbert Elias took a long term view of the development of society, arguing that it is our interdependencies which have brought about the civilising process. As more and more people have become more dependent on more others more of the time, so social functions have become increasingly differentiated. Longer and longer chains of people become involved in sustaining everyday functions and for Elias, changes arise in society in ways which are beyond the ability of individuals, or even groups of individuals to affect, which is not to say that they are unable to take advantage of these changes:

> ... the spurts in the civilising process take place by and large independently of whether they are pleasant or useful to the groups involved. They arise from the powerful dynamics of interweaving group activities the overall direction of which any single group on its own is hardly able to change. They are not open to conscious or half conscious manipulation or deliberate conversion into weapons in the social struggle, far less so indeed, than, for instance, ideas.
>
> (Elias, 1939/2000: 407–408)

Because we are functionally dependent upon each other, for love, for support, for basic needs, for career advancement, we are inevitably involved in relationships of power. As society has become increasingly 'civilised', by which term Elias is implying no value judgement, so greater advantage, by which we might understand greater power chances, is afforded to those who can take what he terms 'a detour via detachment'. That is to say, it is our ability to take ourselves and our involvement with others as objects to ourselves so that we can exercise foresight and restraint, a facility which also interested G.H. Mead. Taking a more detached attitude to ourselves and our involvement with others is not the same as driving out affect, Elias is quick to caution. What has happened instead is that our strong feelings and anxieties which arise as a result of the process of our socialisation, and which previously we might have been quick to express even in the form of violence, have been driven 'inside' where they operate 'blindly' as anxiety and ever-incipient shame. The veneer of rationality that we convince ourselves we have, dams up a reservoir of uncontrollable feeling. We are in our behaviour 'many layered':

> We scarcely realise how quickly what we call our 'reason', this relatively far sighted and differentiated steering of our conduct, with its high degree of affect control, would crumble or collapse if the anxiety-inducing tensions within and around us changed, if the fears affecting our lives suddenly became much stronger or much weaker or, as in many simpler societies, both at once, now stronger, now weaker.
>
> (Ibid.: 441)

I have written a number of narratives in this book which have drawn attention to exactly what Elias is pointing to here: situations in organisations where a particular patterning of relationships, perhaps a challenge to existing power relationships, has provoked strong feelings in some or all of the people concerned, which is often acted out as aggression, shame, or some other affect-driven behaviour.

There are a variety of things to take from what Elias is saying, which I think are directly relevant to thinking about life in organisations and the task of management. I would also argue that there are direct parallels with the insights I have drawn on from the non-linear complexity sciences. First, then, the interweaving of intention by individuals and groups causes particular global and local social phenomena to occur. Thinking globally, particular social relationships of co-operation and competition arise, what Elias calls power figurations, which can express themselves in terms of divisions of

class, ethnicity, wealth or race, or a combination of all of these, which are in
constant flux, and of which no one, or no group, is in overall control. These
figurations tend in particular directions but exactly what changes occur over
time is probabilistic rather than predictable. The figurations arise because
of our functional dependence on each other, our power chances vis-à-vis
each other and the groups to which we belong. At the same time the blindly
operating social figurations of power create our sense of self and our identities
and suppress the public demonstration of our drives and affects, which can
still burst through our defences provoking shame and embarrassment, which
are socialised forms of control. We are both socialised and individualised by
the civilising process. One image that Elias uses to describe what he thinks
is happening in social life is that of the game. So in a tennis match where
one player is significantly stronger than the other, the stronger player is
able to dictate the course of the game. Where two players are more evenly
matched, it becomes much more difficult to predict the outcome of the game
as each player constantly adapts to the tactics of the other. Imagine, then, a
multi-player game, for which we could substitute society or an organisation,
where there are many different interactions going on. What tends to happen,
argues Elias, is that individuals form into groups to promote their interests,
although there are also intra-group rivalries, and the game tends to separate
out into different levels. Elias does not think of these different levels as being
functionally separate, since they are all interconnected and exist because
of and in relation to each other. So there is intra-group and inter-group
co-operation and competition on one level, as well as inter-level competition
and co-operation. The game being played in its twists and turns is mostly
opaque, even to the most powerful players, although there is some advantage
to be gained by those players who are able to take a detour via detachment
and who may be able better to predict the moves of the game they are involved
in one or perhaps two iterations ahead.

Pierre Bourdieu (1998) also takes up the idea of the game as an analogy
with our engagement with social life in his work, and notices the way that
we are invested in the games we find ourselves playing. We find it difficult
to call the game we are playing into question, he argues, because we are
so absorbed in it. We find it important and interesting, and our feel for the
game is imprinted in our bodies, which he calls *habitus*. We are so absorbed
in the game that we are playing, a state he calls *illusio*, we even forget that
we are playing a game. Only when we encounter social games where we are
not familiar with the rules might we find what is going on strange or even
absurd, which is akin to the experience of going abroad and noticing the way

that other societies' customs and habits are different from our own. If we were to take rationality and reason as the only explanations of why people behave the way they do, then we would not require the social sciences to help us understand organisational life.

The idea of the game for me gives a very powerful analogy with organisational life with the functionally inter-dependent levels of board of directors, top management team, heads of department, units and other groupings within many organisations co-operating and competing to achieve whatever it is they are trying to do together. The game changes over time both as result of what everyone is doing in the organisation, but also as a consequence of what similar, competing organisations are doing, and changes in society as a whole. Bourdieu makes exactly the same series of points: that organisations are driven by processes of competition and co-operation between managers in the firm, and between them and managers in other firms. There are regularities to the way the game is being played, and at the same time there are ruptures and developments which no one can have foreseen and of which no one is in overall control. What transpires arises as a result of what everyone is doing and is a heady mixture of detached behaviour and blindly operating affect. If we were to take Elias' ideas seriously when thinking about managing and leading organisations, then it would pose a direct challenge to the idea of rational, choosing managers who can make up their minds about the game being played and even decide on the rules for the game. Instead, we might think of managers and leaders as being more powerful players of any particular organisational game, but nonetheless as much caught up in it as everyone else, and subject to the same blindly operating wall of shame and anxiety which will influence whatever stratagem or tactic they find themselves involved in. To understand organisational life, then, means paying attention to the negotiation of power, which we might understand as politics, as well as the strong feelings that are provoked in different organisational contexts. We would also be concerned to notice how things move and change, rather than being insistent upon identifying first causes, or the fixed structure of things. Neither power, affect nor processes of flux and change figure prominently in the dominant discourse on management, and in the narratives and the commentary on narratives which I have provided in this book I have tried to demonstrate the ways in which fluctuating figurations of power relations within groups of people have a dramatic effect on what transpires.

CONVERSATIONS OF GESTURES: THE SOCIAL SELF AND THE IMPORTANCE OF LANGUAGE

Where Elias has helped me better to understand the broad sweep of social development and the way that organisations might best be understood as fluctuating relationships of power so G.H. Mead and Bourdieu can assist further in opening up Marion's 'black box'. How might we think about the daily interactions between people which both sustain existing patterns of behaviour, the social regularities that we observe, but at the same time hold the potential for transformation and change?

Mead and Elias are in perfect agreement about the proposition that we are intensely social selves, and that self and society are two sides of the same coin. Central to Mead's argument, however, is the role of mutual responsiveness, particularly but not exclusively through language in the creation and re-creation of mind, self and society. Because of our unique physiology, Mead argues, we are able to take ourselves as objects to ourselves, we are able to see ourselves as others see us. We gesture and respond to ourselves, using what Mead (1934) terms 'significant symbols'. A symbol is significant when it calls forth in someone else the same response that it calls out in ourselves. In a conversation of significant symbols with ourselves, which we have learnt through the socialisation process, mind arises, and in conversation with others we gesture and call out a response in ourselves and in the other person at the same time. We are able, he says, to anticipate how someone else is going to react to our gesture because of our bodily and affectual resonances with each other, but also because we both inherit a generalised sense of how to behave with each other as we exchange significant symbols. We are responding both to our spontaneous sense of self and a generalised other, both at the same time. For Mead, meaning does not reside in what one party intends with their gesture, but rather emerges in the back and forth gesture and response between one party and another. As we respond to what we ourselves are saying, and to the responses of the people with whom we are communicating, we are capable of calling out surprising reactions in ourselves and in others arising out of our particular histories and experience. We may not know what we think about something until we hear ourselves say it out loud in a conversation of gestures with another.

At the very heart of a conversation, then, lies the paradoxical possibility of continuity and change at the same time: if there were no regularities in social interaction it would be impossible for social life to continue. In general we can anticipate with a good degree of accuracy how someone will respond to what we are saying. However, in a particular conversation with a specific other we cannot fully anticipate how we will respond to each other until we each find ourselves doing it. There are lots of opportunities for misunderstanding and misinterpretation. Pierre Bourdieu (1977, 1990) understands this process as an improvisation on the 'rules' of social life. We are acculturated into an embodied feel for the game, as I indicated in the passages above, but we are still called upon to respond to a specific context of interaction where we will be obliged to improvise on the 'rules' of engagement. I pointed out how current research into brain activity (Ramachandran, 2011), and particularly the way that our brains anticipate our anticipation of another's anticipation, have supported Mead's ideas about how the paradox of self and other arise in each of us. We can become more skilful at noticing the way that these irreconcilable paradoxes influence our daily lives with each other.

The parallel one might make with complex adaptive systems theory, which I discussed earlier, is that generalised social patterning and a particular expression of it are present both at the same time Bourdieu says that 'the body is in the social world, and the social world in the body' (1982: 38), forming and being formed by each other. In local communicative interaction there is the potential for variation and spontaneity, improvisation on the generalised 'rules' because of the diversity of experience of those engaged in gesture and response and their particular embodiment of generalised social tendencies. This is how the patterning that we recognise as stability in organisations becomes replicated over time, but also how, in everyday interaction with each other as we talk about the work, there is a possibility for transformation and change. However, it is rarely a transformation that we plan in advance often one that we only recognise in retrospect.

Mead's theories may also help us understand how it is that different collective phenomena, such as workshops or company conferences, can turn out differently, even if they are planned in exactly the same way. Though Mead does not take up the idea of power in exactly the way that Elias does, he nonetheless argues that social objects, a generalised tendency for groups of people to act in particular ways are shaped and formed by a struggle over the 'life process of the group'. A different collection of people meeting in a different context are likely to produce both similar and very different outcomes from other groups, even if they are following the same agenda or workshop plan.

I have taken up these ideas as a way of thinking differently about a variety of different aspects of leading and managing which are written about very differently in what I have been terming the dominant discourse.

IMPLICATIONS FOR THINKING ABOUT CONSULTANCY

In the chapter on consultancy (Chapter 2), I noted the way that many books on consultancy assume that the consultant is a detached observer who can come into organisations, and on the basis of an objective 'diagnosis', can intervene to put things right using the necessary frameworks. A consultant's job is to rise above politics, or at least to manage them towards predetermined ends. They are supposed to help to 'drive change' and work in an environment of certainty – if employees resist change it is simply because they do not realise, or appreciate, the benefits which change will bring. As an alternative I set out the view that the consultant is neither objective nor detached, and is as constrained by the political interactions in an organisation as anyone else who works there, and will be obliged to a large degree to operate within the client organisation's view of the world. It is simply not possible to call everything into question, and there will be expectations about the way a consultant works. Borrowing a phrase from Mead which I used in Chapter 3, the consultant and what they do is a social object: that is to say that to a degree they will be expected to conform to a particular understanding of what a consultant is and does, which has built up over time.

I drew extensively from the work of the sociologist Norbert Elias to make a case that what happens in organisations is due to the interweaving of intentions of the many different people who work in them, including for a temporary period, the consultant. Because we are interdependent, and because we are only partially in control of a 'wall of deep rooted fears' which are caused by our upbringing and our need for others, bringing people together to achieve something will always result in struggles of competition and co-operation. They will always provoke strong feelings. Rather than something to be ignored or covered over, then, strong feelings might be something to pay close attention to as a consultant intending to undertake an intervention in an organisation, since they might give important clues as to what is going on in any particular situation. I offered this in contrast to the idea that a consultant is an objective technician, bringing rationalist tools and techniques to re-engineer an organisation, or pull particular organisational levers to set in moving in a different gear. I have not made an argument necessarily against bringing to bear experience from other organisations, since it could well be relevant. However, since all situations are unique we cannot guarantee that ideas derived from previous experience will necessarily be applicable.

The consultant becomes part of the power relationships they are trying to affect, since consultants often come with an aura of expertise and expectation about what they bring. There will inevitably be a struggle over what the consultant says and does, and an attempt to engage them in the ideological world view of those working in the organisation. The consultant is likely to be involved in negotiations from the first minute of involvement with their contractors to the last minute of finishing off their report or recommendations. By negotiating, and by drawing attention to the negotiation process, the consultant may be able to bring things into view, ways of understanding what is happening in the organisation, taken for granted assumptions, which will be helpful to the client in thinking about how to work differently.

One very practical role of a consultant, then, is to work with groups of managers or leaders to become more detached about their involvement in organisational life, to help them pay attention to what is most closely concerning them. Helping managers to think about how they are thinking and how their actions and assumptions to date have helped contribute to what they are currently experiencing can be a very powerful way of supporting groups to develop themselves. A consultant can help a group of managers identify, and find ways of describing, the games that they find themselves in which they find themselves caught up. Managers are neither entirely in control of the patterning that arises in organisations, nor are they merely subjects to it.

IMPLICATIONS FOR RESEARCHING ORGANISATIONS

If it is not helpful to think of an organisation as a fixed system transitioning between one stable state and another, but rather as a constantly fluctuating patterning and re-patterning of themes of organising, how can a manager or a consultant know how to act?

By drawing on analogies from complex adaptive systems theory, and the way in particular that these have been taken up in the work of Ralph Stacey and his colleagues Doug Griffin and Patricia Shaw, I made an argument for paying attention to what people are actually doing together in organisations and the way they are talking about the work. By talking about work in the organisation I am claiming, drawing on both Stacey and the ethnomethodologist Deirdre Boden (1994, see Chapter 3), employees are talking the organisation into existence.

So the way people are talking and acting is not a distraction from the big picture, it is the way the 'big picture' of organisational life comes into existence. The local and global are both present at the same time. This would also involve paying attention to moments in organisational life when strong feelings are provoked since these may be indicative of important organisational processes coming under scrutiny. The emergence of strong feelings is not necessarily a 'failure' on the part of managers or consultants to control something, or to bring about harmony, since novelty arises in the exploration of difference not in covering it over. By drawing on the theories of G.H. Mead, I made the argument that small differences emerge even as we talk in an everyday way with each other, as we adapt and respond to each other. In every situation where employees come together to talk about the work there is the potential for both continuity and change.

So for leaders, managers and consultants who are concerned to take an interest in what is happening in their organisation I am drawing their attention to the everyday, the contextual, the conversational and the micro, in the way that talking about the work shapes the work. What is particularly useful when talking to staff in organisations is the stories that they tell about what they are involved in. I set out a number of reasons why narrative is useful for understanding the complex interactions in organisations: they have a time frame in which a plot unfolds, which need not be linear, they admit to multiple interpretations at the same time as calling out resonances in the reader, and in doing so they afford more opportunities for reflection on action. They also call out responses in the listener or reader about what the particular incident being described means for them. The way that organisational life is narrated does not necessarily lead anywhere: it may not result in a new way of working, and particularly not a grid or a framework. What it may do, however, is open the possibility for further reflection and the conceiving of new possibilities of working together.

One of the things that I think leaders and managers and leaders could be doing in organisations, then, is to continue to open up possibilities for those they are working with, particularly when a situation may seem stuck or blocked. Trying to recover some of the richness of experience, of its potential is another way of trying to find a way of going on together without concluding that a new tool is needed, or an appeal to 'best practice' which originates elsewhere. It is also a way of practising accountability. Rather than having a narrow interpretation of what accountability means, that is, simply stating whether one has or has not fulfilled one's objectives or met one's targets, we might reframe the exercise as a form of mutual account giving, as one narrative account is reframed by another. Of course, there are power implications for this way of proceeding, since in the exchange of accounts a leader or manager is ceding some of their authority as being responsible for the ultimate account.

IMPLICATIONS FOR LEADING ORGANISATIONS

I have already been claiming in the above paragraphs that leaders have an important role in drawing the attention of the people they are working with to the games everyone is playing together. In using the word 'games' I am not using it in any pejorative sense, but am borrowing the idea from both Elias and Bourdieu as an analogy that much more appositely represents the fluid, complex, fast-changing environments in organisations, or within a domain of organisations, where there are rules of engagement, but even these rules may change as a result of the way the game unfolds. I have been arguing that paying attention to people's narrative accounts of what is happening, including the way that leaders and managers narrate their own experience of leading, is a powerful way of both understanding and influencing organisational life.

One of the organisational games that is played out involves the idealisation of leaders and leadership. In the chapter on leadership (Chapter 4), I pointed to the vast literature on leadership which helps to shape our expectations of what a leader is and does. These tend to be highly individualised accounts of special talents that leaders have immanently, based on unique insight that is granted to them as leaders. I tried to point to some of the socio-economic and historical reasons as to why this might have come about. But, as we have explored in previous chapters, it is impossible just to discount this kind of literature which provokes these expectations, because the ideas it sets out are actively taken up by staff in organisations. We are likely to experience people differently when they become leaders and to have greater expectations of them: this is something that new leaders need to be aware of. In writing about the metaphysical aspects of leadership, although they may do so in highly reduced or instrumental way encouraging leaders to mimic the supposedly great characteristics of other inspirational leaders, there is something important that is being written about which we should not lose. Leading groups is a complex social phenomenon which stirs up strong feelings in people. We are dealing with rich, complex value-laden territory which involves concepts such as trust, honesty, legitimacy, authority and authenticity.

Rather than stressing the individual nature of leadership I have tried in this book to point to the highly social nature of leadership as an experience between people. And in doing so I am siding with G.H. Mead who thinks of a leader as an individual who in the process of being socialised, has particularly enhanced abilities of recognising and articulating the potential of the particular patterns of relating in the community in which they are part. They have the ability to take the attitude of a large number of others to themselves and to articulate this in a way in which these others are able to recognise themselves in what is said. It is a highly social, group-oriented ability and is discovered and recreated moment by moment. In other words, leadership is an experience that arises in groups of people who have come together to try and achieve things, where the leader may have a particular role, but is informed in their actions by their reading of the game in which they are participating.

IMPLICATIONS FOR THINKING ABOUT 'VISION' THAT A LEADER 'HAS'

One of the special skills that a leader is presumed to have in contemporary organisations is that of vision, a unique ability to see into the future and divine what it is that the organisation needs to become. I have noted in the book the way that this concept has become prevalent through use: management scholars write about it because other scholars have written about it, meanwhile it has become a reality in organisational life and something that staff expect of their leaders. After Deirdre Boden, we have talked this idea into existence.

In Chapter 5 I put forward the view that the idea of vision is strongly tied to an expressivist and romanticised concept of our 'true self', which a leader is capable of articulating because of their proximity to their own true selves. It speaks to our religious imagination and a yearning to be part of something greater than ourselves. I have also pointed out the similarities between the idea of a leader or manager as objective and detached organisational engineer or doctor, with the concept of leader as seer, 'seeing' a unique future for an organisation which is revelation as truth. It is much more difficult to contest what we can see. Another way of thinking about vision, then, is as a form of social control where the vision is understood to be a moral necessity.

Collective visions are an important part of beginning new undertakings together with others: in making a joint commitment we can, after Hannah Arendt, dispose of the future as though it were the present. It can generate a sense of excitement and commitment to a joint undertaking. Moments such as these can be temporary islands of certainty in otherwise uncertain times.

However, there is nothing about a highly idealised abstraction, a vision, for us to know how to go on together every day, in particular contexts. Visions need working out between people, negotiating, to discover what they mean in everyday work environments. It would be a mistake to believe that an imaginative construction can really map out the future: unfortunately is also has the potential for creating oppressive relationships between people if they forget the imaginative dimension of what they are doing. It is very important not to become swept away unthinkingly by what everyone else is doing or thinking.

In the rest of the book I have been pointing to the importance of paying attention to, and engaging in, the politics of everyday life in organisations. One of the great dangers of visioning exercises in organisations, is not just that it seems to invest enormous power in a leader if it is thought that it is the leader who 'has' the vision, but also there is great potential for closing down debate, difference and contestation, the normal politics of organising, with some spurious appeal to an envisioned truth.

IMPLICATIONS FOR THINKING ABOUT VALUES

Values are an important part of who we are and what we aspire to. In contemporary organisations which are replete with metrics and rational ways of managing, employees may still yearn to be part of something greater than themselves. In Charles Taylor's terms, we live in an increasingly secular age, so it can be no surprise that organisations are partially understood as potential sites for spiritual renewal. For Taylor the appeal to the religious imagination in contemporary society is also a rebellion against the sense of a flattened world.

So there can be no surprise that orthodox theories of management treat values as an important area of enquiry and investigation, but they do so, as with vision, as an instrument of management. Values are often confused with norms, which are their conceptual twin, as a way of cajoling and disciplining employees to align their behaviour with the expressed ends and ideals of the organisation. However, as noted in our discussion about vision above, values are highly idealised and abstract: there is nothing obvious about a value that enables employees to know how to go on together in a particular context with particular others without some form of negotiation. Values must be functionalised. Moreover, there is a good deal of philosophical speculation that higher human values are impervious to rational intervention: they are part of who we are. In this sense they are pre-cognitive and come to us as part of our inter-subjective formation, provoking very strong feelings in us. Values are how we understand the world and the more we try to manipulate or grasp them, the more elusive they become.

There are a number of dangers of trying to corral values, particularly into some idealised notion of organisational unity. The first is that we cannot know the variety of responses that an appeal to values may call out in employees: it may provoke feelings of an enlarged sense of self and purpose, but it may also be experienced as exclusionary, calling out cynicism or rebellion. Additionally, if there is an attempt to cover over value differences this may dampen down the very conditions which are necessary for renewal and for novelty to arise, which we have already claimed arises out of the exploration of difference. Instead of encouraging feelings of unity and harmony, the taking up of values as cult, in the terms of Collins and Porras as well as Mead, can be experienced as totalitarian.

In this book I am claiming that values are highly social phenomena that emerge daily in interactions between engaged human beings and will provoke strong feelings and questions of identity. They are a vital part of who we are and what we care about, and cannot be denatured and decontextualised without much being lost. This is not a terrain that a manager should enter into unthinkingly or lightly.

IMPLICATIONS FOR UNDERTAKING STRATEGY

I have been investigating the claims of what I have been calling the dominant discourse on management, which are based largely on the notions of predictability and control. In this sense, the domain of strategy probably poses management orthodoxy its most severe test. On what basis could a theory of management claim to know how the future will unfold, and how would it suggest that leaders and managers could wrestle with unpredictable circumstances, Donald Rumsfeld's 'unknown unknowns', with a pre-reflected understanding of what is best for the organisation?

Theories of strategy have evolved over time and now reflect a far more complex understanding of strategy development in organisations. Despite the fact that the literature on strategic planning has diminished significantly over the last decade, nonetheless, strategy development is something that almost all organisations do, and managers would not feel part of the managerial club if they could not produce a strategy document for their organisations. It is a sign of belonging and being professional. It is also a way of reducing anxiety in organisations and creating a process in which employees can recognise themselves and what they are doing. There is value in strategy development at least for the temporary stabilising effect that it may have on a group of people struggling to define who they are and what they think they are doing.

Contemporary managers are much more prepared to accept that they can create the future of their organisations through interpretation and imagination, but often accompany this with linear planning and design tools. According to Tsoukas (2004), theories of strategy lack a robust concept of creative action, and cannot account for what Stacey (2007) calls 'transformative causality' in their own terms.

As an alternative I pointed to the way that strategy emerges in the interplay of intentions of those engaged in the strategy process, as managers both compete and co-operate for status, access to resources, and the development of meaning. It is an imperfect process and constantly evolving, not just in the form of strategic documents, but in the way the ideas in these documents are then taken up in particular contexts and functionalised by employees. Inevitably all kinds of things will happen which were not envisaged in the strategy document, some of which will be more 'successful' than what was originally intended. If we take the insights from the complexity sciences seriously, then it is likely that innovation will occur because of bizarre and eccentric improvisations on the plan, rather than because of the conscious intentionality of those involved in implementing a strategy. It will be brought about by those obliged to perform what Bourdieu referred to as the 'necessary improvisation' on the rules. In order to develop a more complex understanding of what happens when people undertake strategy development in organisations depends, then, on introducing a different understanding of time, which is iterative rather than linear. A strategy is unlikely to proceed with if-then causality like a physics experiment, but will be constantly reinterpreted in the present, drawing on the past and in expectation of the future.

In this book I have argued that strategy development is a provisional, fallible and probabilistic undertaking where what we understand to be 'success' needs to be constantly reviewed and re-evaluated. There is no such thing as an optimal strategy, at least not for very long. Because we act into a web of other people's intentions, a particular strategy is very unlikely to be successful for long, since everyone is constantly adapting and adjusting to everyone else's plans and intentions. Drawing out themes which I have described above, it is very important for a group of managers undertaking strategy development to pay attention to the way that they themselves are working, and how their power relationships affect what transpires as organisational strategy. It is not a distraction from the 'big picture'; it is the way in which the big picture arises.

IMPLICATIONS FOR MANAGING PERFORMANCE TOWARDS THE STRATEGY

If strategic plans are provisional and fallible, then it becomes much harder to see the activity of managing staff towards pre-reflected strategic targets as a meaningful activity. It is likely to call out exactly the kinds of gaming and cynical behaviour that is a potential in all areas of organisational life where employees are asked to follow rules which begin to bear little relation to their day-to-day activities and how they recognise themselves in their work. Employees are often caught in a double bind where on the one hand they are encouraged to align, conform and meet their targets, and on the other they are enjoined to be creative, innovative and autonomous. So they will continue to represent themselves to the good in order to succeed in the organisation, no matter how meaningful or meaningless they find the exercise. In any case, as with most areas of management it seems that the evidence for the efficacy of managing the performance of employees is highly contested.

If there is no one best way of undertaking the work, and if there is no way of anticipating what it is that employees will have to deal with in order to get the job done, then this demands a much more provisional understanding of what good performance might mean in any situation. One thing a manager might do with the people they manage is to support them in dealing with radical uncertainty, with the necessary improvisation that they will be required to demonstrate if they are to co-operate with others. Rather than relying on 'thin simplifications' of the work, a manager could encourage staff they manage to give an account of what they have been doing. By this I mean more than simply saying whether they have hit their targets or not.

Additionally, most work requires interdependent workers to co-operate with other workers: this goes against the grain of highly individualised schemes for performance appraisal, which are sometimes accompanied by performance-related pay, which take no cognisance of ensemble performance. One person's targets may well cut across the fulfilment of another person's targets and could undermine team effort, no matter how logically derived from the overall departmental work plan. The more complex the job, the less sensible it seems to set targets for what people are doing. This is no argument for managers neglecting their employees. I believe that a responsible manager will take a close interest in what those staff for whom they are responsible are doing, and will ask them to narrate and give an account of what they have needed to do to get the work done. However, this is a very different form of engagement than 'measuring' results against pre-reflected targets.

Similarities and Differences with Other Critical Voices

At the beginning of this chapter I mentioned that there is a substantial minority of critics of the dominant discourse on management in which I count myself. How would I distinguish what I am saying, drawing on the work of Stacey, Griffin and Shaw and the theory of complex responsive processes of relating in organisations, from what they are saying? In what way am I claiming that this approach is radical? Exploring the work of an eminent exponent of critical management studies (CMS) such as Mats Alvesson as an example, we would find a lot in common. Both are concerned to engage in critical reflection on institutions; both resist the strong pressures of normalisation; both would entertain the idea that all knowledge creation is political, value-laden and interest-based. Alvesson's '4 I' framework[2] (identity, institutions, interests and ideology) is a very helpful way for organisational researchers and managers to think about the work they are undertaking (how are identities being constructed in this episode of organisational life; how are people engaged in thinking about the institution; whose interests are being served and what does this say about the ideological claims?). Alvesson encourages reflection and reflexivity as a way of producing complex and rounded accounts of organisational life, accounts which are 'rich in points'. This seems to me to be very helpful for all those engaged in working in, or writing about organisations.

But there are some clear differences between perspectives as well. For example, Alvesson claims that CMS has emancipatory intent. The critical researcher tries to provoke, to draw on a rich repertoire of methods to call into question the normative understanding of those being researched. One of the researcher's questions is to ask: 'what is going on here, and what the hell do they think they are doing?' While being sensitive to the context in which people are working, and trying not to beat people over the head with critical reflection which leaves them bruised and bewildered, Alvesson does not believe it is up to the researcher to work through the critique which has been

---

2   Presented to the Complexity and Management Conference, Roffey Park, UK, June 2010.

offered. Emancipation, then, arises from the production of critical accounts of organisational life as a way of contributing to a wider body of knowledge from the point of view of CMS. The researcher produces knowledge for a community of researchers engaged in the same task.

From the perspective I have been setting out in this book, the manager, the researcher or the consultant is not concerned just to produce knowledge or a knowledge product, but enquires in order to enquire further. Questioning leads to more questioning. There is no 'they' about whom the manager as researcher is perplexed. Rather the question arises as to who 'we' are becoming in the process of researching and working together. So as well as drawing on the critical theory from the Frankfurt School, I have also drawn on the American pragmatists. What interested the pragmatists, amongst other things, is the unity of being, doing and knowing. They took an interest in thinking in practice about practice. For John Dewey (1958) there was no separating the object from the experience of the object, and the task of philosophy was to find ways of describing both which made the object and the experience of the object more 'luminous'.

For the tradition of complex responsive processes the community of enquirers (a phrase borrowed by the founding pragmatic philosopher Charles Sanders Peirce (1984)) is broader than the academic research community, but involves leaders, managers and consultants as well. If there are emancipatory intentions, then these revolve around the ways in which 'we' can continue to stay engaged in discussion together. Staying in conversation, with all the conflict, co-operation and compromise that this involves (perhaps what we might term this the three 'Cs'), and taking into account the otherness of others, involves an identity shift in oneself. We are obliged to adapt to those with whom we try to stay in engaged conversation. This describes a particular quality of reflexivity which is not just concerned to reflect in a detached way about how one might be thinking about others, but pays attention to the shifts in one's own identity that arise in the necessary interaction with other engaged enquirers. The question of identity arises not just for 'them' but for us as we engage in a dialectical back and forth between self and others.

The important themes derived from the alternative approach that I have tried to set out in this book are the following:

ON UNCERTAINTY

Taking uncertainty seriously involves radically rethinking management which is predicated on theories of predictability and control, even to the extent of trying to control theories of uncertainty (if managers are thought capable of 'unleashing emergence', or 'harnessing complexity' in their organisations). It becomes a much more probabilistic exercise, fallibilistic, emergent and open to radical doubt, challenging taken for granted assumptions of best practice, industry standards or effective working. The management of people involves experiment and a greater openness to experience, paying attention to what is emerging in the flux and flow of organisational life. I would argue that to act with the assumption that the future cannot be known implies a move away from the hubris of managerialism, or certain outcomes and 'effective working', towards a greater humility on the part of managers.

ON PARADOX

Whereas in most orthodox management literature everything can be conceived as a 'problem' which requires a solution, I am suggesting instead that there are many areas of human experience that are paradoxical. True paradoxes have no solution, like non-linear equations, but can only be iterated and investigated and perhaps made more comfortable through investigation. So when people try to achieve things together in organisation there will always be processes of inclusion and exclusion which will provoke strong feelings; in particular situations employees will be taking up general prescriptions, such as strategies; in reflecting on what they are doing together, groups of employees will be trying to be more detached about their involvement as they compete and co-operate both at the same time. Organisational life is a constant encounter between the self and other, and this paradox manifests itself even in the way we become who we are in the constant dialectic between 'I' and 'me'.

ON POLITICS

Rather than producing static, reduced grids and frameworks I have been borrowing from both Elias and Bourdieu to reflect upon how we are absorbed in the game of organisational life, and I have been suggesting that the rules of the game evolve in the playing of it. I have put forward the idea that this might be a more helpful way of thinking about the fluctuating, complex of organisational life than thinking of an organisation as a whole disaggregated into parts. Rather than taking a systemic view and assuming that somehow managers can stand outside the game and direct from the touchline, I have instead put forward the idea that we are involved in influencing the game as we engage with each other in the playing of it. There is no engagement without politics since we are interdependent: as long as we need things from each other, so there is the potential for withholding, the clearest manifestation of power relationships. I have been talking about management as a radical engagement with the everyday politics of organisational life, which I am terming the proper exercise of power. If our grasp of reality is always partial, fragmentary and incomplete, then proceeding with others requires negotiation and agonistic interaction.

ON THE IMPORTANCE OF EXPERIENCE IN EVERYDAY INTERACTIONS

As an alternative to 'big-picture' representations of organisational life, on the ubiquitous abstractions and schemata that figure in many management books I have been using narrative ways of knowing as a way of writing and thinking about how the macro manifests itself daily in micro-interactions between people. This turns the focus of much contemporary management literature on its head. This is a challenge to the usual dualism of 'task' and 'process' which are often considered separable aspects of any undertaking: I am arguing instead that the way groups of managers undertake whatever it is that they do together will directly shape what it is they are doing. So I am arguing that paying attention to the way people are working together is an important part of knowing how to go on together:

> Zeal for doing, lust for action, leaves many a person, especially in this hurried and impatient environment in which we live, with experience of an almost incredible paucity, all on the surface. No one experience has a chance to complete itself because something else is entered upon so speedily. What is called experience becomes so dispersed and miscellaneous as hardly to deserve the name. Resistance is treated as an obstruction to be beaten down, not as an invitation to reflection.
>
> (Dewey, 1934/2005: 46)

ON REFLECTION AND REFLEXIVITY

In urging managers and leaders to pay attention to how they are interacting with others I am also pointing to the importance of reflection and reflexivity. Neither aim for optimisation: there is no abstract quest for the ideal system, or ways of working based in 'best practice'. Reflection dwells upon lived experience with the intention of intensifying it, and in doing so the reflector can sometimes come to understand themselves and their relationships anew: they become reflexive. The kind of knowledge that is most likely to arise from reflective practice, both individual and collective, is self-knowledge, rather than the instrumentalised understanding that one can sometimes derive from knowledge-oriented writing that somehow all knowledge is action or problem-oriented.

Reflection is not necessarily inclined towards answers, solutions and conclusions, but rather to doubt, questioning and uncertainty. This is in no way a despairing uncertainty however, simply one which implies further openness to experience. It assumes that things are mutable, ever-changing, without permanent foundations. In this sense there is a profound discipline here, and a dialectical method of never being satisfied with answers that would close off further questioning. Being open to new collective meaning-making is recognition of our inter-dependence and the otherness of others. In reflecting with others we are using our conscious and self-conscious capacity which is what most distinguishes us as being human, our ability as G.H. Mead (1934) said, to take ourselves as an object to ourselves.

Reflective and reflexive practice will incline us towards doubting the very instruments of management that have become so ubiquitous in organisations that we have come to take them for granted. In order to respond to the new and the unexpected, our inevitably changing circumstances, we may want to explore instead managing without foundations.

In conclusion I would argue that there is nothing more practical for a manager to be doing than to pay close attention to how they are working with others in everyday work situations; to find time to reflect with colleagues on how they are working and thinking, and to have the courage to stay engaged with each other as they negotiate how to go on together.

References

Bourdieu, P. (1977) *Outline of a Theory of Practice*, Cambridge: Cambridge University Press.
—— (1982) *Leçon sur la Leçon*, Paris: Editions de Minuit.
—— (1990) *The Logic of Practice*, Cambridge: Polity Press.
—— (1998) *Practical Reason*, Cambridge: Polity Press.

Dewey, J. (1934/2005) *Art as Experience*, New York: Penguin.

—— (1958) *Experience and Nature*, New York: Dover Publications.

Elias, N. (1939/2000) *The Civilising Process.* Blackwell, Oxford.

George, M., Maxey, J., Rowlands, D. and Upton, M., (2005) *The Lean Six Sigma Pocket Toolbook: A Quick Reference Guide to 70 Tools for Improving Quality and Speed*, London: McGraw Hill.

Kant, I. (1790/1978) *The Critique of Judgement*, Oxford: Oxford University Press.

Mead, G.H. (1934) *Mind, Self and Society from the Standpoint of a Social Behaviourist*, Chicago: University of Chicago Press.

Olson, E. and Eoyang, G. (2001) *Facilitating Organizational Change – Lessons from the Complexity Sciences*, San Francisco: Jossey-Bass.

Pascale, R. (2007) *Surfing the Edge of Chaos: The Laws of Nature and the New Laws of Business*, London: Crown Business.

Peirce, C.S. (1984) *Writings of Charles Sanders Peirce: A Chronological Edition*, vol. 1, Bloomington: Indiana University Press.

Prigogine, I. (1997) *The End of Certainty: Time, Chaos and the New Laws of Nature*, New York: The Free Press.

Ramachandran, V.S. (2011) *The Tell-tale Brain: Unlocking the Mystery of Human Nature*, London: Heineman.

Senge, P., Schwarmer, C., Jaworski, J. and Flowers, B. (2005) *Presence: Exploring Profound Change in People, Organizations and Society*, London: Nicholas Brealey Publishing.

Stacey, R. (2007) *Strategic Management and Organisational Dynamics*, 5th Edition, London: Prentice Hall

—— (2010) *Complexity and Organizational Reality: Uncertainty and the Need to Rethink Management After the Collapse of Investment Capitalism*, London: Routledge.

——, Griffin, D. and Shaw, P. (2000) *Complexity and Management: Fad or Radical Challenge to Systems Thinking?*, London: Routledge.

Uhl, M., Marion, R. and Meindl, J. (eds) (2008) *Complexity Leadership: Conceptual Foundations Part 1*, New York: Information Age Publishing.

Wheatley, M. (1999) *A Simpler Way*, San Francisco: Berrett-Koehler.

Index

inclusion and exclusion 157–58
on parts and wholes 44–45
emergence 61, 194, 245
The Emergence of Leadership (Griffin)
112–13, 155
emotions 37, 45, 90–91, 117, 124
employees
performance management, *see*
performance management
resistance 222–23
to change 31–32, 34, 100–102
to domination 165–66
enactivism 178
The End of Certainty (Prigogine) 216–17
engagement, radical 51–56
essential nature 124
ethnomethodology 64, 76
evidence-based management 17–20,
175
Experience and Nature (Dewey) 160
expressivism 125

figurations 41, 247–48
Flawless Consulting (Block) 48
Fletcher, C. 210–11
Flyvbjerg, Bent 80–81, 189, 221
Ford, J. 96
Foucault, Michel 132, 153
foundationalism 123
From Higher Aims to Hired Hands
(Khurana) 93

Gadamer, H.G. 77–79
game, playing the 43, 103–6, 177–78,
205, 248–49, 255, 263–64
gestures 71–72, 165, 250–52
Geuss, Raymond 21–22
Giddens, Anthony 80, 123, 137
Griffin, D. 49, 112–13
Guest, D. 211

Habermas, Jurgen 81–82
habitus 193–95, 197–98, 215, 248
Hall, L. 211
Hall, T.D. 207
Harding, N. 96
Harvard Business Essentials 207–8
Harvard Business School 94, 212
Hedström, Peter 191–92, 192, 241
hermeneutics 76, 77–78
double hermeneutic 80, 123
House, R. 119, 121–22, 123
The Human Condition (Arendt) 133
humanistic psychology 124, 169
Hyde, P. 211

identity
collective 94
inclusion and exclusion 158,
162–63
and leadership 96, 110, 188
shifts in 262
threats to 39, 53, 90, 158, 224
and values 155, 164, 258
ideologies 8, 14, 22, 119, 157
improvisation 72, 104, 194–95, 196,
205, 216–18
In Search of Excellence (Peters and
Waterman) 3
individualisation 73, 124–25
individualism 125, 129–30
interaction 4, 46, 104–5, 129–30, 264
agent-based computer models
60–61
Allen's model of 189–91
Bourdieu's *habitus* and
improvisation 193–95, 197–98
and collective promises 133–35
communicative 7–8, 63, 65, 74–75,
89, 113, 130, 251
consequences 22